WRSYDHT

we rock
so you don't have to

THE OPTION READER #1

EDITED BY

scott becker

Incommunicado Press
P.O. BOX 99090 SAN DIEGO CA 92169 USA

©1998 Incommunicado
Contents © Supersonic Media, Inc.

ISBN 1-888277-07-6
First Printing

Art direction and book design by Gary Hustwit
Cover photo by Lori Eanes

All rights reserved. No part of this book may be reproduced or transmitted in any form or by any means, electronic or mechanical, including photocopying, recording, or any information storage and retrieval system, without permission in writing from the copyright holder.

Printed in the USA

contents

introduction 9
BY SCOTT BECKER

sonic youth 15
BY STEVE APPLEFORD

chumbawamba 24
BY CHUCK CRISAFULLI

radiohead 32
BY STEVE APPLEFORD

cornershop 40
BY LARRY KANTER

jon spencer blues explosion 45
BY JOHN LEWIS

afghan whigs 52
BY GINA ARNOLD

patti smith 58
BY HOLLY GEORGE-WARREN

new bomb turks 65
BY CHUCK CRISAFULLI

meat puppets 69
BY MARK KEMP

superchunk 78
BY EDDIE HUFFMAN

the flaming lips 84
BY GINA ARNOLD

daniel johnston 92
BY JASON COHEN

the jesus lizard 100
BY LORRAINE ALI

liz phair & lou barlow 106
BY JOHN CORBETT

pavement BY JASON FINE	119
beck BY MARK KEMP	128
green day BY GINA ARNOLD	134
hole BY LORRAINE ALI	143
the breeders BY GINA ARNOLD	153
screaming trees BY JASON FINE	163
melvins BY LORRAINE ALI	170
mike watt BY JASON FINE	177
the jesus & mary chain BY DAVID SHIRLEY	184
thurston moore & mike d BY MARK KEMP	194
dinosaur jr. BY JASON COHEN	210
my bloody valentine BY MARK KEMP	221
nirvana BY GINA ARNOLD	232
fugazi BY TAEHEE KIM	241
mekons BY GORDON ANDERSON	252
contributors	262

For Jenny

introduction

BY **SCOTT BECKER**

HISTORY, WE'RE TOLD, is written by the winners. Does anybody ever wonder what the losers have to say for themselves?

Losers are way more interesting. They embody qualities no winner could ever hope to possess: the vain idealism of the romantic, the failed bitterness of the vanquished, the inner fortitude of the downtrodden and the hollow ache of the chump. Losing isn't about giving it the old college try; it's about risking everything in exchange for nothing. It's about watching the undeserving other side — the smug, happy ones with more friends, fewer scruples and bad taste besides — walk off with the prize.

Back in the dim recesses of rock history — around '92 or so — somebody queried the writer Gina Arnold as to the meaning of Nirvana's explosive, unpredictable success. Gina, a friend of mine who's at times the most perceptive of rock journalists, got caught up in the moment, lost her head and giddily declared: "We won."

Ah, but Gina, I know you know better. Punk rock and its offspring — umpteen generations of post-punk, indie, alternative and/or grunge bands — were always fueled by resignation and bad attitude. *Loser*: from a slogan on a Sub Pop T-shirt to Beck's half-ironic anthem, underground rockers reveled in their Loserhood. The loser might prevail in an occasional skirmish, but the war was always a lost cause. So Gina — you might have been a little bit right (all those poodle-haired bands never again figured out which way was up, destroyed by a single spritz of Teen Spirit), but you also forgot: in the long run, by definition, losers never really win.

This book is history from the losers' perspective. Taken collectively, these stories — all of which ran in the pages of *Option* between 1991 and 1998 — represent the alternately glorious and futile efforts of the decade's most intriguing rock bands. All of these artists have made good music. Some of them have had moments of greatness. But they also represent a colossal folly: the imbecilic notion that the hue and cry of a million losers, armed with distortion pedals and vintage amplifiers, could ever triumph in the rock'n'roll marketplace.

Yet that's what so many of us wanted to believe as the '90s dawned. We — the rock'n'roll geeks and indie freaks, the anti-social, record-collecting, fanzine-reading, thrift-store-attired, music-obsessed mini-multitudes — had watched from the bench for 15 years as every other form of despicable, earsplitting, cheesy pop music ruled the world. Disco trumped punk; horrific mutations like new wave and hair metal devoured our valiant, pathetic heroes. In this losers' paradise, A Flock of Seagulls and Ratt made hit records while Swell Maps and Live Skull wallowed in obscurity.

Even as Nirvana hit big-time paydirt and our secret army of negative creeps rose up to proclaim victory, we were being undermined by a force bigger than any conspiracy nut could possibly imagine: the feeble, flickering tastes of the smiling masses. A trillion college girls put rings in their belly buttons, their boyfriends went out and got tattoos, and the nighttime raids of a half-dozen multinational record companies plundered the "talent" of a thousand screaming indie labels as cannon fodder for the Lollapalooza masses. The alternative became the mainstream and imploded under the weight of self-contradiction.

Do I resent the commercialization of underground rock? Nope. If the idea of a magazine like *Option* was to call attention to music on the fringes — music that was in many ways "better" than what average listeners had foist upon them by corrupt disc jockeys, chain record stores and the glossier rags — then the increased exposure and availability of that music had to be a good thing. (I never bought into the indier-than-thou economic/political agenda. Little labels can be as scummy as big ones.) It's just that when the music of scowling outcasts becomes a soundtrack for the in-crowd, something's bound to get lost in the translation. And you can't have it both ways: the only thing more repulsive than a whining rock star is a satisfied, successful one.

The death of alternative rock was foretold by its growing popularity. We rooted for the Slits, the Minutemen, the Pixies; Pearl Jam, the Smashing Pumpkins and Stone Temple Pilots went platinum. We stood by Pavement and Sonic Youth. We got Weezer

introduction

and Third Eye Blind. I've made the claim in the past that Nirvana's *Nevermind* wasn't the origin of alternative rock's triumph, but its climax; the music was all downhill from then on.

From the vantage of the Summer of '98, compiling these stories was a trip back in time. Since *Option* was conceived exactly 14 years ago, so much has changed. If *Option* were an animate, sensient being — a living teenager — how would "he" look back at his lifelong obsession with music? Certainly the earliest years would be a dimly perceived fog, the years when he struggled to walk, to talk, to find his way amidst the giants. After that would come years of discovery and wonder, his interests alternately expanding and focusing with each moment of revelation. Finally would come the painful shift into adolescence, a know-it-all scrim masking the insecurity of looming adulthood. His perspective would be distorted by the intensity of recent events, by the blur of activities just a few years distant and a time frame all too short to impart real wisdom. The changes in his world would be barely apparent to him. Could he know that rock's best years had come and gone?

To help myself as editor — and so you, the reader — look back at the music through *Option*'s adolescent eyes, you'll find the stories here arranged precisely in reverse chronology. There's a fitting logic to beginning this volume with Steve Appleford's profile of a mature Sonic Youth. Here's a band that's been around for longer than the magazine itself; they first appeared on *Option*'s cover in 1986 and returned in 1998. One of the most creative, self-aware acts in rock history, the arc of both their music and career is uniquely graceful: from Lower East Side art-rockers to indie darlings, then alternative heroes back to major label art-rockers. Now that's cool.

Yet every other act in this book charts a bumpier, less predictable path. There's Chumbawamba, an all-but-unknown collective of anarchist ex-punks who basically told us in a 1993 *Option* story that they were going to use pop music to reach the masses; five years later they made good on that threat. There's Radiohead, a grandiose band with a stupid name, who could easily have become '90s alt-rock one-hit-wonders, yet clawed their way to credibility. And there are a dozen or more bands here — from Superchunk and the Jesus Lizard to the Meat Puppets and My Bloody Valentine — whose careers have been messier still. In certain cases,

SO YOU DON'T HAVE TO **11**

disaster followed success; in others, frustration led to deeper frustration; in still others, artistic brilliance was followed by years of silence. Some ran from stardom; others were destroyed by it.

Certain pieces from the pages of *Option* proved remarkably prescient. Gina Arnold, in particular, has had an uncanny set of antennae. Through the winter of 1993-94, she worked on a profile of Green Day that chronicled their momentum prior to the release of their breakthrough LP, *Dookie*; she also foresaw that the marketing muscle of Warner Bros. would propel them to wider success. None of us knew how right she was until the story hit the stands as the band was going multi-platinum. (In that context, some readers thought we were crucifying the group for selling out; actually, Gina's sympathetic story gives Green Day the last word on the subject.) Gina also rang the bell with an early cover story on the Breeders, whose subsequent record was a million-seller. But she outdid herself with Nirvana.

Already a fan, Gina got hold of an advance tape of *Nevermind* and proposed a cover story several months before the album's release. I was skeptical about a cover, but we put her on the case. Hearing the record myself shortly before its debut made me a believer; seeing Nirvana perform to a packed house in a cavernous club in Tijuana gave me religion. Most acts at their level play to a papered house of 150 people even in Los Angeles; here were a thousand kids on the brink of pandemonium just weeks after their first major label album appeared in stores.

Gina's story had been bumped an issue to make room for an overdue Fugazi article, but by the time Nirvana ran, a cover was inevitable. Oddly, the whole piece is from a frozen moment before Nirvana broke — before their watershed album came out, before its massive success, before anyone had seen the janitor playing air-mop in the video, before the whole epic tragedy of the last great rock band played itself out. In light of what was to come, rereading the story gave me chills.

Maybe Kurt Cobain, in his sweet, pathetic way, was the ultimate loser — a kid who desperately clung to his loser's status, the guy who walked out on stardom and wealth and a generation of followers with all the finality and conviction he could muster. Kurt saw where the vortex of success would take him. He just couldn't

introduction

go there. He hated the winners so much he refused to be one.

This book could end right there: depending on your view of Nirvana's arrival as superstars, *Nevermind* marks both the beginning and the end of alternative rock. But we couldn't leave off without going two steps further back in time. Fugazi and the Mekons were *Option*'s cover stories from the issues prior to Nirvana, and in retrospect it's curious that two of the most defiantly independent acts would precede the band whose major label breakthrough transformed the music industry. Maybe you could call Fugazi a pack of losers for their sheer failure to cash in when they had their best chance; the Mekons are a whole other story.

Part of the original generation of English punks, the Mekons thwarted their own success as much as their friends in Chumbawamba coveted it. They did their dance with the majors at least three times. Each was a greater disaster than the time before. They've changed labels, altered their sound, shifted their line-ups and scattered to different cities. They've fallen in love, broken up, made solo records, and worked on books and art projects on the side. They tour, release brilliant albums, and perennially fail to connect with anything broader than a tiny cult audience. They can be exasperating, drunk and funny, usually all at the same time. Twenty years on, though hardly anybody knows it, the Mekons are the greatest rock'n'roll band ever.

Sometimes losers have the last laugh. It's the best feeling in the whole world.

Scott Becker
Publisher & Editor, *Option*
August 1998

SO YOU DON'T HAVE TO **13**

sonic youth
BACK TO THE GRIND

BY STEVE APPLEFORD

THIS STORY IS TRUE, more or less. And this is where it happens, upstairs from the writhing and grinding of the New York Dolls strip club, up here in rooms crowded with the frustrated young cannibals of Wall Street and the nearby World Trade Center towers. They come slouching in after work, to remove their neckties, to plug in their electric guitars, to shout and rumble with overwrought fury through endless renditions of "Sympathy For the Devil" or something by the Doobie Brothers or Fleetwood Mac or some other faded icon. And for some, that is enough. This is paradise.

This is also home to Sonic Youth, veterans of the avant-garde and punk and No Wave and wild improvisational noise. The quartet's new studio and headquarters is sandwiched in this ancient brick building between floors rented to Manhattan's rock'n'roll hobbyists. It's a sign of the band's unity after more than 16 years together, making music equally profound and grating, monstrous and pure, even if they can't agree on what to call the place: Tribeca Recording Studio? Echo Cañon? Second Home? Steve's Place?

But now, all Sonic Youth operations momentarily stop as producer Wharton Tiers pauses to listen to the shouting and labored drum rolls coming from the floor below. "Is that the chick singer," he asks with a wicked grin, "or the guy who sounds like a chick singer?"

Not that it matters. Guitarist Lee Ranaldo is just hoping it stops, as he prepares to overdub another delicate layer of noise onto "Woodland Ode," a song tentatively set to appear on Sonic Youth's next album, *A Thousand Leaves.* He untangles a cable and plugs it into an electric guitar. "One of the worst things about this place is that you have to hear the worst fucking riffs over and over," says Ranaldo, rolling his eyes to the ceiling, "both below and above you."

He's not complaining exactly, since the hapless playing here every weeknight is more amusing than irritating. Much of the building acts like a kind of dating service, putting like-minded musicians together to live out their adolescent rock fantasies after a long day chasing profits. Mediocre guitarists are introduced to bad drummers. Incompetent singers meet sloppy bassists. A fine idea, really, and one that rarely conflicts with the serious work of Sonic Youth, who do their recording in the daylight hours. But the band's self-imposed deadline for finishing their album is only weeks away, with most of the vocals and the usual tinkering yet to be done. Which suggests things are somehow no different now than when Sonic Youth began as a quartet of young, atonal punks playing cheap pawnshop guitars.

"In some ways we're just as inept now as we were then, and it might be a saving grace," says Ranaldo, graying now at the temples. "We know how to work together pretty well, but it never seems to get formulaic." He describes the band's creative trajectory as "a really jagged line. We're not, in some sense, professional technicians at what we do. We work off what's in our heads. So it comes out different every time."

Different, but recognizable. In a moment, Ranaldo is bent over his guitar, picking and strumming, working out the song's final bits of inflection, mood and cascading melody, built upon an exotic alternate guitar tuning known only to himself and the notebook at his feet. With a sound both contemplative and aggressive, Sonic Youth still trades in the same kind of howling feedback, the same tangled chaos of electric guitars that launched them at the beginning of the 1980s.

Sonic Youth had its brief fling with the mainstream, back when the confusing success of Nirvana seemed to open a door for rock rooted in the raw esthetic of punk. Sonic Youth flirted with traditional song structures, toured with Neil Young & Crazy Horse, headlined Lollapalooza and even scored a modest hit with "Kool Thing." But the pop breakthrough never came. So now guitarists Ranaldo and Thurston Moore, guitarist/bassist Kim Gordon and drummer Steve Shelley have set all that aside, returning casually to the bold exploration of their earliest days. With most of them now in their forties, the band members are crafting some of the most challenging music of their career.

Clues to their present direction emerged over the last year on a trio of self-produced EPs quietly released on their own SYR label. The music was impossibly jagged and frayed, all white noise and harmonic intensity, somehow managing to sound both twisted and rollicking on wayward instrumental tracks that often stretched beyond 20 minutes.

"It's always been important to us to keep challenging ourselves," Gordon says. "Every band, when they start writing new songs, there is a certain amount of suspended disbelief that goes on, where you have to feel like you're starting for the first time. This record, I really felt like we were in our first rehearsal space, and just playing with that certain amount of freedom and lack of self-consciousness."

Look no further than Sonic Youth's new clubhouse for signs of growing independence from the rock'n'roll marketplace. They've been here less than a year, but the place already feels like home. A row of 29 battered electric guitars is stacked against one corner. Christmas lights shaped like chili peppers dangle above Shelley's drumkit. And the walls are covered in posters and fliers: of a young and inscrutable Joni Mitchell, of punk heroines Patti Smith and Lydia Lunch, of a vintage Jermaine Jackson in full Afro, shirtless and reclining on the beach. In the bathroom is a signed portrait of damaged Beach Boy Brian Wilson, looking typically uncomfortable: "To Thurston, Many thanks for all the kind words in my movie!"

A Thousand Leaves slowly emerged here amidst the scattered cables, amplifiers, microphones and the band's 16-track recording equipment. It's a scene that was unimaginable a decade ago, when the band rehearsed in grim isolation for the acclaimed *Evol* album in an eight-by-ten concrete bunker. And it reflects the rare economic freedom Sonic Youth enjoys as a proud part of the Geffen roster. They've survived at the label largely as a prestige act even as other bands of their ilk and sales figures (never more than 300,000 worldwide) have been let go elsewhere. The strength of Sonic Youth's influence, reputation and longevity now allows them this headlong return towards the most dissonant of pop, recently earning them standing ovations during a mostly instrumental performance at New York's prestigious Lincoln Center.

The usual pop music venues hardly seem appropriate, not for Sonic Youth or the generation of art-damaged punks that have followed them. "Sleater-Kinney doesn't need MTV. Sonic Youth doesn't need MTV," insists Ranaldo, though his own 12-year-old son is a dedicated follower of the Wu-Tang Clan. "It's just a different thing. There was a time when success meant selling a lot of records, and having songs that everybody knew. At this point, a lot of people have come to realize that it doesn't matter."

NOISE. THIS IS NOISE. Thurston Moore is in the midst of a free-form jam without pause or explanation, sitting in during a visit to Los Angeles with a band led by guitarist Nels Cline. Also onstage is Mike Watt, in bushy beard and buttoned-up pea coat, plucking at his bass in sweaty ecstasy. The sound is confrontational, painful, self-absorbed, *loud*.

"I don't understand it," says a cocktail waitress with a shrug. Near the back of this small club, one man is taking it all in from a fetal position, curled up on a couch. And maybe there is nothing to understand anyway. Here beneath the mirror ball, and facing a crowd of mostly mute, blank faces, the quintet is playing a jarring, perhaps unlistenable racket. Some of the elements are recognizable from the work of Moore and Watt, but it's not what earned these players their reputations or what probably drew this sold-out crowd. This isn't pop or punk or even songs. And when it's over, half the crowd is already gone.

"I had no idea it was going to be so relentless," Moore says with a smile after stepping off the stage, his straight blond bangs hanging over his eyes. "Mike Watt just wanted to play all night."

Here was the old approach of free-form improvisation via electric guitars that Moore has embraced again. It's an important part of his repertoire, during the occasional live session with the likes of Nels Cline, or when playing with his own trio in New York, unraveling his guitar against the beat of two drummers. For Moore, these moments are less about the jam and more about instant composition, finding a harsh beauty within the chaos. But he's not surprised that much of tonight's L.A. crowd drifted off. "Regardless of whether they loved it or hated it or it didn't mean anything to them, it was a different musical experience than they would have had otherwise," he says. "So I didn't feel bad about it."

Weeks later, Moore is still thinking about all this in a room filled with bookcases devoted to volumes on the Beat generation and punk rock, in the East Village apartment he shares with wife Kim Gordon and their daughter, Coco. He's watched this music develop across two decades. Now sitting at a table and sipping water from a plastic Winnie-the-Pooh cup, he can still talk excitedly about the early New York punk scene he witnessed as a teenager: Television *(the short hair!)* and Patti Smith *(the poetry!)* and the Ramones *(the sound of the street!)*. The wrecked ambience of CBGBs was home then.

The door slams and there she is, barely three feet tall and trailed by her nanny. "Hey, Coco!" her father says cheerfully. Coco Gordon Moore steps into the room chewing on a granola bar after her first day of roller skating. Three years old, she wears a red bow in her bright blonde hair and a faux-leopard skin coat over a pink shirt. "You didn't fall?" Moore asks her. "You know what, Coco, we can go ice skating, too."

She seems to take the suggestion well, even if that's a minor thrill for a toddler who's already seen the road from a Lollapalooza tour bus. Later, she's running back into the room, shouting "Daddy, watch this!" as she attempts her splits and slides slowly to the floor, whispering "Uh-oh."

Lollapalooza is a prized gig for any young band. But headlining the 1995 festival proved a strange quandary for Sonic Youth. As pioneers of the indie underground that had made the careers of Jane's Addiction and Nirvana possible, Sonic Youth was an obvious, proper choice. But even after the MTV success of "Kool Thing," the band was still better known among critics than casual rock fans. So in some cities, many fans exited after watching the exploding celebrity spectacle of Courtney Love and Hole, leaving the mighty Sonic Youth to face a less-than-packed house.

"Each step of the way I go in not expecting very much," Shelley says of the band's career. "And when something bad, like people leaving during your show, happens, it's like: 'Oh well, I wasn't really supposed to be here in the first place.' It's sort of like we got into the music business as spies."

Lollapalooza was also the band's last version of a straight rock show, with lights, effects and stage decorations. It was also the last time fans will likely hear the band's earlier work performed live. "We will never, ever, ever play 'Kool Thing.' Just never," insists Moore. "A lot of it has nothing to do with disliking the material, but it's just not feeling relevant to our current life. We're not a Las Vegas band that does all the hits.

"Another factor is that we have to relearn the songs, and the songs are really unorthodox. They're in different guitar tunings, we use weird guitars, and we hot-rod our stuff. Sometimes it's really hard to figure out what the fuck you were playing. God, which guitar was I using? What the hell notes are those?"

Now Moore uses words like *bubblegum, cornball* and *tacky* to describe the music labeled "alternative," whether it's the empty rehash of Brit-pop or the prefab grunge of Bush and the like. The music Moore helped usher into the '90s is unrecognizable, leading veterans like Sonic Youth to seek new inspiration.

"That has a lot to do," Moore observes, "with giving up on punk rock as any sort of an identity, and going towards more radical and sophisticated musical ideas, such as free improvisation, jazz and 20th century classical stylings — and also absurdia. We've become more influenced by this whole development in the underground of more experimental ideas. When we first started out, that's totally where we were coming from, completely breaking down any rock convention. We became more conventional as time went by because it was interesting becoming conventional." He laughs. "But now we've gone through it and we can do whatever we want."

SONIC YOUTH LANDED at Geffen at the end of the '80s after releasing numerous groundbreaking albums on a variety of independent labels. Following a trio of acclaimed transitional LPs for the once-great SST — home to a roster that included the mighty Black Flag, Hüsker Dü, the Minutemen and the Meat Puppets — Sonic Youth recorded *Daydream Nation* for Blast First. Their most sophisticated and strangely accessible album yet, it demonstrated a searing, ambitious voice that the major labels could no longer ignore.

In 1991, Geffen released *Goo*, which continued the band's

move towards containable song structures. The followup, *Dirty*, was the first Sonic Youth album to be released in the wake of Nirvana's breakthrough, when it still seemed possible to connect with a larger audience. By now, Moore was himself under the spell of Nirvana's balls-out approach, and reminiscing about his pre-teen love for Black Sabbath and vintage hard rock. "I was trying to explain to Lee about it: when I write chord changes I have Sabbath on my mind as well as the Velvet Underground," says Moore. "He's like 'No you don't! How can you say that?!'"

Like *Nevermind*, *Dirty* was produced by Butch Vig and mixed by Andy Wallace. After the album was finished, Sonic Youth got a call from Courtney Love, who heard an advance copy with Kurt Cobain. "Oh, man, this is going to be massive," she told them. "That's so great you guys did this record! It's going to be huge!"

In the end, even Sonic Youth's attempts at traditional song structures were inevitably yanked back towards the avant-garde through their relentless use of bizarre tunings and a detached vocal style. Time demonstrated that Nirvana had not opened a door for the kind of music Cobain identified with at all, but for a post-Nirvana ocean of manufactured grunge led by the likes of Alice In Chains.

"There were certain expectations which were so ridiculous," Gordon says now. "Maybe it was because *Dirty* was our most produced record. But every interview was like 'Well, do you think your record is going to be really big?' And we were like, *no*." She laughs. "We've always had our own niche."

Like the rest of the band, Gordon reveals no hint of frustration on this subject. By now, she's taken Moore's seat at the dining table, smiling through her weariness from a party the night before. In a few days, Gordon would be out again, in her platinum hair and ruby slippers, joining her husband for a gathering hosted by the New York subculture magazine *Index*, which just put the couple on its cover. The mainstream, she suggests, is not necessarily a friendly place, as Sonic Youth discovered while touring with Neil Young in 1991. During three months on the road, audiences and even some crew members reacted against them.

"That was the first time we really felt confronted by the mainstream, and it was ugly," Gordon says. "There'd be these guys with long hair and beards sticking their tongue out at you, giving you the finger, or holding their ears. Some of them were smiling. Friends of ours in the audience would tell us that people would get really angry at them for clapping for us. It was really interesting. It was the hardest half-hour. It was exhausting. It was kind of a blast in a way. We'd just go out there and explode.

"It was really intense. And there were a couple of people on Neil's crew who really didn't like us, were just freaked out by us. Most people were really nice, but they looked at us like we were kids, which was funny. They thought we were these punks who were going to give them attitude, and they kept waiting for it."

After years of being sheltered within the mostly gender-blind culture of indie rock, Gordon was taken aback during the arena tour, where crew birthdays were invariably celebrated with the appearance of a local stripper. "That was pretty typical, rock'n'roll sexist kind of stuff going on," she says. "It was eye-opening for me. It really made me think of Joni Mitchell; those songs were all about those guys, and she was in such a boy's club and totally alone in a way."

THE AFTERNOON FERRY from Hoboken, New Jersey, to Manhattan is nearly empty of passengers. Just a handful of commuters and Steve Shelley, bundled up in a thick wool coat, his straight brown hair cut into a neat bowl shape. He carries a canvas bag filled with papers and other business for Sonic Youth and the label he runs out of his apartment, Smells Like Records. Outside, the silhouette of New York grows ever closer.

Shelley first hit New York from Michigan in early 1985 with a couple of pals. "We didn't know if we'd be staying or not," he says. "We all knew we wanted to play music, but didn't know how to go about it."

Within a year, Shelley joined Sonic Youth, which had already been through two other drummers. By now the band was beginning to build a national reputation on the strength of a few independent releases. Gordon had arrived from Los Angeles and art school in 1981, expecting to live as a painter before discovering the energy and freedom of live music. Moore and Ranaldo landed earlier and met as members of Glenn Branca's experimental guitar army. "New York had a big part in the way everything came together," says Shelley. "The chemistry of the different people."

That chemistry has so far survived, even as each member has busily pursued a crowded schedule apart from the band. Gordon maintains another active group, Free Kitten, with Julia Cafritz; they've just put out an album, *Sentimental Education* (Kill Rock Stars). Ranaldo has released two solo discs just in just the last few months: *Amarillo Ramp* (Starlight), a collection of archival ephemera, and *Clouds* (Victo), a live recording with drummer William Hooker. And both Moore and Shelley keep busy with a variety of side projects, most of them recorded in Sonic Youth's new studio.

"It definitely benefits more than anything, because it gives everyone an outlet for things they feel they can't do in the band," Gordon says of the group's open structure. "It's hard for the band to be everything. It's like a relationship with someone; you can't expect one person to fulfill everything. But it's really healthy to integrate all that stuff back into the band, and not keep it so separate."

Which indicates that as the band nears completing its second decade together, Sonic Youth is only preparing for more. Commercial pressures have failed to either make or break them. "It's gone on long enough that, why would it end next year? Or why would it go on another ten years?" says Ranaldo. "It's really hard to say. I think we're going to try to put ourselves in a position where we can continue."

January 1998

chumbawamba

WANNA BUY A REVOLUTION?

BY **CHUCK CRISAFULLI**

ALICE NUTTER has four straight white males befuddled, bewildered and enraged. Nutter, the blue-haired vocalist and primary tub-thumper for Britain's pop-anarchists Chumbawamba, is a guest on late-night TV's free-for-all *Politically Incorrect*, where volume tends to trump reason and outrage is encouraged. Tonight, the outrage is all directed at Nutter.

Surrounded by acerbic host Bill Maher, conservative author Petru Popescu, the plump stand-up comic Jeff Garlin and actor Michael Madsen (perhaps best known for slicing the ear off a cop in *Reservoir Dogs*), Nutter calmly and quietly tries to answer their dimly indignant questions about her radical politics. No, an anarchist is not the same as a Stalinist; no, she does not view police as friendly keepers of the peace; and yes, even anarchists would go to war against another Hitler.

Repeatedly trying to make the basic point that the political and economic status quo leaves most people in the world miserable, Nutter can barely complete a sentence before being hooted down. It's mob rule in microcosm: Maher sneers at Nutter's idealism with undisguised contempt, while Madsen grumbles cranky non sequiturs that suggest he's recently been beaten over the head. Popescu stares dumbfounded at Nutter, as if observing some repellent form of insect life. And the comic joins the pile-on by loudly referring to her band as "Chubba Hubba."

The more mean-spirited the attacks, the more composed Nutter seems — though it might well be justified, she will not be baited into telling the fellows to go fuck themselves. Backstage, Nutter does seem a little rattled, but she is still gracious enough to give an autograph and words of encouragement to Popescu's young daughter.

The comic wanders over. "Hey, I didn't mean to give you a hard time. I was just trying to be funny." Nutter offers him a steely gaze and a nod.

Popescu still stares at her, puzzled. "You're an innocent," he says. Nutter takes a deep breath. "No," she counters, "I've been involved in politics for almost 20 years. I am not an innocent. I just think it's worth talking about some better ways of doing things. It is possible that there are better ways."

The author slowly nods. "That's a point of view," he grudgingly concedes.

UNTIL LAST YEAR, the Chumbawamba point of view seemed likely to remain unheard, with the band a barely acknowledged footnote in the slim annals of political pop. The eight-member, self-described "collective" — whose recent album *Tubthumper* has sold at least three million copies in the U.S. alone on the strength of the ubiquitous hit "Tubthumping" — formed in Leeds in the early '80s, inspired to mix message and music by such hometown forebears as Gang of Four and the Mekons. One of their earliest singles was a piss-take of "We Are the World," and their first album, 1986's *Pictures of Starving Children Sell Records*, derided the self-congratulatory rock-star beneficence of Live Aid.

Since then, the band has released a steady flow of singles and albums — first on their own Agit-Prop label and later on the prominent U.K. indie One Little Indian — taking sharp pokes at classist divisions, political hypocrisy and rampant consumerism. Among their output is 1995's *Show Business*, a two-CD set which paired a high-spirited concert recording with profound lecturing by the political iconoclast Noam Chomsky. A six-track 1996 CD by the group was available only as the attached musical accompaniment to the glossy book *Portraits of Anarchists*. And in the rather prodigious Chumbawamba catalog, perhaps the hardest item to track down is what would have been their fifth album, 1991's *Jesus H. Christ*; attempting to subvert mainstream pop by unabashedly giving other people's music the Chumba twist, the band ended up with a record that was legally unreleasable.

Curiously, as the group's explicit outsider politics have sharpened, their music has gone from aggressive Brit-punk to become more inviting, more danceable and, in a word, poppier. Given their massive, unexpected success and the band's subsequent household-name status, it's tempting to think they've executed a cunning Trojan Horse strategy, hiding anarchism inside undeniable dance-beats as a means of subverting the mainstream.

"No," laughs Nutter, rolling up a cigarette on a patio outside the TV studio. The 36-year-old singer — pale, slender and intense — pays almost fierce attention to whomever is speaking to her. But she's not a dour revolutionary. Nutter is quick with a wisecrack and even quicker to poke fun at herself. "We're winging this," she says. "We're definitely winging it. It's taken a lot of group meetings to talk it all out."

Meetings are a hallmark of Chumbawamba's collective approach. Each member of the group has an equal voice in all band decisions. There's been a lot of "talking out" to do this week as Nutter, along with vocalists Lou Watts, Danbert Nobacon and Dunstan Bruce, guitarist Boff, trumpeter Jude Abbott, bassist Paul Greco and drummer Harry Hamer, find themselves taking a mid-January break from a European tour to spend a few days in Los Angeles — the belly of the capitalist, pop-culture beast — for a variety of promotional appearances. They've roused a somnolent *Tonight Show* audience, and on the Keenen Ivory Wayans show, sent producers scurrying when they altered "Tubthumping" lyrics to plead for the freedom of controversial death row inmate Mumia Abu-Jamal (Wayans himself approved of the change).

"I have to keep reminding myself that there's a point to all this — becoming a minor celebrity, I mean," says Nutter. "It's not as bad as becoming a major celebrity, but it can still fuck your head up. We have to remind ourselves that, yes we are talking about other ways to organize, and different value systems, and it's great having access to the media. But it's not been our dream to be pop stars or be rich. We just think that if we've got ideas that are valid, why not be addressing everybody rather than some little ghetto of leftist punk rockers? If everybody laughs at you, fine."

The band's new music, which blends classic pop structures with infectious house and techno beats, has gone beyond pop-chart success into the realm of cultural phenomenon. English soccer crowds regularly burst into choruses of "Tubthumping"; it's becoming a favored saloon sing-along on both sides of the Atlantic. But separated from the guilty pleasures of their frothy pop hooks, the group's political agenda is still subject to laughter, if not scorn, as Nutter's drubbing on *Politically Incorrect* displayed.

"Yeah, look, I'm a woman with blue hair. I must be stupid," she shrugs. "You become this comedy/hate figure just for opening your mouth. On a personal level that's difficult. But I know that this attention is only going to last a short time. So take the fuckin' opportunity to speak — you won't get it again. So what if somebody thinks I'm a crackpot? I happen to think that capitalism is crackpot. It's vicious. Being something like the owner of Nike doesn't mean you're a superior human being. It means you're a successful bastard."

CHUMBAWAMBA'S Jude Abbott and Boff are relaxing in the semi-posh lounge of the Universal Hilton, respectively sipping Perrier and ale. While Nutter was dressed for her TV date in an electric blue vinyl shirt and stylishly chunky platform shoes, these two are in Chumba's de facto uniform: black slacks, black shirts, black accessories. They also sport nearly matching heads of bleached hair. Abbott and Boff are less naturally charged up than Nutter — there's a reason she gets the TV spots — and they nod knowingly as the tale of Nutter's *Politically Incorrect* appearance is told.

Both seem less than surprised that she spent most of her time explaining that she was not in favor of rioting and looting, and so could not go into detail as to how an anarchist might keep the streets clean. "Did they ask her who would take out the trash?" laughs Abbott, 35. "You bring up anarchism and people always want to know who's going to pick up their garbage."

"One of the problems with anarchist politics," says the 36-year-old Boff, "is that you can spend a lifetime addressing people's misconceptions about what it actually means, never mind getting down to actually organizing. For us to be going on TV and radio all over the world talking about anarchy is fascinating because most anarchists have not had the chance to say that this is not about chaos and being angry punks. We like the fact that we've gotten that chance."

"Even if we don't really get a political message across," adds Abbott, "we know we leave some people thinking a little harder. All these people in the mainstream press always say, 'Oh, you're really nice. You're so polite.' They expect you to kick stuff around and vomit. The fact that we don't is one little step towards getting people to think about their preconceptions."

With the idea of anarchism having been defined, refined, debated and declaimed over the last century by voices as varied as Prince Kropotkin, Emma Goldman and Johnny Rotten, it seems only fair to press Chumbawamba for a definition of terms.

"It's interesting," says Boff. "Lately, we're getting asked, 'What's an anarchist?' at seven in the morning on these radio programs. In a nutshell, you need to describe the way we work together and this other larger idea of political systems and social interactions. The easy way out in describing Chumbawamba's idea of anarchism is that the eight of us split everything eight ways. We don't put things to a vote — we discuss things and work out compromises. That way you don't have these small cliques of dissatisfied people all the time, which is what happens in democracy and what happens in most pop groups.

"Considering that most people think that anarchy is about being chaotic," he goes on, "we're probably the most organized bunch of people you could find in the music industry. And I suppose the fact we've stayed together so long without having to travel in separate vehicles says something positive about our approach."

Abbott points out that when dogmatic purity and music-making collide, the music takes precedence. "There's a history of collectives in which the fact that everyone had an equal voice made it really hard for anything to get done. It would be really hard for a band to take that approach, and stand around in the studio saying, 'He got to play guitar last time, so I should get to play an equal amount of guitar this time.' The point is for everyone to do what they're best at, and it gets pulled together in a collective spirit."

FOR ITS PART, Chumbawamba has put its money where its collective mouth is. On tour, members of the road crew get paid the same share of profits as band members do. And while some of

Chumbawamba's long-time fans have grumbled that the group's embrace of chart-scaling success is a sell-out, the band has not so much sold out as facilitated a redistribution of wealth.

When "Tubthumping" was used on the soundtrack for the inexcusably commercial *Home Alone 3*, the band promptly cashed its check from Hollywood and used the money last spring to fund a leftist conference held in Britain. In Italy, the group appeared in an advertisement, and then handed its fee over to socialist radio stations. And Nutter plans to use her royalties to purchase the house in Leeds where the band squatted together in its early years.

"Take the money and throw it away," she laughs. "We get three or four film offers a week now, and we don't refuse anything on artistic grounds. Come on, *Home Alone 3* was dross! But we refused *Mr. Magoo* because we didn't want to be part of making fun of the disabled. And we were offered one where two women pretend to be raped to get money. Uh — wrong. No way is that something Chumbawamba's going to get involved in. We discuss all the offers coming in now, and if there are real objections on principle, we say no. But if it's just plain crap? Yeah, bank it."

You can see why Gang of Four or Dead Kennedys would never have been offered a slot on the *Mr. Magoo* soundtrack: angry politics presented with furious sounds haven't ever stood much chance of floating down the mainstream. Likewise, the long tradition of explicit radicalism espoused through somewhat dreary folk music has rarely traveled well beyond coffeehouse walls. But Nutter and Chumbawamba believe that anarchist notions can be communicated and powered by the uplifting, commercially viable sounds of danceable pop.

"We don't just play pop to push ideas," she says. "We play pop music because we love it. Our anarchism ties in with the idea that people should spend their lives in enjoyable ways. And, after all, you want your politics to improve the quality of your life. You don't want your politics to make you even more miserable."

Yet with the band's music being embraced by a mass audience, and with Chumbawamba itself being spun through the gears of the pop machine, is there fear that the band's politics will be distorted, misunderstood, decontextualized and neutered?

"Pop music is basically a conservative idea," smiles Boff. "So for us to take big social ideas and reduce them to three-minute things with nice choruses does seem strange sometimes. But I do think it's a great way to lead people in. And, even as an explicitly political idealist, I still think it's fantastic to have been part of writing something that people for no reason at all will sing together at a football match or in a bar. They pick up on the idea that it has to do with making the better of something. It doesn't have to make a huge intellectual point.

"I'd feel a little odd if we'd cast off our politics and had a hit with some classic heterosexual love song — it would have been corny getting in that way," he admits. "But we did it with something a little more open. People who hear 'Tubthumping' cotton on that it's not about some powerful politician being down and getting up again — it's about those people in the bars and at the football matches. There's a point to encouraging people to wake up in the morning and say, 'Things could be better.' We're not absolutely certain what the other way would be — but this way isn't working out too well. Getting that across is enough for a start."

"Actually," adds Abbott, "apart from the record sales and the measurable successes and all that, one of the nicest things for us has been simply that the phrase 'anarchist collective' has had to be addressed in some way by the mainstream press. They may not get it, but at least they've had to say it."

"I'M STILL SHAKING," says Nutter, rolling another smoke outside the *Politically Incorrect* studio. "That was nerve-wracking. They really didn't like that shoplifting idea, did they?"

On the show, Maher confronted Nutter about a tongue-in-cheek suggestion on the band's website encouraging people to steal their CDs. Nutter's response would have nationwide reverberations in weeks to come. Chumbawamba wouldn't mind, she said, if poor fans stole their albums from record shops; after all, that expense wouldn't come out of the band's pocket but off the ledgers of the retail outlet in question. But she instructed potential shoplifters not to pick on mom'n'pop stores which might be struggling to survive — they should instead nick the goods of retail giants like Virgin Megastore.

Nutter's fellow panelists made it clear they thought that was a silly idea. But Virgin was even less impressed. After the show aired on January 20, the retailer announced that Chumbawamba records would be sold from behind the cashier's counter. The chain has taken down promotional posters of the band and no longer offers *Tubthumper* at sale prices.

As an anarchist, Nutter probably wasn't concerned about the negative consequences of tangling with Bill Maher. She takes another drag off her cigarette and shrugs off her unnerving TV experience. "Ah, look — people just assume you're a loonie, and you can only fight it so much. I'll give you an Einstein quote: 'The first thing people do when you say something against the established order is laugh at you. The second thing they do is use violence against you. And the third thing they do is say they've always agreed with you.' No matter how shaky I feel about four blokes having a go at me, at least I am talking about anarchism on the airwaves.

"People get angry because they know you don't have the big answer worked out. But we don't want to make it up ourselves. The point is to make it up with other people — to come together and have some faith in each other. If we get together and talk we can actually set something different up — some kind of workable alternative. There has to be some kind of an alternative to this, because this" — she gestures dismissively at the media center around her and, by extension, the whole of the status quo — "this is crap."

January 1998

radiohead

ANGELS & ALIENS

BY **STEVE APPLEFORD**

THERE HE IS, the man with the guitar and the crooked stare, standing amidst the fog and spooky lighting, set to begin another anguished sermon on the endless pain, embarrassment and occasional triumphs of daily life. It's an exercise Thom Yorke has learned to endure and even to enjoy. Tonight the crowd is swooning at his feet, erupting with every burst of guitar and mournful lyric Radiohead has to offer. But there in the front row, standing crushed against the barrier with his arms reaching to touch the stage, is some wild-eyed pilgrim with razor-sharp sideburns, looking up at young Thom not as some fabulous rock'n'roll hero, but as God himself.

Yorke's no messiah. And if he is, what does that make Jonny Greenwood over on stage right, painfully thin and doubled over his guitar, snapping at the strings with furious abandon? Or the rest of the Radiohead quintet, hopped up on the adrenaline of their third encore? God is not standing center stage this late summer evening at the 9:30 Club in Washington, D.C. But if He were, He would see the small swirl of moshers, the crying young girls being rescued from the crush, and the sweaty young pilgrim lunging desperately towards the band with an expression of utter nirvana that has even the bouncers looking worried. Yorke's not the first rock star to be called the Almighty, but maybe he doesn't need someone to remind him that he isn't.

"Calm down, man," he says with a wave of his hand. "Calm down." But soon Yorke is actually dedicating a song to *him*, something called "Motion Picture Soundtrack," a song so obscure, so old and unknown, that even the most devoted Radiohead flock have only heard it on the rarest of bootlegs (even though the sorrowful chords and lyrics can be found on any Radiohead web site). And when the night is finally over, Yorke stops for a moment to chat with the pilgrim and his girlfriend, perhaps as much to help him cope with it all.

"They looked like they'd been through something real traumatic," Yorke says later. "Not looking really happy."

By now, the members of Radiohead are decompressing beneath the fluorescent splendor of their dressing room. A mostly untouched case of Guinness sits on the floor, and Yorke is entertaining a trio of giddy BBC radio contest winners with tales from the road. The band's music, equal parts euphoria and torment, has now delivered these five boyhood friends to places like Manhattan and Los Angeles more often than back home to Oxford, England, during these last four years. Which is quite all right for now, and Yorke is marveling with his guests at the impressive array of weaponry so readily available across these United States. "In practically every truck stop in America you can buy a handgun magazine," he says, leaning forward, "and it tells you how to pull it faster from your holster, and how to hide it in your boot."

That hasn't yet scared the band away, even if America remains an unpredictable environment for Radiohead. Their newest album, *OK Computer*, is a sprawling epic of dark, aching intensity, ready to soothe and increase your stress about the accelerating chaos of modern existence. The album's nearly eight-minute suite, "Paranoid Android," sets Yorke's words of longing and contempt against layers of guitar, electronic effects and psychedelic flourishes that suggest a depth of feeling '70s art rock once claimed but rarely achieved. None of it was exactly what the master tacticians at Capitol (their U.S. label) wanted or expected from a band that had once hit the lucrative Top 40 with the melodramatic "Creep."

"When the record company heard the album, they downgraded their expectations," says guitarist Ed O'Brien, laughing now of the label's sales predictions. "Down from two million to 500,000."

Adopting a dim American accent, Yorke says: "'Oh God, it's *weird*, no one's going to buy that shit!'" That blend of expectation and uncertainty from the proper authorities is an ongoing concern to the band. "I don't think you ever get used to it. It's still sort of like arguing with your parents or something. You just try to see beyond it."

THE WINE BOTTLE BY THE WINDOW is conspicuous by its presence. It's a wonder to behold, all tinted glass and golden foil, the unpopped cork a monument to great expectations. But Room 535 of the Hollywood Roosevelt Hotel isn't exactly the happiest place on earth tonight. It's December 1995, and not even Yorke's smile can hide the weariness on his face, as he sits by a window overlooking the seedy glamour of Hollywood Boulevard. This is just another stop on the endless Radiohead roadshow, and now he's facing yet another unannounced interview, squeezed in before the night's gig across town, where Radiohead will again work to put the curse of too much success too soon finally behind them.

Yorke looks at the bottle, a special gift from Capitol Records president Gary Gersh. The argument for Radiohead's seriousness, ambition and growth was already made via 1994's *The Bends*, their second album. Nothing less was needed after Radiohead's massively popular 1993 debut single, "Creep," a tale of utterly believable self-loathing that somehow connected so deeply with mainstream listeners that the quintet were perversely branded a nice little pop act, or worse, a one-hit wonder: a band destined for nothing more than a spot on the inevitable *Hits of the Nineties!* compilations to come. But *The Bends* redefined Radiohead, taking them beyond the mixed blessing of that first album, *Pablo Honey*, with new tracks that were wrenchingly beautiful.

"It's exciting to have people coming up and saying that they really like a record you've made. It was great for a while with 'Creep,'" says Yorke, the band's singer and lyricist, who remembers how crowds would thin out as soon as they had played the big hit. On the bed behind him sits a mountain of clothing awaiting to be picked through for tonight's show. "But to have an album means I can sleep at night. And it feels like I can let go more. The next record will have a sense of release."

Gone now is the sensitive blond boy that Yorke seemed when Radiohead first arrived in Los Angeles in 1993, for what the band generally remembers as a disastrous gig at the Whisky A Go Go in front of the assembled press and record company execs. Today Yorke seems harder-edged, his hair sculpted into short red spikes, as if fighting off the polite media image that's dogged them from the beginning: foppish, bridge-playing tea-drinkers.

By now, both the Pretenders and Tears For Fears had helped turn "Creep" into a modern standard of obsessive, hopeless love by making it a regular part of their shows. The pressure to repeat, or at least approach the success of "Creep" had sent the band into a panic during early sessions for *The Bends*. What bogged them down wasn't a lack of material, but direction. The most dread for Yorke, Greenwood, O'Brien, drummer Phil Selway and bassist Colin Greenwood (Jonny's elder brother), came from worrying about taking the wrong step, playing the wrong note. The stakes were now too high: the pressures of their own expectations and those of fans hoping for a dozen more "Creeps" on the next LP.

Amid rumors in the U.K. music press that the band was on the verge of a breakup, Radiohead created a harsh, expressive brew. New songs like "Bulletproof...I Wish I Was" and "Bones" were more wrenching than anything they had done before, setting the vaguely industrial tone of Greenwood's lead guitar against the band's grim pop swirl. If Oasis was about pure escapism, then this was something closer to confession and disorientation.

"*The Bends* was an incredibly personal album, which is why when it came out I spent most of my time denying it was personal at all," Yorke says with a laugh. "Since then people have regularly accused us of being miserable fucks from hell. I don't really mind that."

Yorke spent his early childhood in Scotland, but by age 7 his family had moved to Oxford, where all of Radiohead's members live still. Even today he has mixed feelings about the place, its privileged student population, its fading industry and his solidly middle class upbringing. "I hated Oxford for a long time," says Yorke, now 28. "I still do, actually, a little bit. It's a very beautiful place, but a bit weird."

His parents sent young Thom to a boarding school ten miles away in Avington. There he first met the other future members of Radiohead, who soon formed a band that performed under a variety of unfortunate names, like Shindig, Gravitate and On a Friday. They experimented with a variety of styles, from country rock to something approximating the Pixies. One version of the band even had a horn section. "We were like nice boys, we went to a nice school. We were not particularly bad off at all," says Yorke, who nonetheless suffered through five eye operations before the age of six. "We were very lucky, and that's always been an acute source of embarrassment.

"At school I went through a really bad period," he remembers. "And my parents worked themselves into this state and were convinced I was going to get expelled. They got things slightly out of proportion. So they were really shocked that I actually wanted to go to college."

At Exeter University, Yorke studied English literature and fine art, but continued rehearsing with the band. It was nearly four years before Radiohead played a single live gig. "My dad wanted me to go into advertising," Yorke says. "He felt I had talent for advertising. It was always very embarrassing. He was always calling up advertising agencies for me, saying 'Do you need anybody to wipe the floor for three months?' But Dad, I want to rehearse! Or, Dad, I want to sit at home and feel miserable!"

Something of those years remains in Radiohead's deeply personal sound. "What you hear is the isolation, the solipsism of the music," says Colin Greenwood. "We don't really mix with other groups, in terms of going to London and going to parties. So there is this sense of being on a little island."

While Radiohead's songwriting is always credited to the full band, the lyrics remain Yorke's special domain. He's already made the misery of unrequited obsession and the dissatisfaction of youth a key element of his work, though Yorke has yet to fully explore the events of his adolescence in any specific way. "I wish I was actually able to write more about how I felt when I grew up. I don't find I can that well. That would probably be a really good way of dealing with it."

THE MAKING OF *OK COMPUTER'S* sci-fi gothic began at home. The sophistication demonstrated on *The Bends* earned Radiohead the right to record their third album anywhere, and with anyone they chose. So the band purchased its own mobile recording equipment and sessions began last year in their Oxford rehearsal space, a one-time apple storage room overlooking nearby hills and a power station.

"We have a peculiar horror of professional studios," says Jonny

Greenwood. "It doesn't feel very healthy to be part of that production line."

Among the tracks recorded in Oxford was "Subterranean Homesick Alien," a quiet, spacy ballad that imagines, longingly, extraterrestrials examining the lives on earth. Yorke sings: "I wish that they'd swoop down in a country lane...Take me aboard their beautiful ship/show me the world as I'd love to see it."

"When I was a kid I was always very confused about the difference between angels and aliens," says Yorke. "I couldn't see that there was any difference. I had a very proud theory when I was a child that they were the same people. I just loved the idea of someone observing how we live from the outside and running home with home movies to show their friends at parties and sitting there pissing themselves laughing at how humans go about their daily business."

Yorke denies any unifying theme for the lyrics to *OK Computer*, but the dehumanization of society from encroaching technology is a recurring motif. On "Fitter Happier," a computer voice reads a Yorke poem that hauntingly spells out the logical, productive behavior expected of the ideal human. ("Not drinking too much... regular exercise at the gym... getting on better with your associate employee contemporaries... no paranoia...")

"It's the most upsetting thing that I've ever written. The reason we used a computer voice is that it appeared to be emotionally neutral," explains Yorke. "In fact, it wasn't, because the inflections that it uses made it to me incredibly emotional. It brought out something that I thought was essentially flat, it brought it to life in a really fuckin' eerie way.

"I have this thing about my own voice on record anyway. No matter what I sing, it sounds really serious, and I sound self-loathing or whatever, which was just driving me nuts because that's not what I was writing."

Sessions for *OK Computer* ultimately left the band's apple shed at the outskirts of Oxford ("There was nowhere to eat or defecate, which are two fairly basic human drives," says Jonny), and moved to the library of an 18th century manor just outside Bath. The entire recording process took about three months, spread over the course of a year, with the band entering the studio only when inspiration dictated.

Binding the album together is the often harsh, melodically expressive sound from Radiohead's formidable trio of guitars played by Greenwood, O'Brien and Yorke. The subversive elements emerge from a mix dense with ideas: the found radio signals, the vaguely bossa nova passage within "Paranoid Android," the melancholy vocal melodies suitable enough for string quartet.

In this era of electronica, Radiohead is notably a band that understands the emotive power of electric guitar. Jonny Greenwood comes closest to filling the role of *lead guitarist*. He remains a skinny, wiry presence onstage, but with arms rippling with strange new muscles, a brace on his right wrist from repeated abuse.

"It's a very difficult thing to do well, to use volume and noise, and white noise," says Greenwood. "It's a very easy thing to overuse. We're very careful how and where we use dynamics."

Greenwood is standing backstage after a short charity set in Los Angeles, but he's still wired. As he talks, his arms move nervously, almost spider-like up and down his rail-thin torso. "I never listened to guitar playing in any band, ever," he says. "I still don't, really. Worshiping guitarists is all about buying guitar magazines. Anybody can play guitar, but writing songs is a far harder challenge. I'd rather idolize someone like Elvis Costello than I would Steve Vai."

That dismissive attitude towards guitar heroism hadn't stopped Greenwood from helping shape a desperate beauty within the chaotic pop of *OK Computer*. "You knew you were on to something, because I started to get this fear, probably some induced paranoia, that the tapes would be lost or stolen," Greenwood says. "I was really worried about it, which suggests that I knew it was good. That was a good sign."

IT'S ONLY A SHORT, QUIET DRIVE from their hotel to the 9:30 Club, but the members of Radiohead are not wasting a moment. The quintet is rolling through the capitol, past the monuments and the boarded-up apartments, in a rented tour bus with scenes of tropical paradise painted on each side. Inside, assorted plans and schedules are being considered, discussions about some requested EP for Japanese fans, about some T-shirt designs gone wrong. Resting on the shelf above Yorke's head is an alien doll, slouching in the summer heat. "It's so hot!" moans Colin Greenwood. "I can't believe this is your legislative center!"

The show is still hours away when the bus pulls up to the club, but already awaiting Radiohead on the sidewalk is a quartet of teen girls, who will keep a respectful distance with their snapshot cameras as the band exits the bus.

As the driver guides the bus up towards the door, Jonny Greenwood stands behind him, urging him closer to the old brick building. There are customs to uphold, appearances to consider. Move ever closer to the door, Jonny jokes, "So that we don't have to touch the ground."

November 1997

cornershop

CULTURE CLASH

BY **LARRY KANTER**

TJINDER SINGH AND HIS BAND CORNERSHOP are onstage at Spaceland, an indie rock dive in L.A.'s Silverlake district. Clad in old jeans and a purple T-shirt, with thick dark hair falling into his face, Singh looks tense as he cradles an acoustic guitar and begins to strum a dark, Velvety minor chord. Soon, sitar and tamboura join in, their separate tones weaving a dense, warbling drone. A percussionist pounds on a large bank of bongos, tablas, bells and chimes as the band locks into a deep groove. Standing ramrod straight, Singh starts to chant. Unfamiliar syllables clang together, dancing in and out of the groove as the ecstatic din builds behind him. His dark eyes blazing with the intensity of a cleric, Singh looks like a man struggling to communicate in a language no one can understand.

In fact, that's exactly what Singh is doing. The lyrics of the song, "6 A.M. Julander Shere," from Cornershop's Woman's Gotta Have It (Luaka Bop), are delivered in Punjabi. And it's a safe bet that few, if any, of the hip young Angelenos in the audience speak even a word of the North Indian language.

Fortunately, you don't have to be fluent in Punjabi to understand Cornershop. The band's music — an organic blend of scrappy guitar rock and the exotic tones and textures of Indian ragas and Punjabi folk songs — speaks eloquently for itself. The ten songs on *Woman's Gotta Have It* describe a world in which technological advances and waves of immigration render traditional notions about borders, both political and cultural, increasingly archaic. In Cornershop's music, Hindi religious chants, washes of looped feedback, aggressive rock riffs and dense layers of African and Indian percussion co-exist in lo-fi cacophony. With lyrics in English, French and Punjabi, the group's musical mosaic is as meaningful in

cornershop

Los Angeles as it is in the group's hometown of London — or, for that matter, as it would be in any of the world's major cities perched uneasily on the edge of the 21st century.

STANDING AT THE CENTER of this heady mix is the 28-year-old Singh. A first-generation Briton born into a tight-knit Sikh community near the industrial city of Birmingham, he straddles the same disparate worlds as his music. He is among the first of his generation to resist intense community pressure to go into business or shopkeeping, instead choosing to pursue a life in the arts — a decision which has caused considerable grief for Singh and his immigrant community.

His father, a schoolteacher in the Birmingham suburb of Wolverhampton, refuses to see Tjinder perform. Instead, Singh says, his father clings to the wish that his ambitious son choose a less risky career path. It's for that reason he named his band Cornershop. Yet Singh has not been embraced by the Anglo world, either. Despite several generations in their adopted country, South Asian immigrants continue to bear the brunt of a particularly nasty strain of British racism. Even in the ethnically diverse Archway neighborhood of London, where Singh lives in a flat above a fish and chips shop, he regularly faces verbal abuse and even physical attacks from people put off by his dark complexion and his white girlfriend. It's a compelling paradox: even as Cornershop's music embodies the increasing irrelevance of cultural borders, Singh's story demonstrates that the old boundaries still assert themselves with brutal intensity.

"It was always there, in the air — from being chased by motorbikes to being beaten up just for the sake of it. It was always there." Singh is sitting in a crowded Mexican restaurant in a Sunset Boulevard mini-mall. Between mouthfuls of huevos rancheros, he explains what it was like growing up in England. Exhausted from a late night party following a gig opening for Porno For Pyros, he answers questions politely but without much enthusiasm. Ben Ayers, Singh's songwriting partner in Cornershop, sits beside him, and is even quieter. It's clear that both have quite a bit of partying to sleep off.

Nonetheless, Singh patiently explains that, as a kid, racism was a constant concern. And, in many ways, he adds, it wasn't much easier in his own community. Like many English kids, Singh and his brother, Avtar, were interested in playing cricket, listening to rock music and keeping up with the latest fashion trends — all of which were frowned upon by Sikh immigrants who seemed only to value qualities of hard work and enterprise.

But Singh says he knew from an early age that, just as his father had left his native India, he would have to leave his own cloistered community. As a child he says he would often sing and play the *dholki*, a small Indian drum, during services at the local Sikh temple. "Half the building was owned by the Sikhs, and half the building was owned by the black, gospel church," he recalls. "We used to open the door and listen to their music. It was great, good old rousing shit. And they would pop into our section as well."

But Singh didn't start making his own music until 1988 when he met Ayers while attending college, and the duo began bashing out songs on acoustic guitars. "We banged around on old pots and pans and stuff," says Ayers. Eventually, Singh got a bass and an old amp. Ayers got a drum machine. They began adding sitars and samplers, and things slowly fell into place. It became apparent to Singh that the band could use music to mirror the racial tensions he had grown up with. "Asians in England are seen as not contributing anything to the community, as keeping to themselves," Singh explains, aimlessly stirring his coffee. "We wanted to use instruments like the harmonium or the sitar to represent how Asians are seen as being passive, just living their own lives. And on the other side, with the guitars, we wanted to just fuck it up, to show how Asians actually feel. We were trying to counter the rage felt by Asians with the serenity of Asian culture."

Cornershop released a series of 7-inch singles, but didn't gain notoriety until 1992, when the group launched a high-profile assault on — of all people — Morrissey. The former frontman for the Smiths had been flirting with skinhead imagery and writing allegedly racist songs, such as "National Front Disco" and "Asian Rut." Cornershop burned pictures of the singer onstage and at a press conference in front of EMI Records' London office — which many in the English music press dismissed as a cheap publicity stunt.

"Morrissey was mouthing right-wing sentiments," Singh says. "It was very dangerous, especially at that time. It was a very tense moment. There was a lot of hostility and there had been some racial killings. We still stand by what we did. And we'd do it again."

Nonetheless, Singh bristles at the notion that he's some kind of role model or spokesman for the Asian community. Cornershop, he insists, "is just a reflection of what I've gone through. A lot of people say there's a lot of pressure on my shoulders, because a lot of Asians will be looking up to me. I'm not speaking out for no one else. I'm just speaking out for myself. I'm just reiterating what happened to me. I don't want any part of the rock'n'roll thing," he says, using a tortilla to mop up the last bits of his breakfast. "And I don't want any part of the role model shit, either."

WE PAY THE CHECK and head out into the bright summer sunshine. Singh and Ayers appear ready for little more than a nap. But they perk up at the suggestion of stopping into a few thrift shops on the way back to their hotel. "We can't afford to buy new music," Singh says excitedly. "All our best stuff comes from charity shops — choir music, children's records, bird songs, sound effects, stylus-testing records, classical music, '20s jazz, '70s reggae, Punjab folk music and a lot of hippie shit as well."

The first couple of stops turn up nothing. But at the Children's Hospital Thrift Store in East Hollywood, Singh and Ayers head straight for the racks of dusty used records. Rifling rapidly through the stacks, Singh pulls out a French record called *The Singing Nun*, and sets it aside. "Can't pass that," he says with a grin. Singh leaves Ayers and the records behind and moves quickly through the store, fingering a dark tweed suit on a rack, asking a salesman to take an old vintage Kodak from the glass case. In the luggage section, he picks out a fine-looking straw suitcase. "For my CDs and guitar leads and stuff," he says. After some confusion over American currency, Singh pays for his goods and we climb back into the car.

Soon we're stuck in traffic, idling near the intersection of Sunset and Vermont. Long, slender palms arch over the wide, congested boulevard, and in the distance the Hollywood sign peeks through the summer smog. Salsa music, dense with percussion and punctuated with shrill trumpet riffs and raucous singing, pours from the car stereo.

Singh sits in the passenger seat with his purchases cradled in his lap, smoking a Marlboro Light and nodding his head to the unfamiliar music. "This is some kind of dream, isn't it?" he says, looking out the window at the scenery. "Some kind of dream."

July 1996

jon spencer blues explosion

MEMPHIS BLUES AGAIN

BY **JOHN LEWIS**

ON A ROOFTOP HIGH ABOVE New York City's West Village, Jon Spencer sits amidst strewn camera bags, half-empty bottles of seltzer water and dozens of thrift store shirts and sports jackets arranged neatly on hangers. Like his Blues Explosion bandmates, guitarist Judah Bauer and drummer Russell Simins, Spencer is dressed in a black gorilla suit. Nearby, several yellowjackets buzz laconically; a topless woman sunbathes, oblivious to the activity around her; and photographer Brian Velenchenko stands on an overturned milk crate and peers into the viewfinder of an old Brownie.

With Bauer and Simins looking over his shoulder, Spencer examines a vintage "Battle of the Blues" concert poster featuring Howlin' Wolf and Muddy Waters, a gift from a visitor to this surreal scene. Spencer studies the poster's crude design, runs an index finger over its rough print, then looks up and flashes a grin. "You know what it should say?" he asks. "It should say 'Howlin' Wolf vs. Muddy Waters vs. the Blues Explosion.'"

Such cool confidence has long been Spencer's trademark, and it serves him well. With looks that wouldn't be out of place on a fashion runway, he's created a persona that's equal parts Jerry Lee Lewis and James Dean. It's a mask that can be daunting, but with expectations high for the Blues Explosion's new disc, *Now I Got Worry* (Matador), Spencer seems more contemplative than irascible these days. Maybe even a bit humble.

After the four-hour shoot, the group makes its way to Gansevoort Street in the meat packing district in search of a place to unwind. Past loading docks, dozens of parked falafel carts — one of which sports a Hoffa '96 sticker — and the Flavor-Rite Provisions Co., they eventually settle into a table at Florent, a favorite diner. Just around the corner from the former Waterworks studio, where the Blues Explosion recorded its last disc, *Orange*, Florent is decorated with dozens of strands of pearls across the ceiling and miniature cardboard Eiffel Towers on the Formica counter. Donald Fagen plays on the sound system. Bauer and Simins order beers; Spencer asks for a glass of seltzer and a cup of coffee. "This is where we always go after late shows," says Simins.

Professing their love for more traditional blues musicians — Howlin' Wolf, Hound Dog Taylor and R.L. Burnside top the list — the group is quick to address the issue of authenticity that's plagued the Blues Explosion since its inception. "We got a really bad review in the *Village Voice* when *Orange* came out," says Spencer. "It basically said that we were making fun of not so much the blues but white blues bands from the late '60s. Other people compare what we do to what Quentin Tarantino does, as far as his infatuation with blaxploitation and use of the word 'nigger.'"

"Who compared us to Quentin Tarantino?" asks Simins.

"English people," says Spencer, a bit defensively. "But if you've got a pulse and you're not a fuckin' uptight asshole and you see us play, what we do makes sense, it works. People may get hung up with the name of the band. The word 'blues' is in there, and there is an element of the blues in our music, but it's not traditional blues. There's a lot of stuff going on in our music. You can call it post-modern, or whatever you want to call it, but I'm not hung up on stuff like that. I just like playing with Judah and Russell."

"People have to pigeonhole," says Bauer. "'This is the blues. This isn't the blues.' That's what we're busting up against."

Finally, Simins says, "We're a rock band."

TO THE CONSTERNATION of some listeners, no musical reference is safe in the Blues Explosion's hands. They embrace cliché, blow it up real big and stretch it to the point of distortion, then burst it wide open. Deftly, the Jon Spencer Blues Explosion frames its plundering with fresh conception, sharp design and irrepressible enthusiasm, and the results are often thrilling. For nearly six years,

jon spencer blues explosion

the band has been defibrillating the heart of rock'n'roll with a jolting blend of rockabilly raveup, Stax-Volt soul, hip-hop braggadocio and punk intensity. With a bassless, two-guitar line-up patterned after Hound Dog Taylor's, the group looks to the future by strip-mining rock's past. "New York City is our bass player," says Simins. "New York is the fourth member of the Blues Explosion."

A New England native, the 31-year-old Spencer grew up in Hanover, New Hampshire, home of prestigious Dartmouth College. "With college kids there, it's not totally isolated," he says. "I certainly never felt like, 'God, I'm trapped.'" Spencer left Hanover for Brown University, convinced that he wanted to study film. But his cinema career was quickly jettisoned when he discovered that, "Playing rock music was a lot more satisfying. It wasn't so much the idea of playing rock music — although that's what I was totally in love with — it was being on a stage. Me, here, and the audience, there. Rather than working a long time on making a movie and then having somebody look at it, I was interested in doing something more immediate."

Spencer got his mojo working in 1985, when he formed Pussy Galore with Julia Cafritz, future Royal Trux guitarist Neil Hagerty and former Sonic Youth drummer Bob Bert. After a brief stay in Washington, D.C., the band settled in New York. Spencer describes Pussy Galore's music as a "mix of industrial music and '60s garage punk imitating the Rolling Stones imitating blues artists."

Besides the Stones jones, the Pussies were known for being obnoxiously excessive. Songs such as "Kill Yourself," "You Look Like a Jew" and "Don't Give a Fuck About You," and the albums *Right Now!*, *Sugarshit Sharp* and *Dial M For Motherfucker* provided ample shock value, and a self-released cassette cover version of *Exile On Main Street* — played in its entirety — underscored the band's unflagging audacity.

In 1990, Pussy Galore imploded and Spencer gigged as a sideman with tweaked roots-rockers the Gibson Brothers and the crazed New York underground band Honeymoon Killers. Both experiences proved vital. "I learned a lot from the Gibson Brothers," says Spencer. "Other people would say, 'stole.' They turned me on to a lot of music I hadn't heard before, a lot of blues

SO YOU DON'T HAVE TO

and rockabilly stuff." Around the same time he began jamming with Honeymoon Killers' drummer Russell Simins, who brought along his roommate, Judah Bauer. The trio's jams inspired Spencer to again front a band, and the Jon Spencer Blues Explosion was born.

After a solid, self-titled debut on Caroline in 1992, the Blues Explosion jumped to Matador and hit its stride with *Extra Width* a year later. Recorded with Doug Easley and Davis McCain at Memphis' Easley Studios — the same studio used by R&B artists like the Bar-Kays and Bobby Womack — it was a gutter-soul workout. *Extra Width*'s high-octane fuzz replaced the debut's hollow clang, and propulsive head-bobbers such as "Afro," "History of Lies" and "The World of Sex" hinted at a stylistic shift to come.

Released in 1994, *Orange* was a great leap forward. Sticky and stinky as a Delta ditch in the heat, it sizzled with a funny, frazzled funkiness that bordered on pop. Warmer-sounding than its predecessors, the songs flayed Memphis soul bare — sometimes to the point of abstraction — then crystallized it and warped it with clotted guitar riffs and elastic beats. Through it all, Spencer injected a twisted anthemic vibe, punctuating songs such as "Sweat," "Blues X Man" and "Flavor" (featuring Beck on background vocals) with Elvis-inflected shouts of "Blues Explosion! The blues are number one! Blues Explosion! New York City! Blues Explosion!"

With *Orange*, the band expanded its cult following. "Our audience suddenly became a lot larger," Spencer acknowledges. "Different types of people started turning up at the shows."

"Oh shit, I gotta tell you what I saw the other night," interjects Simins. "I was riding in a cab on Avenue A, and there's this college kid in a Datsun next to me, and his music was blaring. I rolled down the window because it sounded like the Blues Explosion. He was singing along to every word. Then I realized it was 'Write a Song.' This kid was screaming, 'I'm gonna write/I'm gonna write/I'm gonna write.' It was so amazing, man. Then, he turned around the corner, still screaming, 'I'm gonna write/I'm gonna write.' That made it for me, man."

"YOU DON'T HAVE to have wallowed in dogshit in rural Mississippi to understand the Blues Explosion," says Robert

jon spencer blues explosion

Gordon, author of *It Came From Memphis*. "In fact, I wish every bar blues band took their approach because what they're doing is real vital. They're able to take seemingly different musical languages and blend them perfectly."

Producer Doug Easley hears something similar. "Usually, this type of music doesn't get out of Memphis," he says, "so it's great that Jon comes down, scoops it up and shares it with the world. Jon's thing is about trying to fuse the old Memphis locals with his thing. We love that."

During the recording of *Now I Got Worry*, the Blues Explosion had the opportunity to work with one of Memphis' local legends, Rufus Thomas. "When we got to town, we had a song called 'Chicken Dog,'" recalls Spencer. "You know, what are you gonna do? You gotta call Rufus Thomas."

Now 79 years old, Thomas pioneered the funky chicken dance craze and had the first hits ("Bear Cat" and "Cause I Love You," respectively) for the Sun and Stax labels. He also made an appearance in *Mystery Train*, the Jim Jarmusch film shot in Memphis.

The afternoon Thomas spent with the Blues Explosion was a memorable one. "When he said he was coming in, I was scared," says Spencer. "After all, he's a legend. He walked in drinking from a bottle of Scope and complaining about a water pipe breaking in his house. He was having kind of a bad day."

Thomas listened to the instrumental take of "Chicken Dog," which the band had cut earlier in the day. Then he got a piece of paper, wrote out lyrics, and "had the whole thing worked out in no time," says Easley.

"It was an honor," says Spencer, who recalls Thomas's parting words as, "I'll sue ya later."

Spencer and his mates speak in similarly glowing terms about R.L. Burnside, the veteran Mississippi bluesman who sometimes tours with the band. Over the past few years, Burnside has opened numerous Blues Explosion shows, mostly on the East Coast and in the South. "It's been really cool to see people coming to Blues Explosion shows really getting into R.L.'s set," says Spencer. "Most of the people in the audience probably have no idea who he is, but they go for it."

Burnside often transforms Blues Explosion encores into

SO YOU DON'T HAVE TO

impromptu jam sessions — "We can't keep him away," Spencer jokes — so collaborating on a record seemed like a logical move. In February, the Blues Explosion, Burnside and guitarist Kenny Brown holed up in a hunting lodge not far from Burnside's home for a day of recording. Undeterred by the lodge's lack of heat and running water, they set up amps around a huge fireplace in the living room, plugged in and went at it.

The resulting disc, *A Ass Pocket of Whiskey* (Matador), plays like a juke joint fantasy come true, as Burnside leads the Blues Explosion through ten gritty, spontaneous songs. Burnside cracks jokes, tells tales about the signifyin' monkey and gets lowdown as the band vamps and boogies mightily, shadowing his every move.

"They play good music, up-tempo, with good rhythms," says Burnside of the collaboration. "It doesn't always sound like the blues but it has a blues foundation. I'm getting them back to the blues."

THE AFTERNOON AFTER his rooftop photo shoot, Spencer sits in a coffee shop at 19th Street and 2nd Avenue, around the corner from the apartment he shares with his wife, Boss Hog singer Christina Martinez. Sipping coffee and eating a raisin bagel, he talks about the upcoming release of *Now I Got Worry*. Produced by Spencer and Jim Waters, and recorded in Tucson, Los Angeles and Memphis, it will be Matador's first joint release since selling a 49 percent stake in the company to Capitol. "The label's looking for a bigger push with commercial radio and MTV and stuff," says Spencer. "That's cool, but when I think about what this record is like, it's kind of ridiculous."

Stylistically, *Now I Got Worry* is both funkier and more adventurous than *Extra Width* and rawer than *Orange*. Slack-stringed guitars and distorted no-fi vocals crowd together, electricity surges, circuits short and imaginatively crafted sound sculptures take shape to become bracing rock songs. Spencer says songs like "Skunk," "Wail," "Sticky" and a cover of Dub Narcotic's "Fuck Shit Up" were built around accidents in the studio. "If something was fucking up, or something weird happened, or something suggested itself, Jim [Waters] and I usually just went with it," explains Spencer.

jon spencer blues explosion

"Accidents play a big role in the making of Blues Explosion records."

While the success of similar-minded artists such as Beck and the Beastie Boys may bode well for the Blues Explosion, Spencer isn't banking on *Now I Got Worry* becoming a commercial breakthrough. "It's such an off-the-wall record," he says, "and it was such a hard one to make. At one point I did feel a lot of pressure, but after I stopped worrying about what the record was going to be like, it just became what it is."

July 1996

afghan whigs
SOUL SURVIVORS

BY **GINA ARNOLD**

ON THEIR LAST PASS through California, the Afghan Whigs rolled into Sacramento for a show at the El Dorado, a tacky metal bar plopped in the middle of a suburban shopping mall. It was May of 1994, six months after the release of the band's widely acclaimed fourth album, *Gentlemen*. *Backbeat*, the Beatles biopic featuring Whigs singer Greg Dulli as the voice of John Lennon, was still in the theaters. The very next night, the band would play a triumphant sold-out show at the Fillmore in San Francisco. But here they were in the state capitol, sandwiched between a do-it-yourself dog-wash and an auto parts store, in front of a sparse and disinterested crowd, at a bar decorated with posters of girls in tight jeans, bending over.

Snootier indie bands would have wilted under the bright lights and bad vibes of the place, but the Afghan Whigs took the stage in another spirit altogether — symbolized by the fact that drummer Steve Earle walked onstage buck naked. Over the next two hours, the band played mostly covers, including "Black Boys On Mopeds" by Sinéad O'Connor, "Everything Flows" by Teenage Fanclub, Iggy Pop's "I Wanna Be Your Dog" and a killer version of "Straight Outta Compton," which segued magnificently into the Whigs' own "Debonair." The whole thing culminated with a splendidly deranged rendition of "Helter Skelter" which ended with Dulli swinging from a light fixture, clapping his legs around guitarist Rick McCollum's neck, bringing him to his knees and then staggering backwards into the audience, Sub Pop style, circa 1989. It was just five weeks after Kurt Cobain's suicide, and that show single-handedly revived my interest in rock'n'roll.

afghan whigs

TWO YEARS HAVE PASSED since that night in Sacramento — two years during which the Afghan Whigs didn't tour, lost their drummer and moved to four separate states. But things are gearing up again for the band, whose new album, *Black Love*, is out on Elektra.

Tonight, while the rest of America recovers from the Super Bowl, the Whigs' John Curley and Greg Dulli are ensconced in a tastefully appointed suite at the Beverly Hills Nikko Hotel, listening to John Coltrane and sipping burgundy. The Whigs have just flown in from New York, where they played an opening night party for the movie *Beautiful Girls*, on which Dulli served as executive music director. Tomorrow they begin shooting the video for "Honky's Ladder" with "Smells Like Teen Spirit" director Sam Bayer, and on Thursday, it's off to Europe for a round of interviews.

The Whigs have always had a reputation for being difficult, but tonight they seem relaxed and easygoing. In fact, as the evening progresses it becomes clear that there's much more to Dulli than the preening prima donna lampooned in a Chicago fanzine called *Fat Greg Dulli*, or the bitterly debonair gentleman who emerges from the love/hate songs he writes. Dulli, who at one time aspired to be an actor, knows the value of a carefully cultivated persona.

"I think of myself as an entertainer," he says. "When we go out to play, I'm definitely me, but I'm an amped up version of me. I'm not a character or anything like that, but I infuse the parts of my personality that are most attuned to being onstage, and I kind of inflate them a little bit. Because when I go to see shows, no matter what it is — opera, or a punk rock bar, or an R&B club — I want to see that performer, you know. Nail me to them."

Since their formation in Cincinnati in 1986, the Afghan Whigs have played some of the most powerful and creative — albeit mid-tempo — rock music of the post-punk era. As their Sacramento show proved, the Whigs are willing to take risks and be moved by the moment. In fact, that spontaneity got them a record deal with Seattle's Sub Pop label in 1989, after Sub Pop co-founder Jonathan Poneman saw them play a blistering set at the Seattle club Squid Row.

Unlike most of the Seattle-based "grunge" bands that dominated the label at the time, the Whigs inspiration was derived not so much from the MC5 and the Stooges but from a far broader sonic palette, including R&B and soul artists like the Isley Brothers, Al Green, Solomon Burke and Wilson Pickett. Live, the band often covers the Supremes, N.W.A, Prince and (lately) TLC, reshaping the music to match their own dark vision of life, love and loneliness. Although the band's commercial trajectory has been less than supersonic, their creative growth has far outstripped most bands that emerged from the grungy late '80s. If the Whigs' 1990 Sub Pop debut, *Up In It*, was the first indication that grunge could be replicated outside of Seattle, each successive album has grown more mature than the last, taking the band deeper into a world of moody sound all its own.

IN 1983, WHEN GREG DULLI LEFT his hometown of Hamilton, Ohio, for the University of Cincinnati, he brought two posters to hang on his bedroom wall. One was of Aerosmith. The other was of Earth Wind & Fire. He soon became immersed in punk rock — turned on to bands like Hüsker Dü, the Damned and the Ramones by two older roommates who were film students. But those posters still summarize the attitude of the Afghan Whigs, the band he would form three years later with John Curley, Rick McCollum and Steve Earle.

"Punk rock didn't make it to Hamilton," says Dulli. "When I was in high school, I would go to just about any concert that came to town just 'cause it was something to do. I think I saw Judas Priest five times. I saw Nugent a couple of times, Aerosmith a bunch, I saw AC/DC... But when I moved up to Cincinnati when I was 18, I caught up real quick."

Dulli dropped out of college after a year and a half and moved to Los Angeles, where he tried unsuccessfully to become an actor. Instead, like many a hayseed-gone-Hollywood, he worked in a record store and saw bands like the Dream Syndicate, whose live shows inspired him to start playing guitar. Eventually Dulli moved back to Cincinnati where he formed his first band, the Black Republicans.

"We were *baaad*," says Dulli now. "I mean, really bad. Some of the things we'd do to pass off as songs would be like, the Hail Mary done to the tune of the Cramps' 'Goo Goo Muck.' And we had this true-life crime song called 'DUI' about our old bass player Steve who got a DUI while me and the guitar player were in the car. And we'd do a lot of Who covers and Pogues covers.

"We were bad, but we were kind of outrageously bad," he adds. "There's still people in Cincinnati who say, 'Man, you'll never fuckin' top the Black Republicans, dude, you should just pack it in.' They should have come see us in Sacramento. That was kind of a Black Republicans night."

The Black Republicans had a tiny draw — about 100 people on a Saturday night, Dulli recalls — and John Curley was their biggest fan.

"Mostly I would go because Greg would always do something outrageous, like taunt somebody in the audience, or break something," Curley says. "They had like maybe ten songs, but they'd play for like three hours."

By 1986, Curley had joined the Black Republicans on bass, and the band evolved into the Afghan Whigs. They recorded their 1988 album, *Big Top Halloween* on their own Ultrasuede label and played around the South and the Midwest. One night the band's manager, Scott Halton, who ran a club in Louisville, Kentucky, played their demo tape during sound check before a Fluid show, and later members of the Sub Pop band told label boss Poneman about the Whigs. Ten days later, Poneman called up Dulli with an offer to do a one-off single. Poneman and partner Bruce Pavitt, working under the seemingly deluded idea of creating a new Motown-like sound factory, brought the Whigs to Seattle to record at producer Jack Endino's studio.

Things weren't easy for the Whigs, though, coming into the tight-knit scene from out of nowhere. "Yeah, we made a lot of Seattle scenesters a little uneasy," Dulli says. "It was definitely tough coming in there. We had a few allies — the Nirvana guys liked us and Tad liked us. But the rest of them were a little cool to us when we first went to those parts."

Dulli even admits that for a while the band tried to compete with local grunge rockers. "It wasn't like we heard that sound and said, you know, 'That's what we gotta be like,' but I think I was definitely trying to live up to some kind of Sub Pop sound," he says. "It was the first time we tried anything that abrasive. But I think we were heading in that direction."

The Whigs signed to Elektra in 1992; flippant press information included with promotional copies of *Gentlemen* claimed they "were on Sub Pop to get laid, Elektra to get paid." Though their last Sub Pop album, *Congregation*, sold just 30,000 copies, its 1993 followup, *Gentlemen*, was a remarkable and haunting album which both explored and expiated some of the violent impulses underlying American life. It drove Dulli to dig even deeper for the next one.

"A lot of people are satisfied with making the same record over and over again," says Dulli. "I'm not. I've never been interested in that. We could have made *Gentlemen Part II: Ladies* but it wouldn't really fly. No one would have been satisfied."

Last year marked the end of the Whigs' association with drummer Steve Earle. "We didn't feel like he was progressing with us emotionally or musically, and that makes it tough for people to hang out day in day out," says Dulli. "It was hardest for me because Steve was my roommate, and at one time, a very good friend of mine… But you cannot base friendships on nostalgia, in my opinion. Friendships have to always evolve and that one had ceased to evolve for quite a long time."

The Whigs replaced Earle with drummer Paul Buchignani, who they met while recording *Gentlemen* at Ardent Studios in Memphis. Dulli says that Earle's departure won't affect the band's sound, since he often writes songs around drum parts himself. *Black Love* bears this out: it is not a sonic departure from *Gentlemen*. But where the last record centered around a dysfunctional relationship, *Black Love* concerns a person who questions his own duplicity; who at least tries for moral rectitude, even if he doesn't always achieve it.

Black Love is a record about personal responsibility: about a man who can't decide whether to lie or tell the truth. Over and over the question is repeated in the songs "Crime Scene Part One" and "Blame, Etc.": "A lie… the truth… which one should I use?"

"This past year was very tumultuous for me personally," Dulli says. "I never write songs when I'm in a happy mood anyway, because I'm out being happy. But I'm not really an unhappy person — it's so strange that people I talk to that know the music we play expect me to be like Morrissey or something.

"I think I've been pigeonholed a little bit as some kind of angst merchant," he adds, "and I disagree with that perception of me. When I think of an angst merchant I think of Lou Barlow and I don't think of myself in those terms. It's not that I'm insincere, it's just that I'm probably a bit cynical. And I think this time I let that slip down a little bit."

Though the Whigs have captivated a sizeable following over the years, there's something a bit too sharp about the romantic gloom their music generates to make them likely rock stars. Now that grunge is considered thoroughly passé and Brit-pop is ascendent, it remains to be seen whether *Black Love* can reach a broader audience. Dulli says he doesn't really care either way.

"It's not like we're some alien band, but we are kind of unto ourselves," he says. "I'm proud of our group because of our singularity, but it could fuck us in the end."

March 1996

patti smith
SHE IS RISEN

BY **HOLLY GEORGE-WARREN**

"I was feeling sensations in no dictionary
He was less than a breath of shimmer and smoke
The life in his fingers unwound my existence
Dead to the world alive I awoke."

"I NEVER DID MISS FAME," says Patti Smith. "What I really missed was a good cup of coffee." Sipping a double latte at the recently opened Java House near her home in suburban Detroit, Smith is talking about the reclusive life she's led since leaving New York in the late 1970s. Though her name is etched forever in the rock'n'roll annals, her reputation here amounts to little more than her daily order of a cinnamon bun and two double lattes. The cafe's proprietor used to offer her free food, assuming from her usual attire — old jeans, work boots and a baggy shirt — that she was broke. Only when he spotted Smith on MTV with Michael Stipe did he realize his most loyal customer had been famous in a previous life.

"In the '70s I actually enjoyed the privileges and the excitement and some of the danger of being a rock'n'roll star," Smith says. "It was very intoxicating at that time in my life. But it wasn't enough."

In fact, Smith has lived several completely different lives over the past five decades. Growing up in small-town South Jersey, she escaped to New York City at 20 with dreams of becoming a painter. She soon began pouring her energy into writing and performing her brand of visceral, hallucinatory poetry — inspired equally by French symbolists, the Beats and the Rolling Stones. Fronting the Patti Smith Group, one of the most visionary rock bands of the '70s, her lyrics mixed mystical poetry, sexual imagery and populist politics, which she delivered in a raspy voice that

patti smith

contained more fury and abandon than any female rocker had ever dared.

Raucous stints at downtown dens like Max's Kansas City and CBGB earned Smith a loyal following and a deal with Arista, and her 1975 debut, *Horses*, captured the rapturous anarchy of Smith's live shows. Three years later, her third album *Easter* contained the hit "Because the Night" (co-written with Bruce Springsteen), and rocketed Smith from cult artist to pop star.

Then Smith chucked it all for love. She moved, in 1979, to the hometown of her paramour, ex-MC5 guitarist Fred "Sonic" Smith. The Smiths married in 1980 and had two children, Jackson, now 14, and Jesse, eight. And while Patti Smith talks about life in Detroit with obvious fondness, the past seven years have been wracked with pain. In that time she has dealt with a string of deaths that began in 1989 with the passing of Smith's longtime soulmate, the photographer Robert Mapplethorpe. The death of her friend and former pianist Richard Sohl followed the next year. Then, in November of 1994, her 44-year-old husband died of heart failure, and a month later her younger brother Todd also passed away.

Resurrection, however, has always been a theme in Smith's work, and 16 years after largely vanishing from the public eye, she has returned. Along with original Patti Smith Group guitarist Lenny Kaye and drummer Jay Dee Daugherty, her old friend (and former Television guitarist) Tom Verlaine and several others, Smith spent the past year recording *Gone Again* (Arista), her first album in eight years, a collection of urgent, emotional songs that capture the sadness of Smith's struggles as well as her intense will to live through it.

In addition, Smith recently published *The Coral Sea* (W.W. Norton), a lengthy, imagistic prose poem dedicated to Mapplethorpe. This summer, she plans to move with her children back to New York City. And during the past year she has begun to perform again, making a surprise appearance at Lollapalooza last summer, an emotional homecoming in Central Park, and opening for Bob Dylan on his ten-date tour last December.

"I perceive that there's a lot of people who have their own troubles, whether they've lost a friend or a lover or they don't know what to do with themselves," she says, sounding more like an ex-hippie than a punk provocateur. "Maybe together we can have a good night, rise up and have a treaty on troubles, then hopefully go back a little more energized to get through another segment of life."

SITTING IN THE JAVA HOUSE on a warm May afternoon, Smith carries herself with a compassionate, maternal air. She openly reflects on her life during the past 16 years, particularly the carefree, reclusive days when she and Fred Smith embarked on their life together.

"We set certain tasks upon us and achieved them," she says. "Mine was to develop my prose writing; Fred wanted to study navigation and aviation. I like to write by the sea and was working on a character study of a man who just roams the beaches. So Fred charted all the places where he could take flight lessons at small airports along different seacoast towns. In the early '80s, when Jackson was small, we'd pack up the car and go up and down the coast and stay in little motels. We lived very frugally. I wrote; he studied aviation and eventually flew. It was a happy, J.G. Ballard existence — if a J.G. Ballard story was ever happy."

Though they shared the same name even before they were married, Smith and Smith were in many ways opposite in character. "Fred was gifted at driving motorcycles, race cars," she says. "He had great instincts, he was quick, the same way he was on guitar. If he put himself into a weird corner, he'd get out of it in ways other people wouldn't even think of." She, on the other hand, is scared of heights and is often stricken with motion sickness while flying. In the decade and a half she's lived in the Motor City suburb of St. Clair Shores, Smith never learned to drive a car. "I have that syndrome where I have to school myself about which is left and which is right," she explains. "I have to write my name in the sky and look to see which is my right hand."

The couple recorded one album together, *Dream of Life*, in 1988. "Fred wrote all the music," says Smith. "He was so prolific musically and had a lot of complex patterns and preferred to write his own music. He loved my lyrics and was real supportive of my writing. Quite often, he chose the title and concept of a song, then

I wrote the lyrics. The song 'People Have the Power' was really important to him. That's where Fred and I really entwined in a song. The concept and title was his, then — as I'm wont to do — I brought in a biblical reference. Fred had a lot of ideas for more politically oriented songs. He liked to remind people that each individual is of worth and that their collective powers are infinite."

Smith gave birth to their daughter Jesse around the time of the album's completion, and the couple chose not to tour. "We took Jesse and Jackson through their formative years and were very close-knit," she explains. Though *Dream of Life* featured "Power" and other memorable songs, including the upbeat "Looking For You," the bittersweet "Paths That Cross" and "Jackson Song," the album was a commercial failure. Perhaps that experience fueled her husband's bitterness toward the recording industry. "He was cynical about the music business and business in general, but he had a lot of faith in people in the abstract," she says. She describes her husband as "a private man who could be difficult," but, with watery eyes, adds that "he was a really wonderful father, and though he did keep to himself, he was extremely kind."

During the last months of his life, Fred Smith taught his wife to play guitar. "I really wanted to be able to write my own songs, and I only knew how to play sounds, feedback," she explains. "I wanted to learn chords so I could sit down and write melody lines. So he gave me guitar lessons every night after the kids went to bed. I was slow, but he was very patient. He taught me chord after chord and how to structure songs."

She pauses and laughs at the memory. "He used to tease me, though, and tell me I wasn't allowed to tell anybody! I'd play a song really poorly and I'd say, 'I can't wait to tell people my guitar teacher was Fred "Sonic" Smith!' and he'd say, '*Don't* do that, Patricia!'" When Smith died, he had already begun making plans for the couple's next recording. "Fred wanted us to do a rock'n'roll album," she says. "I didn't want to do that because I was starting to write songs on acoustic guitar and I was feeling more reflective. But it was funny, he really felt I did rock'n'roll well."

After Fred's death, Patti's brother, Todd — who worked on the Patti Smith Group crew in the '70s — came to her aid. "He tended to everything. He got me back on my feet," she says softly. "He said, 'You're going to do it, you're going to work yourself out of this, people will help you, they'll make you feel better. I'll be there.' Then he passed away within days of telling me all that."

She stops and stares off. "The interesting thing about it is that I could go two ways: I could think of him and go into this sea of complete desolation, or dip into the positive, that joy he exuded and the self-confidence that he developed in me. Instead of focusing on the loss of individuals, I've found that it's very helpful to consider one's privilege to have had those individuals in your life."

SMITH'S POSITIVE OUTLOOK was apparent when she performed before 9000 people in New York's Central Park on a hot July evening in 1995. Joined by Kaye, bassist Tony Shanahan and her sister Kimberly Smith on acoustic guitar, it was a powerful reunion for Smith and her audience — which contained everyone from yuppies and middle-aged ex-punks to riot grrrls and green-haired boys who were toddlers during Smith's heyday. "I've always found New York the most friendly town I've ever been in," Smith says. "That night, the response brought tears to my eyes."

It also encouraged Smith's decision to return to the studio and the stage. During live shows she often performs poems and songs inspired by departed loved ones. It's an emotional experience to hear her proudly introducing "Babelogue" as her brother's favorite or dedicating the poignant "Farewell Reel" to her husband or improvising the verses to "About a Boy," declaring "this was writ for Kurt Cobain and a multitude of others — and the boy within us all."

These impassioned gestures communicate not so much grief, but strength. If Patti Smith's stage persona in the 1970s was remarkable for its raw fury, in the '90s her performances are just as powerful in their calm reflections on loss. "What I most like about performing at this stage of my life," she says, "is to be in a place with these people and it's a meeting ground, instead of an arena for rock'n'roll stars. I like how it's evolving so that we get to spar a little. We communicate."

Nowhere was this more apparent than during her gigs opening for Bob Dylan at New York's Beacon Theater in December, 1995. After Smith's 40-minute set, she joined Dylan for a duet on "Dark

Eyes" that was likely one of the most inspired performances either musician has ever given. "Getting to sing with him was one of the most treasured moments of my life," Smith says. It was Dylan's music, in fact, that helped her get through the bleak days following her husband's death. "I was playing [Dylan's 1993 album] *World Gone Wrong* over and over," she recalls. "It was the theme music of my life at that time. It actually inspired a lot of the songs on *Gone Again*. By listening to it, I started writing songs myself."

PATTI SMITH IS CRUISING through the streets of St. Clair Shores, listening to the final master of *Gone Again*. "Turn it up! Can we hear that one again?" she asks excitedly from the passenger seat as the hallucinatory "Fireflies" comes through the car stereo. "That's Tom Verlaine playing his guitar with a screwdriver!"

Passing rows of tract houses on the way to a Middle Eastern restaurant, Smith gets so caught up in the music she forgets to give directions. Her thoughts are focused on the album's upcoming release. It's still undecided which song will be the first single, but Smith is thrilled that the choice is between "Gone Again" and "Summer Cannibals," two rockers written by her husband. "This obviously isn't the record that Fred and I were going to do," she says. "But he got his word in, though, because the two real rock songs on the record are both his — the last songs he wrote."

Strangely, the title track was a last minute addition to the album. "Fred and Patti had worked on 'Gone Again' the summer before he died," relates Lenny Kaye, who co-produced the album with Malcolm Burn. "But we lost the tape and constructed the album without it. At the last minute, Patti was feeling agitated one day, walking around the house, kind of restless. She opened up a drawer and there was the 'Gone Again' tape as if by magic. We recorded it quickly, and all of a sudden it seemed to be the glue around which everything else could find its place." Kaye mixed into the track a rough tape of Fred Smith singing the melody line, audible in the background of the finished song as a kind of primal, chanting drone.

The genesis of the playful, spirited "Summer Cannibals" dates to Fred Smith's days as leader of Sonic's Rendezvous Band in the '70s. "He'd written part of it but never recorded it," Smith recalls.

"Like 'Gone Again,' he had the title and the music and told me about the concept. When I sing it, it's as if I'm him — it's his attitude toward the music business, although I've tasted the same kind of lifestyle. For him, the whole business was people shoveling drugs, champagne, promises of fame, money, just to keep them working so people could make money off of them. He really perceived the whole journey into fame, which he had tasted when he was younger, as very destructive. It's dangerous to work for those kinds of ends — fame and fortune will turn on you. If there's anything negative on the album, it's that song. But it's got a sense of humor, in the way I sing it, because I survived it all. It didn't have an unhappy ending for me. It's a survival song."

Throughout the album, Smith expresses her will to survive in a cornucopia of voices, from lush, resonant singing to a scratchy growl — often all in one song. Instrumentation varies too, from the eerie sound of a musical saw on "Summer Cannibals" and the effervescent vocals by Jeff Buckley on the atmospheric "Southern Cross," to Verlaine's imaginative guitar work on four tracks and sister Kimberly's mandolin trills on "Ravens."

Family is the most important thing to Smith, and she includes members in her work whenever possible. Just home from school this afternoon, her lanky 14-year-old son plugs in and works up the guitar line from Deep Purple's "Smoke On the Water" on his mom's Fender Duo Sonic, while his sister races to an old upright piano to join in. Riffing away gloriously, the two look like junior versions of their parents.

At the same time the music is cranking, the phone rings off the hook with calls from record company honchos asking Smith to make decisions about tour itineraries, video directors and various upcoming TV appearances. Rather than being overwhelmed by all the attention, Smith seems to be enjoying the excitement. Having survived the death of so many loved ones, life is clearly something she relishes. The afternoon light is fading, and even though she's tired, Smith's blue-gray eyes still sparkle. "I think the key to everything is to just wake up each morning and think, 'I'm alive, I can feel the blood in my body,'" she says. "Just take it from there."

May 1996

new bomb turks

GEEK CHIC

BY **CHUCK CRISAFULLI**

A FRIEND OF NEW BOMB TURKS frontman Eric Davidson recently asked him if he'd predicted the Return of Punk Rock. The singer cocked his head and winced. "'Well, no,' I said. But I didn't care. I thought there were great punk bands five years ago, like the Didjits, the Supersuckers and the Devil Dogs. The fact that we're playing the kind of music we play now isn't because we've been following some punk rock world domination strategy."

There may be little strategy behind this Columbus, Ohio, quartet, but the New Bomb Turks' music consistently unloads well-targeted, punked-up punches. And given their penchant for fast, loud, masterfully raw songs that focus on dread, self-doubt and various other sinking feelings, it might appear as though the band timed its noisy ascent to coincide with the much-hyped, mid-'90s punk rock resurrection.

"I don't care if Green Day sells millions," says Davidson. "It's probably better that there are more Green Day fans in the world than Michael Bolton fans. But you can't let it worry you. We do what we do and we're happy to sell a few records and a few T-shirts at a time."

The New Bomb Turks, whose latest album is the thrashing *Information Highway Revisited* (Crypt), would rather call the gutsy clamor of their music "rock'n'roll" than anything. And they aren't particularly concerned that the brighter, tastier punk of Green Day and the Offspring has set the world afire.

Matt Reber, the band's affable bassist, admits he's baffled by the whole thing. "It's kind of weird that this resurgence has happened," he chuckles, "but I honestly don't think it's affected the sales of our records. It wasn't our mission to reintroduce punk rock to the masses. It's been hard enough to do well in Columbus."

THE FOUR UNASSUMING GUYS who make up the New Bomb Turks certainly don't look much like punk rock missionaries. You could easily mistake them for a bunch of easygoing ex-college DJs, and, in fact, you'd be correct. They're laid-back, friendly, even courteous, and they perk up noticeably when talk turns to *Back From the Grave* garage rock compilations and DMZ bootlegs. For the past five years, whenever these Midwesterners have clambered on to some unsuspecting club stage or plugged in at some tiny, unventilated studio, they've poured forth a primal, rock'n'roll roar that conjures the tang of hormonal sweats, the aroma of beer vomit, the joy of alienation, and the splendor of crappy amps, battered guitars and ugly garages. In short, their music is the stuff of rampant rock'n'roll heroes — the Stooges, the Pagans, the Saints, the MC5.

"I think the stuff that's getting called punk now is pretty much a West Coast thing," says Davidson. "We're not a part of that. The bands that influenced us are from Detroit and Cleveland and New York. Maybe Australia too. The West Coast stuff seems a little British-based and a little naive emotionally. Those bands seem political, but any deeper levels of anger and sex and noise in the music aren't really acceptable. It has to be kind of neat and poppy. And that's not our sound."

The Turks' sound is as fierce and feral as ever on *Information Highway Revisited*. It's their second full-length, following their 1993 debut *Destroy-Oh-Boy* and a fistful of singles. But while the Turks' heavy touring has taken them thundering across the U.S. and Europe, they've yet to get a hero's welcome in the town they call home.

"We've never been accepted by the rock scene in Columbus," shrugs Reber. "We never hit it off with the heroin-snorting grunge crowd, and were never cool enough to hang out with the people who had a shitload of tattoos. We were always seen as a bunch of record-collecting geeks. Now they're finally getting used to us. They still think we're geeks, but now we're *OK* geeks."

It was record-collecting geekdom that brought the Turks together in the first place. Davidson, Reber, guitarist Jim Weber and drummer Bill Randt became friends while working at Ohio State's student-run radio station, the now-defunct WOSR. "We were all listening to tons of records," recalls Davidson, "and I guess we figured out that we liked the same stuff. We tried to do a little noisy New York-type thing when we first got together, but we had a better time when we kept things simple and straight-ahead. We played fast, so sometimes we were called a hardcore band."

Drummer Randt had worked up some fairly mean chops playing along with Black Flag records as a kid, and Reber could handle a bass. But Weber had only been playing guitar for a year, and Davidson had never sung in a band. The foursome's enthusiasm, inexperience, and growing appreciation of obscure '60s garage bands guided them towards their own whopping sound. "We weren't good enough to be anything but what we were," says Reber. "There was no chance we were going to play experimental jazz. But some of the first songs we wrote — 'Tail Crush,' 'Trying To Get By' and 'Outta My Mind' — hold up as some of our best songs."

The newer tunes on *Information Highway* are pretty good contenders. The tightly coiled rage of "Brother Orson Welles" is about the fine line between ambition and misery; "Apocalyptic Dipstick" vents a hearty disgust for self-styled prophets of doom; "Fingernail Chomp" is a finely detailed description of the energizing buzz you can get from a heavy dose of anxiety. It's all done in two- to three-minute assaults of stampeding beats and porterhouse guitar riffs.

The album was made in a similar blitz of recording over a weekend last May. "Our drummer was in grad school and we wanted to record during his spring break, but we couldn't get it together in time," says Davidson. "So we went down to Austin one weekend and got it done. We recorded everything pretty much in one day — 21 songs in nine hours." He pauses. "Actually I guess we did spend a few more hours on this one than we did on the last one."

The Turks' sound is so large on record that the band members occasionally have trouble living up to it onstage. They've been stared down by fans who come to their shows and can't believe that such a formidable noise can come from such fresh-faced regular Joes. "I think we come off a little heavier on record than we do live," says Davidson. "In Germany all these anarcho-punks stood around pissed off at our shows, because we goofed around onstage."

"The music's not goofy," Reber interjects, "but I guess we are."

"We have to remember to try to appear angrier for our fans," Davidson continues. "At least for the anarcho-punks' sake."

The band did oblige one fan request when putting together the new album. For the first time, they included a lyric sheet. The singer still seems uneasy with the decision. "It's something I resisted at first," he says. "But when we were in Europe, kids told us they couldn't understand English at the speed I sang. I can't understand any other language at any speed, but I figured what the hell, I'll put in a lyric sheet. I think it's kind of pretentious, but maybe now people can see that we're not that deep."

Some of their more ardent fans have apparently found more depth than Davidson intends. During the band's last European swing, the Turks were trailed by a British speed freak who insisted on cornering them in bars and screaming their lyrics into their faces. "It was a little disturbing," says Weber. "The guy's eyes are popping out and he's got veins bulging out of his head. It was like, 'Yes that's our song. We like it too. Now stop grinding your teeth.'"

At home in Columbus, the band members are currently taking advantage of their downtime to assemble a singles compilation. They're also preparing for their first trip to Japan. And though Columbus may not recognize the Turks as hometown heroes, the band members aren't planning to relocate. "We don't have to have day jobs here," Davidson explains. "It's a pretty cheap town, rent-wise. The only things we spend money on are going to bars and buying records. It's a simple life here, and we like it. If we lived in a bigger city, even Cleveland, we'd have to work a lot harder."

September 1996

meat puppets
SAVED BY SHOW BIZ

BY **MARK KEMP**

IT WAS LIKE A MIRAGE. The Meat Puppets ambled onstage at the KROQ Christmas Party last December, and nearly every member of the largely teenaged crowd inside L.A.'s Universal Amphitheater knew who they were. The audience went wild when the band tore into its runaway hit "Backwater," and sang along to every word. After 15 years of what the trio's punk rock peer, bassist Mike Watt, calls "econo" touring, the scruffy Meat Puppets had become overnight pop stars. It's not something they're complaining about.

"I fucking *love* show business," growls Curt Kirkwood, the band's singer, songwriter and guitarist. "So many people in this business don't like it. They whine about their success. They get addicted to drugs. They just aren't happy with what they've done." He pauses for a bong hit. "I don't know what to say to them: 'Why'd you get in a band, then?'"

MESA, ARIZONA. High noon in late July. A stuffy 115 degrees outside. Kirkwood is sitting at the table in the air-conditioned dining room of his two-story home, sucking on a Heineken and reloading the bong — a 32-ounce Gatorade bottle with a pipe stem jammed into its side. His girlfriend, Sandy, is stooped on the floor in a semicircle with the band's manager and sound man, kicking their asses in a game of rummy. Elmo, Kirkwood's 12-year-old son, is sequestered in the living room in a bundle of blankets, watching Scooby Doo on TV. Kevin, a brawny, brown-and-white English pit bull, has his two front paws in my lap and is vigorously licking my face. George Jones is on the boom box crooning "Why, Baby, Why?"

The Meat Puppets have just finished recording *No Joke*, their third album for London Records and the follow-up to the trio's surprise hit of last year, *Too High To Die*. That's the one that put the long-struggling cult band over the top, selling 500,000 copies — more than all of the Pups' previous nine albums combined — on the strength of "Backwater."

And then there's the Kurt Cobain connection. In 1993 Nirvana invited the Meat Puppets along for their *In Utero* tour. Later that year, when the band appeared on *MTV Unplugged*, Cobain sang three songs — "Plateau," "Oh Me" and "Lake of Fire" — from the Puppets' 1983 album, *Meat Puppets II*. After Cobain's suicide in 1994, DGC released the acoustic set as *MTV Unplugged In New York*. The album has since sold 3 million copies, and its residuals have made the Meat Puppies — which also include Kirkwood's bassist brother, Cris, and drummer Derrick Bostrom — wealthy men.

Kirkwood takes another hit from the Gatorade bottle. "For me, in terms of what I feel about myself, not much has changed," he says, exhaling a stream of sweet-smelling smoke. "I know who I am, and that's all that matters to me." Wearing a white, V-neck T-shirt and faded blue jeans, Kirkwood looks like your average working class hippie in his mid-thirties. His wavy brown hair is tied back in a ponytail, and his pretty-boy features are beginning to show signs of wear and tear. "The way I look at it is, I fucking caused whatever happened to us with Nirvana," he continues. "They chose to have us come along with them, but I wrote those songs." He pauses and stares blankly at the wall behind my head. "I don't know *why* things happen," he says in a near whisper. "I *have* thought a lot about it — why? why? — but I don't know."

Long considered one of the sexier denizens of the underground — he was recently interviewed by the saucy *Playgirl* magazine — Kirkwood is getting a bit of a middle-age spread: his gut is thicker, and his jaw is not as square as it used to be. But his icy, blue-green eyes are still as piercing. "This new audience of younger kids is like a vacuum," the 36-year-old guitarist continues. "They don't know what the fuck they want, but they know they want something. And if they want anything I've got to offer, cool."

The big question for the Meat Puppets now is whether their newfound popularity was a fluke. *No Joke* will determine that. It's the Puppets at their most bone-crunching, experimental, and melodic — and their most focused. From the squalling lead guitar that introduces the first track, "Scum," to the breezy country-rock of "Chemical Garden," the album is one seamless aural facsimile of the band's distorted observations of humanity. Cellos, piano and chiming acoustic guitars play alongside feedback, the Kirkwood brothers' tangled guitar-bass interplay, Bostrom's deceptively simple beat, and lines like "Under the stones/We find the scum/Under the stars/We find the scum."

"I'm not discounting humanity because I feel like we're scum; it's not a derogatory thing," Kirkwood protests. "To me, it's just fucking reality." His brother Cris sees the Puppets' Dali-esque musical landscapes as a kind of mirror image of society: "We're just a little channel for the horrors of the world."

CURT AND CRIS KIRKWOOD are true children of the American Southwest. Their Catholic parents, Vera and Don, met at the University of Nebraska in Omaha in the late 1950s, and married when they learned Vera was pregnant. In 1958, the couple moved to Wichita Falls, Texas, where Curt was born the following January. They didn't stay long. In 1960, Don, an Air Force man, moved the family west to Amarillo, where Cris was born that October. Three years later, the Kirkwoods were back in Omaha when Curt, then four, had to undergo surgery. That's when the family started falling apart.

"I had a kidney removed and I guess it was just too traumatic for my dad," Curt says bitterly. "My parents divorced right after that."

Vera briefly moved the boys to Acapulco, Mexico, where her father had made millions in the hotel business (she was later cut out of the family fortune). By Curt's second year of school, the family had moved again, to Phoenix, where Vera married a horse racer named Paul White. "He was a total cowboy from Golden, Colorado," Curt recalls. "He wore big cowboy hats and linen shirts." The family settled into a red brick, ranch-style house in the city's Sunny Slope neighborhood, which at the time was a rural area out on the northern edge of town. By 1970, when Curt was 11, his mother had divorced again and married "a rowdy fucking crazy man who liked Bruce Lee movies and was interested in literature about the Third Reich." The man wound up nearly burning the house down.

Curt and Cris began looking for an escape. The elder brother turned inward. "Before I was eight I believed in elves and things," Curt says. "When I discovered they weren't real I started looking into the origin of the myth. My mom always told me, 'You have a good imagination, you should use it.' So that became my world. My imagination is as real to me as anything." He liked music — the Monkees, the Beatles, Bobby Sherman — and his favorite TV programs were the Glen Campbell and Johnny Cash variety shows. But Curt's real passion was motocross bikes. "Racing motorcycles was my life until I was 17," he says. "It was my outlet. It was a major part of both Cris's and my world."

For Cris, motorcycles were just something Curt had introduced him to. "Like a lot of little brothers, I followed him into the things he found cool," says Cris. "He got into motorcycles, I got into motorcycles. I loved it, but what I really loved at the time was playing my banjo." Cris had discovered bluegrass when he saw the movie *Deliverance*. "I was a fat little boy. That was something I could do by myself."

When an accident ended Curt's motocross career, he began focusing on guitar. After a semester of college, in 1977, he dropped out to become a full-time musician. "I'd become kind of an outcast, which was something I could do to replace the bikes. I was really fucking flipped-out."

CURT KIRKWOOD wasn't the only one feeling that way. The '60s were seven years dead, and a growing segment of his generation had decided that the disco, soft rock and arena sounds of the '70s were not addressing their rage. The Sex Pistols' first album landed on U.S. shores the year Curt dropped out of school, and Derrick Bostrom, a new friend from the upper-middle-class neighborhood of Paradise Valley, was trying to persuade the Kirkwood brothers to get with the punk program.

Bostrom's family was unstable too, but nothing like the Kirkwoods. Born in Phoenix, in 1960, he was raised in a liberal intellectual environment. When he was six, his parents divorced, and his medical technician mother, Sandra, remarried a doctor.

meat puppets

Derrick and his brother, Damon, spent their teenaged years living in a sprawling, '70s-style home with a guest house and huge saguaro cacti in the front yard.

Bostrom was an excellent student at Chaparral High, where, as editor during his senior year, he turned the school paper into a sort of *National Lampoon*. "I was a straight-A student, a pothead who had the longest hair in school, and I ran the paper," recalls Bostrom, taking me for a ride around his old neighborhood the next day. "I had more fun that year than I've had at any other time in my life."

His mother and stepfather divorced in 1979, two years after he'd turned the Kirkwood brothers on to the Pistols' "No Future" — and right about the time the three decided to form a band. "I was able to get them somewhat interested in punk rock," Bostrom recalls. "Curt had been in a few non-punk bands and kept getting kicked out because he was too wild. I thought, let's harness some of that wildness."

THE KIRKWOODS were still living at their mother's Sunny Slope home in 1980 when the Meat Puppets recorded their first EP, the feral *In a Car*. On it, the band buzzed through five twangy, avant-hardcore songs in just five minutes. It was the Puppets' ticket into the fledgling punk scene. After a few gigs in the nearby college town of Tempe, the band took its show to L.A. Their unlikely mix of desert weirdness and hardcore spirit so impressed Black Flag guitarist Greg Ginn that he asked the trio to do an album for his new label, SST. The Puppets' raucous, self-titled debut was the label's third full-length release, behind the Minutemen's *The Punch Line* and Black Flag's *Damaged*. It wasn't until *Meat Puppets II*, however, that the band perfected its blend of punk energy with country-rock melodies and experimental, Jerry Garcia-like noodling. Kurt Loder gave the LP a four-star rave in *Rolling Stone*, which, until then, had rarely covered the indie scene, let alone given one of its bands such high praise.

Right around the time *Meat Puppets II* came out, Kirkwood's twins, Elmo and Katherine, were born to his then-girlfriend, Cinda. "Our lives were so fucked up," Kirkwood recalls, shaking his head. "We were into all kinds of weird shit. We were so young. A lot of the stuff on that album has to do with having kids. It was weird, because when I wrote the song 'Split Myself In Two,' we had no idea we were going to have twins."

For the next decade, the Meat Pups were on a long, strange punk rock trip, getting fucked up as often as possible, touring with little money, and watching the wheels of the indie scene gain momentum. The band's audience expanded with 1985's *Up On the Sun*, which added progressive rock- and jazz-inspired moves to the sweet, country-folk melodies. They cranked up the volume on 1987's *Huevos* in homage to ZZ Top. The indie rock faithful couldn't figure it out: had the Meat Puppets sold their souls or was their collective tongue buried too deeply into their cheek?

By the late '80s, the Meat Puppets had watched some of their fellow indie bands, such as Hüsker Dü, make the big leap to the majors. "We weren't ready," Kirkwood says. "Nobody would be ready until after Nirvana. Time has fucking made itself very clear. That's why they call it 'Father Time' and 'Mother Earth.' There are things in this world you gotta be respectful of."

The Meat Puppets' pre-Nirvana major label debut in 1991, *Forbidden Places*, was the trio's first with an outside producer. But Pete Anderson, a country guitar virtuoso whose specialty is his pristine production work for C&W artists, wasn't well suited for the Pups' ragged sound. "He had a certain way of going about it, especially in the area of mixing and getting vocals on tape, which was a serious waste of time and effort and energy for us," explains Bostrom. The band's next album proved to be a giant leap forward, thanks in part to the production of Butthole Surfer Paul Leary. "When we started working on *Too High To Die*," Bostrom continues, "it was largely about finding a producer who wasn't going to do to us what Pete Anderson did."

"I think we just decided to go with the flow on *Forbidden Places*," says Curt. "We thought, we're capable musicians and we're artists, so we can do this. I did my best on it, but I think it would have been a better record if it had been a little less thought out." He pauses, looking down at the lighter he's fiddling with. "Maybe some of the songs were a little tedious, too. But it was hard going from a cult band to a major label, because the majors don't care about your cult status."

meat puppets

WHILE MAJOR LABEL BUREAUCRACY loomed overhead, Kirkwood was involved in another layer of business with SST. The Puppets had never signed a contract with their former label, and they wanted to gain control of their earlier albums and publishing rights. "I just had a gut feeling that my songs would be valuable some day, and I was right," Kirkwood says. "I'm goddamn lucky that I got them back when I did, 'cause right off the bat we got this thing going with Nirvana which happened to be really popular. How did I know that would happen? I didn't. But it happened as soon as I fucking resolved that situation."

Both Curt and Cris have a hard time using words like grateful — unless they're referring to the Dead — but you can see the gratitude in their faces even as they shrug their shoulders. "At that fucking point in my life, for Kurt Cobain to come from out of nowhere... I mean, I had no fucking association with the guy, none whatsoever, until — BOOM! — there he was. When you've been dogged all your life, and all of a sudden some little champion comes through for you... I don't know what to say. I wish my thoughts could come out more completely."

Says Cris, "Before this shit happened, I thoroughly figured it was going to be Burger King for the lot of us for the rest of our lives. I've been pretty blown away by the whole thing. I mean, we were always heralded by the geek patrol — big deal."

After Cobain's death, the Pups were dogged with questions about the impact of the singer's suicide on them. "I don't think anybody has any idea what Kurt Cobain meant to me," says Curt. "To this day I'm completely fucking disturbed by what happened. And yet I totally understand it. I *feel* it more than I understand it. I don't have any questions about it. I'm disturbed because I can't speak my mind about it the way I'd like to; I can't feel the way I want to feel about it, because we live in such a fucking weird society I don't think my point of view would be nurtured."

Kirkwood alludes to those feelings in "For Free," a song on *No Joke*. "It's just a fucking disclaimer, basically. The title says it all. It's not really for Cobain, per se. I did it because I've known a lot of people who've killed themselves in the name of this fucking garbage *scene*" — he spits out the word like poison — "and I think that's such a shitload. I didn't take Cobain to be some kind of huge icon. To me, he was just a person I worked with. That's a rarity for me, because one of *my* icons is work. And when you spend time working with somebody like him — well, that shit's fucking cool, man. It's totally real."

THE WALLS of Curt Kirkwood's home are adorned with his own twisted, soft-colored paintings: a portrait of a death-blue Lincoln with a tiny log cabin in the background, the earthy-looking coffee mug that graces the cover of *Up On the Sun*, the Aztec-like bird from *Out My Way*, and other canvases populated by the grotesque and the distorted. Right now, Kirkwood is sharing a moment with his son. The two are flipping through a fanzine-like booklet called "Bostrom's House of Horrors," a collection of grisly photographs the drummer culled from the Internet, of people who died violent deaths.

"Hey dad, look at this one," says Elmo with a shit-eating grin on his face. "That's cool," Kirkwood responds. "Check this one out."

For some punk rock veterans, looking at corpses might be just another dated pose. But I get the feeling Kirkwood is searching for something beyond the corporeal — his sickness is almost spiritual. Having been through so much upheaval in their lives, Curt and Cris are intensely distrustful of humanity. While listening to "Scum," Curt says, "That's a beautiful song, isn't it? It's like, 'What are we?' I certainly don't know. And I don't care. I don't have a dream for people to be anything other than what we are. But I do like the idea that there's a perfect person out there who we can hold a candle up to. I hope to meet him some day."

Kirkwood distances himself from the idealists of rock's past. "I'm the exact opposite of John Lennon. To me, there is no hope. I love what John Lennon did. He plumbed to the depths what he could about humanity in the early '70s. But I don't agree with him in any way. I don't think 'human beings' exist in the way John Lennon imagined them. I think this world is total fucking slime. It's a fucking human sewer — and I love it." The statement doesn't seem so contradictory when he later tells me that all things "just burn into love at a certain point."

None of the Puppets harbor any lofty visions of humans working together for the betterment of themselves and the planet.

Bostrom laughs. "People don't take well to our ideas, which are just this side of the militia mentality," he says. "We don't espouse kind, compassionate things. We're not really into the whole white man's liberal guilt trip. And we're not all that worried about righting the wrongs of oppression. I mean, why try to save a sinking ship?

"Personally, I'm more into concepts," Bostrom adds. "Freedom. Enlightenment. And I'm more interested in one-on-one relationships than in saving the whole of humanity. I guess I'm basically an anarchist."

For Curt Kirkwood, it's a loner's philosophy. "I don't have many people around me. I keep my family close by" — he waves his hand around the dining room — "the people you see right here."

It's about midnight now and Elmo is running around the house, dancing wildly to the Ministry disc Kirkwood just plopped into the boom box. "My kids are the best things in my life," he says. "You can't get any closer to a person than that. They're the excuse I have for being fucking semi-normal after all I've been through."

He smiles. "I try to stay normal. I've exorcised many demons through this music and I'm still pretty fucked up. I'm real volatile. I'm unpredictable, a total nuisance, really hard to get along with. But I'm a lot better than I was 15 years ago."

July 1995

superchunk
ORDINARY PEOPLE

BY **EDDIE HUFFMAN**

MAC MCCAUGHAN IS THE ANTI-KURT. The frontman of North Carolina's Superchunk is the positive image to Kurt Cobain's negative. Both were born in 1967 and grew up to be skinny guys whose small frames made their ferocity onstage that much more potent. Both found punk rock at early an age and formed bands that combined punk's energy and noise with classic songwriting skills and undeniable emotional conviction. Superchunk and Nirvana both were nutured in fertile college town scenes — Chapel Hill and Olympia, respectively — and found themselves hyped to the skies by the early 1990s. Both McCaughan and Cobain look bad in dresses.

Yet while Nirvana rose from blue collar roots in the Pacific Northwest, Superchunk is Sunbelt and comfortably upper-middle-class. When Nirvana became heavy rotation staples on MTV, Superchunk was lucky to get on *120 Minutes*. Nirvana ended up selling millions of records; Superchunk still sells tens of thousands, tops. And while McCaughan runs Merge Records and tours the world today with his band, Cobain's ashes don't stray from their urn in Courtney Love's house.

"It'd be great to sell as many records as possible," says McCaughan, sprawled in the Merge office on an old couch, below posters of Polvo and Erectus Monotone. He's wearing a tourist T-shirt with a smiling Mickey Mouse on it from his home state of Florida. "I don't think anybody believes that a band doesn't want to sell records. It's just a matter of: 'What do you want to do to achieve the highest sales possible? What are you willing to give up to sell more records?'" In the case of Nirvana and Kurt Cobain, the answer was: everything. In the case of Superchunk and Mac McCaughan: nothing.

superchunk

THROW A ROCK through a window and you've got a reasonable approximation of Superchunk's music, which is loud and bracing, and its output, which is broken up into a thousand pieces. Four years ago the band released a compilation of its singles called *Tossing Seeds*, and that's what McCaughan and company have done since their inception in 1989. They've scattered songs, live shows, singles and albums far and wide from their modest base in Chapel Hill.

That makes their latest album, another singles compilation called *Incidental Music 1991-95*, a rare opportunity to focus on a band whose product often seems too fragmented to afford any kind of focus at all. "I'm kind of excited about the compilation, because we finally got to do a double album gatefold," McCaughan enthuses. "And people can stop writing us asking where can they find this thing or that thing."

Dissect that comment and you'll learn a lot about both Superchunk and McCaughan (pronounced "McCon"), a record geek and one of the premier renaissance men in American independent rock. Superchunk gets to do a two-record set with an old-fashioned gatefold sleeve because two of its members run the band's label. They've released six albums and God-knows-how-many singles in just five years. Superchunk occupies a key seat in the American indie pantheon, one that places them in such demand that they had to put together a double-length compilation to collect all the songs and singles they've tossed out.

Not only is Superchunk prolific, but as the 19 tunes on *Incidental Music* make clear, the band is consistent. On song after song, the walls of guitar noise thrown up by McCaughan and second guitarist Jim Wilbur stand on a solid foundation laid by the rapidly pulsing bass playing of Laura Ballance and the spare, muscular drumming of Jon Wurster. Above it all, McCaughan shouts to be heard.

"I think it would be a mistake to try and force Superchunk to do things that are weirder than what it already does," McCaughan says, alluding to the journalist's tendency to want more than what's on the surface. "It's a four-piece rock band. I think we're really good at that. Sometimes I wish we weren't so middle-of-the-road with the format, but the focus is on the songs, really. I don't think anyone's gonna do anything really revolutionary at this point in music, especially this genre of music. So long as the songs are good, and you're doing an old thing an interesting way, that's what counts."

YOU HAVE TO STEP outside of Superchunk's closed circle to get near its center. Otherwise you end up with interview tapes full of crap like the stuff I got when I had lunch with the band at the Aurora, a modestly upscale pasta restaurant in the small town of Carrboro, adjacent to Chapel Hill. The town is home to several key elements of the Chapel Hill indie scene, including the Merge office, Mammoth Records (which sits above the Aurora in Carr Mill Mall, a converted cotton mill), and Cat's Cradle, the scene's flagship club. As the greatest hits of 18th century European classical music played in the background, the members of Superchunk talked about touring and made jokes about groupies, Johnny Depp, Brillo pads and digeridoos. That was about it.

Ballance occasionally attempted to cut through the bullshit and give straight answers, but even she made it abundantly clear we would not be straying into any open emotional territory. "I get mad about interviews a lot of times," she said. "People ask me bad questions sometimes, things that are personal and offensive and nobody else's business." So much for asking how it felt for Ballance and McCaughan to continue working, playing and touring together after their romance ended.

I didn't get much in the way of substance out of Superchunk until I asked McCaughan to come back to the Merge office and talk one on one. Here, he gives me a concise, comparatively direct overview of his and Supechunk's musical career. "Unless a band starts to get bored, the longer they play together, the better they interact with each other," he says. "There's always the chance of getting burned out, I think, from playing in the same band for so long, but at the same time there are rewarding things. There's something comfortable and familar about playing with the same people that allows you not to think about it so much and just play."

Laura Cantrell, who played with McCaughan in the late '80s New York City band Bricks, confirms McCaughan's need for a family-like musical environment. "He doesn't come from the hired-

superchunk

hand school of music-making," says Cantrell, who now hosts "The Radio Thrift Shop" on WFMU in East Orange, New Jersey. "The people involved in bands with Mac were often people he really dug and loved."

GET PAST THE EXCITEMENT of Superchunk's music and the band's story is fairly boring. Ballance majored in anthropology and geology at UNC-Chapel Hill. She joined Superchunk after her then-boyfriend McCaughan taught her to play bass. Wilbur, an old friend of McCaughan, came down from Connecticut to join Superchunk after the band's original guitarist quit in 1990. Wurster came to North Carolina from Pennsylvania as a teenager in 1985 to play drums, performing with the Right Profile and the Accelerators before replacing Superchunk's original drummer (and namesake), Chuck "Chunk" Garrison.

McCaughan was born in Ft. Lauderdale and moved to Durham, North Carolina, at 13. His father, Ralph, a Duke University staff lawyer who plays jazz and likes the Rolling Stones, took Mac to his first concert — Molly Hatchet, if you have to ask — in the late '70s. Both of McCaughan's parents have wholeheartedly supported their son's music career since his early days with bands like the Slushpuppies and Wwax, which grew out of the mid-'80s hardcore scene in the nearby state capital of Raleigh. McCaughan went on to Columbia University where he majored in history. Today he presides over Superchunk and Merge with businesslike efficiency.

"I don't know when he sleeps," his father says. "He's always been a workaholic. Just very hyper, going at it at 100 miles an hour. Everything, whether it was school activities, or recreation, or whatever. He puts in the hours." It was the same in college, says WFMU's Cantrell, who was a classmate of McCaughan's at Columbia. "I was always amazed at how Mac could be involved in all this other stuff and be a good student too," she says. "The papers always went in on time. He had his shit together."

Apart from the hype that descended on Superchunk in 1992 — when, during the post-Nirvana feeding frenzy, many major labels tried and failed to sign the band — the most dramatic event in the group's history was McCaughan and Ballance's breakup.

That happened about two years ago, and seems to have little effect on the way the band operates today, other than a loaded glare or two across the lunch table. In addition to playing in the band together, McCaughan and Ballance continue to take care of business at Merge, the label they co-founded in 1989. Still, the breakup did fuel some of the lyrics on Superchunk's best album, 1994's *Foolish*. "One good minute would last me a whole year," McCaughan sings in "The Five Part," adeptly conveying the way time seem to slow down during an emotional crisis.

It was actually the group's second major split. The first one came in 1992 — when they decided to leave the ultra-hip Matador Records after the release of *On the Mouth*, their third Matador album. Superchunk's contract was up, and the members didn't want to be on anyone else's label, even with promises of big bucks from the majors. "We've dealt with as few assholes and slimy people as possible in this business, and we haven't given up control of anything that we wanted control over," McCaughan says. "We don't owe anybody tons of money. We're making a living. We don't have to work day jobs. So that's nice."

SUPERCHUNK MAY, as they once sang, be "Cooler than you/And you know it's true," but the band has not made it on 'zine appeal or indie credibility alone; they've made it on their music. McCaughan and his enterprises embody a staunchly indie ethic that means as much to its cult as Ian MacKaye's Fugazi and that band's Dischord label. That's where the real drama and excitement come into play. Listen to the band's sublime sound or attend one of its sizzling live performances and you'll understand the hyperbole surrounding Superchunk.

McCaughan just shrugs. "If it sounds intense," he drily replies, "the only thing I can think is that maybe the experience that generates the lyrics, combined with the volume of a loud rock band, may sort of imply intensity. I hope there's intensity in the delivery, but we don't sit around and stew about our songs or have heavy practices."

Peyton Reed, a Los Angeles filmmaker and UNC graduate who directed or co-directed three of Superchunk's videos, feels too much emphasis is placed on Superchunk's identity as an indie band.

superchunk

"There has been so much written about how Superchunk have stayed indie, and I think it's great that they have," says Reed, whose video for "Driveway To Driveway" is an ingenious black-and-white takeoff on *The Philadelphia Story*. "But I don't listen to Superchunk because they stayed indie; I listen to them because I really like the music."

A lot of people do. The band's sound is the aural equivalent of a Tootsie Pop: hard and crunchy on the outside, soft and chewy on the inside. And it's landed the band everywhere from the cover of England's *New Musical Express* to MTV's *Beavis & Butt-head* — who argue whether the bass player has boobs before realizing that they're watching a bunch of puppets. McCaughan freely admits his debts to earlier bands that mixed punk and pop, like the Buzzcocks and Generation X, and has long pledged allegiance to such New Zealand popsters as the Chills, along with plenty of way-obscure American groups.

But two things separate Superchunk from the indie herd. The first is McCaughan's ability to write lyrically acute songs with soaring melodies and memorable hooks. "We used to call him King of Catchy," Cantrell says. "Whether it was a quote-unquote serious song or not, it was super fuckin' catchy." The band's second distinguishing trait is an emotional center in the music that conveys a sense of vulnerability beneath a veneer of fun. More than anything else — from "Slack Motherfucker" to "Shallow End" — Superchunk has managed to reconcile for the '90s two of the dominant strains of '80s post-punk: the lyricism and rush of the Replacements with the dissonant guitar noise and fuck-you attitude of Sonic Youth.

It's all in the music, though. On the surface, McCaughan would like for you to believe he's about as ordinary as they come; that the most mundane things spark his creativity. He may be right.

"Something has to be powerful on some level, either positive or negative, to inspire you to do it," he says. "It's fun to write songs and play music, and that's an intensity in itself."

May 1995

the flaming lips
THE RIDE OF THEIR LIVES

BY **GINA ARNOLD**

THAT DAY IT RAINED.
The clouds clotted up suddenly and soon were dripping steadily onto the blasted gray surface of Central California's Highway 99. It was 3 p.m. in early October, and we were on our way to the Fresno County Fair to see the Flaming Lips.

It just seemed like the right thing to do. In the same spirit that people went to Egypt to see the Grateful Dead play before the great pyramids, we went to Fresno's Big Fair because we found ourselves inexplicably attracted to the setting. The Flaming Lips have a certain carnival atmosphere that belies its loud metal origins — an atmosphere that's only enhanced by the smell of dead corn dogs and live pigs, and tents housing a petting zoo, a freak show and the World's Largest Living Horse.

The band's album titles alone are like a verbal hall of mirrors, reflecting their warped, trippy pop: *In a Priest Driven Ambulance, Telepathic Surgery* and last year's *Transmissions From the Satellite Heart*. The songs themselves, like "The Spontaneous Combustion of John" or "Maximum Dream For Evel Knievel," allude to strange characters who might be refugees from some perverse rock'n'roll sideshow.

So we drove through the rain, past acres of boxy beige subdivisions, before coming upon a magnificent sight: whirling across a headache gray sky were the giddy pink lights of the ferris wheel. Enhanced by the steady drizzle, it created a wonderfully blurry glow in the dusk.

The Flaming Lips took the stage at 7:30 amid amplifiers wrapped in multicolored Christmas lights. Singer Wayne Coyne's face appeared on a giant video screen framed in a halo of sparkling

flaming lips

pink and green and yellow lights. If you squinted, he looked positively magical, as if hovering, Good Fairy-like, over the entire state.

After Coyne delivers a winding tale about a father saving his toddler from under his neighbor's car by single-handedly lifting the auto off of the child — the point being how love can inspire superhuman strength — the Lips launch into "Superhumans":

*Once in a while the time will come
to surrender everything you have to give
I would have given up for you...*

HOURS LATER, after the show, as rain continues to batter the big top, the Flaming Lips pose patiently for photos in various Wim Wenders-meets-Tom Waits locations somewhere among the corn dog stands, an Orange Treet booth, and the pig racing event. The sky is full of shooting stars: it's all the twirling lights from the kind of abusive, sick-making swing rides they don't bother to bring to big cities anymore. Howling over our wind-blown heads, the dreadful noise of the headlining band, Candlebox, fills the sky: "I didn't mean to hurt you, but I did, but I did, but I did, but I did..."

Meanwhile, 'round and 'round the merry-go-round the Flaming Lips go, and each time they twirl by, people stop to gawk. "What are they, some kind of a group?" someone asks skeptically. Then, inevitably, "Are they on MTV?"

"Yes, but they were on the Lollapalooza tour too," I say to their blank looks. Apparently, the word "Lollapalooza" hasn't penetrated King's County. The only other thing I can think to say is, "And Beavis and Butt-head hate them!"

It starts raining even harder. We all blunder to the backstage room, which is full of cigarette smoke. Candlebox is still onstage, while back here the Lips sit around silently swigging from a whiskey bottle and looking pained. Although the Fresno date is only the fourth on this tour, the Lips are feeling a little daunted by the thought of doing 60 more.

"I'm just going to drink a lot," shrugs drummer Steven Drozd.

"And we're going to buy some great Christmas presents when we get home," adds preternaturally silent guitarist Ron Jones, sucking down his third cone of cotton candy.

Later, on a brief walk through the sheep pens, where some of Fresno's finest sheep are dropping bloody babies every few minutes, the almost pathologically friendly Coyne philosophizes hopefully about the point of doing all this. "It's not so bad, really," he insists. "I prefer this to doing heavy metal crowds, like Stone Temple Pilots. Those people were completely boneheaded. But these kids could easily have good record collections five years from now."

"Anyway, it's not meant for us," he continues. "It's like *Barney*, or religion — if you don't need it, you don't need it."

THAT THE FLAMING LIPS are here tonight entertaining 10,000-plus lukewarm Candlebox fans is due to a confluence of circumstance peculiar to this exact moment in music biz history: the Lips have credibility, which has become a sellable commodity.

Though well-received critically, last year's *Transmissions of the Satellite Heart* (Warner) was released with relatively little fanfare. Always more of a road band than a recorded act, a recent increase in the Lips' accessibility and songwriting skill — combined with a decrease in the kind of horrid sonic abuse that riddles earlier records like *In a Priest Driven Ambulance* (Restless, 1990) and *Hit To Death In the Future Head* (Warner, 1992) — went virtually unnoticed by media outlets. Moreover, since the band had signed to a major in 1990, just prior to Nirvana's massive impact on label dealings, Warner seemed to have forgotten assets it already had on the roster in its subsequent haste to sign the "next Nirvana."

In some ways the Lips suggest the mutant result of some sonic DNA experiment, recombining grunge with some old acid test. Like Nirvana, the music they make is infused with a potent pop sensibility, gobs of clangor and some severe mood swings. But where Nirvana's music coalesced in a punk rock matrix, the Lips are locked in a distorted, Floydian vortex. Making music that is harsh and rocky with lurid, hummable interludes, the group may ultimately be too weird and elusive for mass consumption — which may explain why chart success has given their career path wide berth.

Despite a minor hit with 1993's "She Don't Use Jelly," a small but rabid following around the country, and a ten-year history of lineup changes and indie label nightmares, no one seemed to be paying any attention. The band's ten-day stint on the second stage of last summer's Lollapalooza, however, radically changed the Lips' position in the zeitgeist. They were the all-out favorites of critics, fans and other bands, often joined onstage by members of the Bad Seeds and L7. A nerve-wracking performance at the Reading Festival in late August solidified the band's position among its peers; even the Counting Crows started their own shows with "She Don't Use Jelly."

After Lollapalooza, while the group's cred-factor was having babies, the Lips were planning a fall tour, headlining 1,000-seat clubs. When the Lips were offered the Candlebox tour — 60 dates at $2,500 each, far exceeding what they could earn in many cities on their own — they agreed. Credibility is an aspect of their career that the Lips have always downplayed; besides, they had already opened for such acts as the Soup Dragons, Stone Temple Pilots and Tool with no adverse effect on their psyches.

One night backstage at Detroit's Pine Knob Arena, Coyne speculated dispiritedly that the Lips' popularity at Lollapalooza was due to the fact that they opposed main stage act George Clinton and Funkadelic, a band which lots of midwestern kids did not have the patience for. Whatever the origin of the Lips' success with the kids in Detroit — who mashed against the stage some 5,000 strong, bodysurfing throughout the set — it contrasts with the reaction of the rain-soaked kids here at the Fresno Fair.

ONCE UPON A TIME, in 1985, the Flaming Lips drove for three days straight from Oklahoma City to San Francisco to play their first out-of-town gig at the I-Beam. I was at that gig and I hated them. Steeped in the music of the Replacements, Soul Asylum, the Minutemen, the dBs and the Feelies, I thought the Lips were too hippie-ish, too psychedelic, too bombastic; they were four country bumpkins who had somehow jumbled their Led Zeppelin with their Hüsker Dü. They even played Pink Floyd's "Wish You Were Here" for an encore. I was annoyed.

"But why?" Coyne asks plaintively. It's ten years later and we're sitting in the band's large, comfortable van, the likes of which would not have been carrying the Flaming Lips back in those days. "I mean, I'm sure we did the song badly, but why did just the fact that we did it bother you so much?"

"I don't know — because it was from the wrong era of rock, and I had no sense of humor about it. And it was also too long. I guess I didn't know if it was meant to be funny or a tribute or what."

"Oh, both," says Coyne. "It's like this" — he picks a tape from the van's cassette box — "it's got, let's see, the Au Pairs 'Heading For Michelle' next to Ghoulie Brothers; David Bowie next to Nick Cave; bits of *Reservoir Dogs*. To me, it's all music. I don't care where it comes from. I don't know how anyone can do that — go, 'Well, you're not thinking the way I do, so I can't like where you come from.'

"Back when we began, me and Michael [Ivy, the bassist], we'd be the guys who'd bring the P.A. to gigs in Norman and Oklahoma City," he continues. "We were the P.A. at the first Black Flag show. We did it for free, because we wanted to see the bands. We'd be the only guys with hair, you know? We weren't stupid, we knew we had long hair and that those people didn't like people with long hair. But we'd look around and go, 'We don't care, the music rocks.' We liked it. And I always thought, well, how weird! I mean, how can people who like music say, 'This is the friend and this is the enemy?'"

In Oklahoma City, a person interested in punk rock did not have the luxury of drawing such distinctions; this is the type of city, after all, where the alternative newspaper has only two sections in its personals ads: "Man Seeking Woman" and vice versa. Oklahoma City is the type of place, Coyne says, where "you have to have a car. In St. Louis you could take a cab to a bar. But I think there's maybe only a couple cabs in Oklahoma City. There's just no use for them."

For all its drawbacks, Oklahoma City is also along U.S. 40. "It's one of those spots everybody has to come through," Coyne explains. "Me, I always wanted to be in a band, but I could never figure out how. I saw the Who and was like, 'Wow, how do you get to do *that* for a living? Fuck!' It wasn't until we saw the hardcore shows that we figured out how to do it. We'd say to ourselves, 'These guys pulled up in a van. We could do that. These guys have little amps. Same sort of amps we have at the house. They just do it all themselves.' We were like, 'I see! That's cool!' And we talked to them and said, 'How'd you guys make records?' And they said, 'Saved up money and did it.' And we'd go, 'Oh, I see! We could do that!'

"Before that, I thought you had to belong to some club or something," he adds. "We really wanted to get out of Oklahoma City and see the world, we just had no idea how to do it."

SINCE THEY LEARNED HOW to get out and do it themselves, the Lips have made seven records, four for the hapless Restless and three for Warner, including last year's wonderful *Transmissions* and the more recent *Providing Needs For Your Balloons* EP, which includes the new song "Bad Days" and an unplugged performance of Smog's "Chosen One." In the process, the Lips have transmogrified from the lengthy, psychedelic jam band they used to be — a combo which, as Coyne points out proudly, was equally at ease playing Black Sabbath or the Birthday Party — into a thoughtful, tuneful, carnival-like mix of the surreal and the basic; a band with chops and thoughts alike. I think they now sound like Mott the Hoople or *Something Else*-era-Kinks, though Coyne says he doesn't listen much to either of those bands.

"I've gotten to be a better singer," he admits. "Little by little, I can do different things. Plus," he adds hesitantly, "I've learned that rock has to have a reason for all that hairshaking and buttshaking and shit."

Alas, the reason is still somewhat unspeakable — like the name of God in Hebrew. But you can find it in songs like "Turn It On" and "Oh My Pregnant Head," in "Halloween On the Barbary Coast," and especially in the poignant "Bad Days," whose refrain beseeches you, Ray Davies-like, to hang on for better days.

Nowadays Coyne owns his own home with a lawn, three dogs and a truck on Oklahoma City's north side. Although Flaming Lips albums sell about 50,000 copies each, low by major label standards, he feels assured of a future in music. "When you first start out, you have different reasons for doing it," he says. "Your reasons change so much after a while. But I sort of feel like, what I do, I could probably still do till I'm 70. I could still be a person who writes interesting songs from my own perspective that would still be interesting to hear, rather than just be in some clique or fashion, or cool thing of the moment.

"We've been really lucky," he adds. "If we'd had any success — meaning money or respect, I guess — when we were playing 'Wish You Were Here,' it would have ruined us. Really, it's only through luck and not having success that all the bad elements that surrounded us eventually disappeared. There's no reason to be around us unless you just love the music. So we're surrounded by people who love us no matter what we do. And that's good, because earlier we had some people who just sucked. And it would have sucked to have gone through life with them."

THE FLAMING LIPS PULL into San Jose late, having lost their equipment truck to a detour somewhere near Gilroy. Tonight's gig is at a college basketball court which has been cut in half by a giant black curtain due to low ticket sales. The show's promoter, Michael Bailey, shakes his head as he surveys the crowd: "I can't understand it. The Candlebox record is double-platinum, and we sold out the Fillmore; all the sales came from San Jose outlets." Could this be the beginning of the end for Candlebox? Could the past two weeks, during which the band has been perched at the top of the charts, have been the high point of Candlebox's collective life?

It's certainly possible, perhaps even probable, since the group's sound, unlike that of the Flaming Lips, is not exactly durable. Moreover, during this same period, a shakeup of major label executives has kicked off the slow process of shuffling out some of the post-Nirvana signing-spree bands, the ones on majors who don't really belong there. In the future, the latter part of 1994 might be considered a watershed period — a giant pause for breath.

At 8 p.m., the Lips take the stage to palpable boredom among the ranks. But by mid-set the audience begins to wake up. During "Superhumans" and "Jelly" the crowd is positively perky, and by the time the band goes into "Under Pressure" a half an hour into the show, the throng of Candlebox fans is bopping up and down.

I turn to Michael Bailey sadly: "Michael, how are the Lips *ever* going to get big?"

"Like Soul Asylum," he conjectures. "By default."

Suddenly, I see it: bad bands felled by indifference and defeat, bad bands falling by the wayside, all of them depressed and debauched, hating each other and the lives they lead. One by one they drop off the face of the earth while the Flaming Lips soldier on. Ventura, L.A., San Diego, Vegas; Tucson, Santa Fe, El Paso, Omaha... If they can stick it out long enough, the Flaming Lips might eventually stand alone on the top of the heap.

November 1995

daniel johnston
STARRY EYES

BY **JASON COHEN**

TEN YEARS AGO Daniel Johnston roamed the streets of Austin, Texas, passing out cassettes of his homemade songcraft to just about anyone he encountered. Someday, he told people, his music was going to make him famous. Really famous. It was beyond a simple wish that people would hear his songs — Johnston wanted the glory, the adulation, even the pitfalls of his idols, the Beatles.

So it came as a surprise to everyone but Johnston when he earned a slot on the 1986 all-Austin episode of MTV's *The Cutting Edge*. Yet on the night the segment aired, Johnston was confined in the Austin State Hospital, having attacked his first manager during one of his periodic bouts of delusion.

Since emerging in Austin with his fistful of tapes, he has been a celebrated denizen of the underground, with a particularly impassioned following among fellow songwriters and musicians, from locals Glass Eye and Poison 13 to national acts like Half Japanese, Firehose and Sonic Youth. Dozens of artists have covered his work, celebrating what they consider his essential genius: quavering, disarmingly honest songs that are memorable, intelligent and prodigiously crafted.

FOR ALL ITS POWER and singularity, however, Johnston's music has not been his sole drawing card. A manic-depressive who is gentle, funny, good-natured and even sharp when at ease, he is given to spectacular flights of fancy and frightening violent spells. The tape that first brought him wide recognition, *Hi, How Are You?*, was recorded during a nervous breakdown in 1983. To many, Johnston is simply "that crazy guy," notorious mainly for his bizarre, ultimately tragic adventures that invariably lead to his confinement in a hospital or being left in the care of his aging parents.

daniel johnston

Yet more than a decade and countless crack-ups, arrests and hospital stays later, Johnston is, at least in his own mind, closer to fame than ever before. He has signed with Atlantic Records, and his debut for the label, *Fun*, marks the first time his work has been presented with full-fledged arrangements and better-than-average fidelity. To Johnston, it's a long-awaited opportunity to earn a living from his art. "It's a lot different being in the big time," he says. "It means I'm not making little records anymore. It's a big deal. It's great."

It could also be the worst thing that has ever happened to Johnston, because his life and career seem to mirror the lockstep pattern of his illness. Excessive attention has almost always sent him over the edge, with the best of times being inevitable precursors to the worst. A 1988 recording session in Maryland with Jad Fair was followed by an incident in which Johnston chased a woman out her window because he thought she had the devil in her. Flying home to West Virginia after playing the 1990 Austin Music Awards, his erratic behavior forced the pilot — his father — to distress-land their plane in Arkansas. For fans and friends, the release of Johnston's first recordings in three years is cause for joy. It's what comes after that's worrisome.

IF YOU MOVED Waller, Texas, about 40 minutes to the south, it could be a suburb of Houston. As it stands, the little town's welcome sign identifies itself as something else entirely: "The Gateway To Clean Living." Daniel Johnston, the man who often speaks of communing with the devil, lives here with his parents, in a house nestled a few miles off U.S. 290 and within walking distance of the local Church of Christ that his family attends.

Until 1991 the Johnstons' home was outside of New Cumberland, West Virginia, where Daniel, the youngest of five, was raised. He migrated to Texas in the mid-'80s, but returned home after his first hospital stay in 1986. Meanwhile, several of his older siblings had also been living in Texas. So when Bill and Mabel Johnston retired, they decided to move closer to their progeny, taking up residence in a ranch-style house in Waller with a spacious backyard and a twin garage.

Imagine the inherent awkwardness of a 34-year-old rock'n'roll-playing son living at home in rural America with two highly religious, septuagenarian parents. Factor in Johnston's mental state, bullheadedness and eternal adolescence, and the situation is even more potent. Yet aside from the bleak environs of a public mental health institution, home is the only place the singer's behavior can be controlled, if only because his parents make sure he sticks to his regimen of medication. "Yeah, I take quite a few pills," Johnston says. "Keeps my moods down."

His parents are less successful at restricting their son's junk-food diet. Johnston receives the highest allowable dosage of lithium because the huge amount of soda he drinks flushes it out of his system. As a result of the combination of excess sugar and his drugs' side effects, he's progressed over the years from gawky to stocky to paunchy to overweight.

Johnston's parents have given him half the garage as a music area and bedroom. The space is strewn with comic books and memorabilia from his various records. The walls are littered with snapshots and pictures — one of Jesus from *Jesus Christ Superstar*, the cover of *Hi, How Are You?*, clips from Captain America comics by Jack Kirby, a picture of Casper the Friendly Ghost, sheet music for "Rudolph the Red-Nosed Reindeer" and photos of Johnston with Butthole Surfer Paul Leary, the producer of *Fun*. "Yeah, it's great here," Johnston says. "I just sit and daydream all day, smoke cigarettes and write songs."

JOHNSTON HAS AN OLD Wings album cranked up as his mother announces that visitors have arrived. Immediately aware that there's a car to take him away from the house, he suggests going out in search of french fries. When we stop at Bruno's Bar-B-Q in Waller, he orders his fries and a soda. As he eats — and throughout the rest of the day — Johnston chain-smokes Doral Menthol 100s in disrupted bursts, nervously stubbing out and relighting each cigarette four or five times before finishing it.

Johnston's mental problems often lead people to believe, mistakenly, that his talent is the mark of a primitive. In fact, on a purely musical level, his gift is a wholly natural one, divorced from the demons that occupy his mind and his lyrics.

daniel johnston

"He's got this amazing, raw, untouchable talent," says *Austin Chronicle* editor Louis Black, who has known Johnston since the early '80s. "One of the reasons I respond to him in a real way is it's like responding to Muddy Waters. You can't come up with an idea so abrupt and obscene that American culture can't homogenize it, make it its own in some period of time. But Daniel can't be tainted. Daniel doesn't know how to sell out and be a normal person, and that's his saving grace. What is pure about Daniel is still pure."

His childlike demeanor can make Johnston seem simple, but he's actually quick-witted and self-aware — about his music, about his craziness, about what's expected of him as a semi-public figure. Stuck with total recall of his deluded mental excursions, he'll tell you, matter-of-factly, about a dream he had in which "everybody on the earth wanted to kill me," or how "a lot of my other selves walked out of my body and did a lot of things I was surprised at." Once, he explains, "I believed that the Beatles evolved into roaches, and John and George would come out and scurry about when we got our smoke break in the mental hospital." Then, just as matter-of-factly, he admits, "I've just been talking weird, trying to make things interesting."

Johnston's songwriting is equally as self-conscious. He's written dozens of beautiful, innocent songs in which he expresses his unrequited love for Laurie, a woman he met back in West Virginia. Yet in "Grievances," one of the first songs he ever wrote, Johnston declares, "If I can't be a lover then I'll be a pest," rendering his love from afar at once real and unreal, genuine and neurotic. "The biggest nightmare," he says, "was that I'd been writing songs about her all the time. Then I saw this special on TV about this guy who had been plaguing this woman, and they said, 'Why are you bugging this woman all the time?' He goes [*drops his voice and makes a grim face*], 'I love her.' It blew my mind. I thought: Is that me? Is that what it's like for her?"

Johnston can be just as savvy about the relationship between his problems and his career, having described himself as "a monkey in a zoo" long before he'd ever seen the inside of a hospital or heard the mockery of a skeptical club audience. Still, Johnston exploits himself just as well as any outsider ever could, even as he documents the sweat and confusion that his self-pandering causes.

"Well you heard about the time I was in the insane asylum," he sings in "A Lonely Song," which appears on one of his self-released live tapes, "And you read the magazines/I've been wounded by folklore/But I bet you never knew what I went through/And what I had to do just to bring you/A lonely song."

Johnston is lonely in Waller. When he was in Austin he knew dozens of people, and even the various hospitals there offered comrades-in-arms and sometimes even the occasional girlfriend. "It's kind of fun to get in the hospital," he says. "There's a bunch of girls and a bunch of guys and they're all crazy. It's like *The Twilight Zone*. It's just like going down to the Beach" — the Austin nightclub where Johnston first played — "where everybody was crazy." In Waller he has no one. The only time he's been with a friend recently was when Paul Leary hauled some instruments and a portable studio into the garage to record *Fun*.

For Johnston, all the new attention surrounding *Fun* is sweet revenge. When he first began making his primitive recordings in his parent's West Virginia basement, his mother harangued him mercilessly as his little tape recorder caught her every word. Now, the songs that bugged her are part of an important body of work. And the music he's recorded in his parent's new house is on a major label.

JOHNSTON WAS BROUGHT to Atlantic by Yves Beauvais, a vice president of A&R whose specialty is jazz and reissues. "I'm used to dealing with proven jazz artists and the cream of the crop of the Atlantic catalog — Aretha Franklin, Ray Charles, Ornette Coleman — people who have an immense body of work behind them," Beauvais says. "When I ran into Daniel's music I felt like I was running into a similar body of work. I first bought one cassette, then two, then three, then four, then all of them. I thought this guy was an absolute genius. His great melodicism, and his use of everyday language in a very poetic and appealing way reminds me of Hank Williams."

Beauvais first heard Johnston via "Love Defined," a dance piece by Bill T. Jones set to several of Johnston's compositions and performed worldwide. In 1993 Beauvais brought Johnston's poorly recorded material to the attention of his fellow Atlantic staffers, and presented it without fanfare or legend. Somewhat to his surprise, he met with no hesitation from his superiors.

At the time, Johnston was on the verge of signing to another Time Warner label, Elektra. Much to the aggravation of the label's lawyers, his longtime manager, Jeff Tartakov, had even ensured the contract reflected Johnston's condition. Ordinarily artists are contractually compelled to produce a certain amount of work and cooperate with promotional activities, including touring, in exchange for seeing the work released. Because such activity and attention are not good for Johnston, he was exempted.

"When he gets on these highs it's scary," Tartakov says. "People would say, 'I'm sorry that he feels so bad,' and I'd try to explain that the problem is actually that he's feeling too good."

Unfortunately Johnston was going through precisely one of those periods during the Elektra negotiations. From fall of 1992, when Johnston played three rapturously received shows in Texas, until spring of 1993, he had been in the state hospital as often as he'd been home. He'd been missing for several days. At one point, he lit his mattress on fire and then deposited it, smoldering, in an outside Dumpster. And he had clashed with police. "Yeah, I got in a bunch of trouble," Johnston says. "I beat up a bunch of cops and went to jail and then they put me in the mental hospital." He laughs. "Man, I knocked those guys around."

Clearly it was no time for Johnston to be putting his name to legal documents. But he also needed to sign a management contract with Tartakov, as the two had been working without a written agreement for several years. Terry Tolkin, who was trying to sign Johnston to Elektra, did not want to move forward on the deal without Tartakov's involvement, feeling the singer could not be controlled apart from his manager's participation.

In fact, no one can control Johnston. But Tartakov had been attempting to do so for seven years, tirelessly serving as advocate, banker, friend and babysitter. After years in which Johnston would harass or fire Tartakov routinely, only to change his mind moments later, Johnston suddenly decided he didn't want to sign the contract, claiming Tartakov was ripping him off by giving away tapes and drawings that he should have been selling. In reality, Tartakov was doling out money to Johnston like an allowance, while keeping some revenue for himself to pay back the money he laid out. It was a standard managerial task, really, and one that could be abused; yet no one in Austin who knows the Johnston-Tartakov relationship believes Tartakov is anything less than honest. When I wrote about Johnston for the *Austin Chronicle* in 1992, and asked to keep a drawing provided as an illustration, Tartakov told me I would have to pay $75 just like everyone else.

The situation with Tartakov did not resolve itself. The Elektra deal eventually went away, and one day Johnston walked into the offices of the Austin indie label Amazing, and gave a tape to staffer Tom Gimbel. A few months later he asked Gimbel to be his manager. For a while Gimbel tried to mediate for Tartakov, but Daniel was resolute. Johnston now credits Gimbel with getting him the Atlantic deal "within two weeks," when in fact it was something Tartakov had been aware of long ago.

SO NOW DANIEL JOHNSTON records for Atlantic, label of Led Zeppelin, Phil Collins and the Stone Temple Pilots, and still lives at home. It's a picture of relative stability. But Tartakov warns that it would be easy "to mistake stability for wellness." Tartakov should know, because he, along with most everyone else close to Johnston, has been guilty of making that mistake himself. Atlantic is aware of how precarious the situation is, and the label is doing what it can by keeping him off the road and limiting his interviews. Still, it's easy to recognize the familiar tone of optimistic denial accompanying his care and passion when Yves Beauvais says, "I'm hoping this situation enables Daniel to get better and be better. Hopefully, he'll remain healthy and get healthier, with better medical care, and an improved self-image.

"We're giving him a chance that he's never had before," he adds. "We've already assessed his high creative ability, and our job is to find musicians and make their work heard. Daniel is dying for that chance. Should we not give him that opportunity?"

It's the eternal, unanswerable question. How do you give work like Johnston's the exposure it deserves while preserving the artist's health and integrity? Especially when the artist, for all his talent and brains, wants the exposure more than anyone else, but can't be held entirely responsible for his actions? No matter how carefully people proceed, Johnston will find ways to blow things up. As usual, he acknowledges this in his work. In "Going Down" he sings, "To think of all/All the times/I felt so low/Every time I got feeling better/I got naive/And thought that it would stay."

Says Louis Black, "You get into an awkward question of what is the responsibility to the artist and the art. To both, in a sense, you have an obligation to promote it. Inherent in that is, you're probably going to destroy the person. But where do you have the right to decide that, 'No, we're not going to do this'? Daniel's spent years thinking about music as a career. He can't handle the fame, but I don't think he can handle the rejection either.

"Everything feeds his sickness, the good stuff and the bad stuff," Black continues. "He'll go further and deeper than anybody else. He'll just push himself off the side of the building and say, 'I don't care what happens.'" Black believes that as long as Johnston continues to respond to his notoriety in his usual fashion, "he's going to end up dead. I just hope he doesn't hurt a lot of people in the process."

But for now, Daniel Johnston sits in his garage in Waller, smoking his menthol cigarettes, drinking his soda, and thinking about the double-album he wants to make next.

November 1994

the jesus lizard

PUNK AND DISORDERLY

BY **LORRAINE ALI**

DAVID YOW WRITHES, CONVULSES and foams at the mouth. It's a hot and sweaty night at the Whisky in West Hollywood, and the Jesus Lizard frontman is captivating a crowd of shirtless, drunk guys and curious industry types. He jumps to his feet, teeters on the edge of the stage and whacks several audience members on the head as if christening them. Wearing a pair of sharp, Cuban-heeled boots, the short, compact singer skids and slips haphazardly across the beer-slicked stage as the band seethes with fervent concoctions of nihilistic noise and twisted, driving rhythms. Yow's beady eyes scan the room with reptilian coldness just before he steps off the elevated stage and into the densely packed audience. It looks as though he's walking on water.

The singer ends this miraculous moment by kicking a member of the audience square in the face, jumping back onstage and blurting, "Yeah, fuck you too."

ROCK'N'ROLL HASN'T FELT this dangerous in a long time. The Jesus Lizard actually delivers the menace and mania that the music thrived on from its start but lost over years of pasteurization. While acts such as the Rollins Band pedal dysfunction and Nine Inch Nails packages paranoia, the Jesus Lizard turns the universal feel of primal distress and terror into excruciatingly good punk rock. But there's an important emotional yin and yang to the Chicago quartet that's often overlooked.

A few months after the Whisky show, Yow and bassist David Sims are waxing philosophical at the Powerhouse, an unassuming Hollywood dive nestled among a string of dingy storefronts. The tanked regulars surrounding them at the bar look like melting wax figures as they slouch lifelessly over cheap tap beers. When the

the jesus lizard

jukebox in the back corner segues into a warped version of the soppy '60s soundtrack hit "Born Free," Yow gets pensive. "This movie made me cry," he says, recalling the scene that touched his pre-pubescent heart. "Remember when they set the lion free — free as the wind blows?"

Wearing jeans and cowboy boots, the 34-year-old Yow fidgets in his seat, leaning forward, crossing his legs or messing with his thin brown hair. Sims, 30, possesses a more passive, Zen-like posture, his blue-green eyes thoughtful and his composure content. Both stand about 5-feet-5-inches tall, and carry themselves with little menace. In fact, when Yow snaps out of his *Born Free* daze, he begins reminiscing about his wedding two years ago. "The plans were such a pain," he offers as Sims, who had witnessed the pink-pastel mayhem, nods in agreement like a supportive bridesmaid.

Sims takes thoughtful sips from his Bud longneck and attempts to explain the fundamental dualism that exists within the Jesus Lizard. "Based solely on our music, you don't know who we are personally," he says. "Although it does reflect a side of us, we're actually some of the nicest, most well-adjusted guys you'll ever meet."

Yow looks amused. "We're mean, dangerous and crazy?" He laughs. "Well, Dave and I are little, Duane is old and weak, and Mac weighs about 30 pounds. Look out, here we come!"

The band members' conflicting personas repel and attract, drawing mixed but strong reactions. While England's fickle *Melody Maker* calls the Jesus Lizard a "bucket of shit" and advises them to "please decompose," fellow bands such as Hole and Sonic Youth have referred to Yow and company as inspirations. The group's latest album, *Down* (Touch & Go), continues to provoke such wide-ranging responses, as the Lizard delivers disturbed, churning melodies with Yow's jittery, high-strung vocals flailing over the top. It's feverishly daunting, with just enough catchy hooks to suck you into the melee.

THE POWERHOUSE PATRONS are now swaying to Peggy Lee's suicidal "Is That All There Is?" as a homeless man from nearby Hollywood Boulevard wanders onto the worn carpet that runs the length of the bar. Sims, still attempting to extract the Lizard's essence, continues. "In particular songs of ours, I can imagine a sinister quality. But in playing the songs, I see too many of the wires and mirrors behind it to get the evocative thing in us. I don't really know what it is."

As a listener, the answer seems easy. Where Nine Inch Nails is like a scary but ultimately safe amusement park, the Jesus Lizard slaps out pure, raw distress with no controllable, video game feel. "We're a lot less image-conscious than someone like NIN," says Yow. "Anything you get from us comes from our music, because we don't put it across in makeup or marketing. I think that superficial stuff diminishes it anyway. People know that Trent Reznor doesn't act like that at home. Nobody buys that."

The Jesus Lizard — which includes drummer Mac McNeilly (who is married, with two kids) and guitarist Duane Denison (who is half of the jazz duo Denison/Kimball Trio) — is not just a one-dimensional terror ride. While the catchy hooks grab you and abstract lyrics add a chill, the group also has a crude sense of humor. You won't find Rollins lighting his farts onstage or Reznor pulling his latex pants down and mooning his audiences. Those moves might be too spontaneous — or juvenile — to qualify as dark and disturbing in the current entertainment world.

"In an ideal world," says Sims, "I want things to be engaging on a number of levels so you can get a lot of different people and a lot of different moods. I think in rock music you want to be pretty visceral and physical and engaging on a very sort of primal level. But we also want our music to be well played, well executed, so it can fuel people — on an intellectual level, where people can appreciate the music as music, and on an emotional level that's more gut instinct."

"If you go to one extreme," adds Yow, "you get a lot of jazz noodling that nobody likes except for other musicians. On the other end, you get brainless metal that nobody likes but stoned, 14-year-old kids. I think we want to suck *all* those people in. We want 'em all."

While a lot of bands aim for that balance, the Jesus Lizard hits it. Maybe it's the chemistry — a certain combination of characters that brings out the primal feel. "I have thought that before," admits Yow, "but ever since I can remember being into rock music, bands would say *[in a perfect British accent]*: 'It's the chemistry amongst the four people in the band.' So I've never been able to actually go, 'BLAHHH! — chemistry!"

SIMS AND YOW FIRST WORKED together in Scratch Acid, the legendary Texas noise outfit that began in 1982 and dissolved around '87. Sims was working on an accounting degree at the University of Texas at the time, and went on to play with Steve Albini in the eloquently titled Rapeman before moving to Chicago with Yow, the earlier band's drum technician, in 1988. Denison moved from Austin to Chicago as well, and decided to pull the three together. With a drum machine and producer Steve Albini, they recorded the Jesus Lizard's first EP, *Pure*. McNeilly joined in 1989 to complete the lineup. The band has since released four albums and several singles on Touch & Go.

Growing up in Austin as the son of a jazz professor, Sims was a fan of the Beatles and classical music until he started honing his own tastes through FM radio. "The first album I wanted to buy was the *Saturday Night Fever* soundtrack," he says. "But the local Eckerd Drugs didn't have it. So I got *Double Vision* by Foreigner instead. I was disappointed at first, but eventually I got into it. It was little, pivotal moments like that, that turned me on to rock."

While Sims was rocking out to *Double Vision*, Yow, an army brat, was constantly relocating with his family from such places as Morocco, Las Vegas, England and North Carolina. Yow was such a Beatles freak, he admits, that "I even knew how much they weighed." He met Sims in Austin after his family finally settled there, and both discovered punk early on. After developing a strong hatred for his father, Yow eventually moved in with the Sims family.

"I sold records for beans and beer money," he recalls. "Now look," he says with a burst of laughter, "I'm an internationally famous rock star."

He may laugh, but the Jesus Lizard has begun to pop up everywhere, from *Rolling Stone* to *New York* magazine to the *Washington Post*. Further, the band has been invited to play shows they wouldn't have been caught dead even attending a few years ago. While some of that is due to increasing word of mouth within the indie community, the Jesus Lizard's split-single with Nirvana, "Puss"/

"Oh, the Guilt," gave the band a much higher profile. Since then, several major labels have approached them.

"It really drove that feeling home when we played the Reading Festival in England last year," says Sims. "The crowd had come to see bands like The The, Ned's Atomic Dustbin and James. Needless to say, I had problems connecting."

Sims seems uncomfortable that the Jesus Lizard's audience is no longer filled with just the faces of family, friends and a few avid fans. "When you first start out," he continues, "you've only got a single or an EP, and pretty much the only people that come to see you are like the kids that buy all the fanzines and 7-inches. They are the cutting edge and a gauge of how it's moving.

"At the other end of the spectrum — like a Janet Jackson audience — those people probably only go to two or three shows a year, or buy a few CDs a year," he adds. "They don't care about the music. They just want a good time. Though we're still well into the underground side, I can tell we've moved; that there's a change in the character of the audience. It's a little disturbing. It's not just those intense kids that buy the 45s anymore. It's good, but..." He pauses and taps the table nervously.

Yow finishes: "But if they like it, whether they know why they like it or not, that's fine. Good for them. It's healthy. It's all perfectly valid. I mean, if we were to turn around and make a record just so more sheep would come and join us, that would be a problem."

BRAT PACKERS ONCE TRIED to take over the Powerhouse like they did the nearby Frolic Room, but it didn't last long. The threadbare green carpet and duct tape on the ripped Naugahyde booths were just too dirty, the clientele too repulsive, and the location, well, too scary and hardcore.

Kenny Rogers's "The Gambler" comes on the jukebox, and the motley lineup at the bar sings the words mechanically. The faces are dead, and the mouths move as if it's some sort of "Barfly Jamboree" attraction at Disneyland. When the song ends, the barflies droop back into nothingness, as though the plug's been pulled.

Yow slams another empty bottle down on the table. He knows the base intensity of the Jesus Lizard's music will likely be the final barrier between the band and the kind of mass audience the Smashing Pumpkins has found. "And I don't care," he states emphatically. "I like having an impact to the extent that either you really like us a lot or you just hate us — nothing passive, nothing in between."

November 1994

liz phair & lou barlow

LO-FI ALL-STARS

MODERATED BY **JOHN CORBETT**

GRINNING WIDELY, LOU BARLOW opens the door to a room on the eighth floor of Chicago's swanky Meridien Hotel, and the sweet smell of hash incense wafts into the hallway. Inside, a slightly dazed Liz Phair bobs up and down on the queen-sized bed, where she'll remain for much of the afternoon.

Barlow, 28, is a soft-spoken latchkey kid from the Boston 'burbs. Growing up with parents who were unusually supportive of his musical endeavors, he opted to postpone college and live at home until he was 21. After leaving Dinosaur Jr. early in the band's career, he has recorded under a variety of monikers, including Sebadoh, Sentridoh, Lou B., and the Folk Implosion. A confessional lyricist, he pours his soul into aching songs about lost love, found love, uncertain love. Though much of his music is recorded at home on a four-track, Sebadoh's latest album, *Bakesale*, is the band's most accessible yet.

Phair, 27, is the daughter of a Northwestern University research physician and an instructor at the Art Institute of Chicago. A product of suburban Chicago, she is self-possessed and conversationally savvy. Her songs — obsessive, compulsive, neurotic, flip and always sexually charged — also focus on love, though with a knowing wink. On the cusp of superstardom with her much-anticipated album *Whip-Smart*, Phair is living up to her startling 1993 breakthrough, *Exile In Guyville*, and her earlier, self-released, lo-fi *Girly Sound* cassettes.

Throughout their conversation, MTV flickers in the background as Phair easily coaxes Barlow out of his self-imposed shell, freely responding to him with her own flamboyant, THC-fueled metaphors. She even offers Lou advice on how to propose to his girlfriend: "Don't be a fucking dork — walk out and get a ring! With a decent-sized diamond in it!"

PIGEONHOLED

LIZ: No one ever asks me about my guitar playing. No one's ever fuckin' asked me about how I write songs. I have all these things to say about that, but no one cares, 'cause it really doesn't matter what I play on guitar. Even if I play really interesting guitar songs, the only thing they care about is what it's like to be an upper-middle-class cute girl with smart parents singing dirty words. You know? No one wants to talk to my band. I know why they like me. I know what they want. And that's depressing, 'cause then it's a job. It's not a quest for change. But the music is what got us into this room today. It's what we're here for.

LOU: I'm just getting to the point where I'm trying to ignore what the printed things say. It's like, OK, they've pigeonholed you, but there's nothing you can do about it, so ignore it. I mean, it doesn't matter how much you do right, 'cause in the end the people decide.

LIZ: It's like a political campaign.

LOU: Yeah, I was thinking about that today. I'm some kind of fucking weird politician and I can't believe that. Through default I found myself in this position of being a strange politician and spending most of my time talking about something that I don't have time to *do* anymore. It just totally sucks.

LIZ: This is what happens. This is the truth of the game. I had a fucking breakdown about two weeks ago and I figured it all out. It hit me like a big old ugly hammer. I was exhausted from something that most people would consider a really cushy job, and I just couldn't figure out what was wrong, and then I got it. I got everything that I do and why I was asked to be here. It's just so surreal. In entertainment they don't tell you the job until you're there.

LOU: I don't know, 'cause I'm not in your position at all.

LIZ: Yeah you are. You're in exactly the position I'm in. You're saying the exact same thing that I'm saying.

LOU: Yeah, but the pressure on me is less than it is on you. I guess I still don't feel claustrophobic, 'cause I still feel that there's not very many people listening.

LIZ: It really changes your life to feel claustrophobic. It means you have to take active measures. It's a matter of deflecting. Earlier we were talking about being the center of attention. Really, the change in my life has been being paid so much attention. The money thing — I lived better as a child. Well, not really. I don't know. But it's like deflection. I don't have a good pro-active measure to protect myself from being the center of attention. I have good passive-aggressive measures. I don't look at who's in the room anymore. I don't even try. I used to be a person who would make eye contact with people. Now I can very easily slip in and out of places without ever knowing who else is in the room.

LOU: See, I just spent my whole growing up looking at the ground. I'm serious. I would look down all the time, and it's taken me up until the last couple of years to even be able to look at people.

SEX IN CYBERSPACE

LIZ: It's a computer world. My boyfriend is totally Internet. Well, we don't have Internet yet, but we want to get all that stuff. We've got America Online.

LOU: It's kind of exciting. It's like, I don't believe anything's sacred, you know? I don't think anything should be any particular way just because it always has been. You know, there's Internet sex, and it's all just sex. It doesn't matter.

LIZ: But there'll never be a substitute for personal interaction, I don't think. Phone sex? I don't even relate. I don't even know anyone who has phone sex. Do you have phone sex?

LOU: No, I never have.

LIZ: Have you seen this software — it's the weirdest thing — where you can couple this woman with lots of different little things, like bondage partners. On a computer nobody can interfere with your enjoyment. Anyway, one of the things she has is this little 8-ball lover — which is so sick. To this day I ask people what it means. It's a guy with the head of an 8-ball, like a pool ball, and he's about up to her knees, and he comes running up between her legs and just starts fucking her. I've got a great imagination, but I have no idea what that means.

There are some things that *are* sacred — like real sex. I guess there's the danger of feelings. If you're more into using a computer than getting down, then don't have kids — and that's just as well. As I see it, we can stand to strain our gene pool. Fuck it. Those people — we don't want their genes. Don't propagate!

LOU: That I understand. I like that.

SOCIALIZING

LIZ: I wasn't extremely social when I was in high school.

Lou: But you said you made eye contact with people when you met them.

LIZ: Well, yeah, all right, so I was *extremely* social. But I knew people who were more social than I was.

LOU: It's not a bad thing to be social. I think it's kind of good.

LIZ: My mother's extremely social. But I was as much of a closet academic geek as anybody.

LOU: You'd have to be. I mean, your music indicates that you'd have to have spent some time, like, thinking about shit.

LIZ: Sure, yeah. But it pays for me to be one thing and not the other. There's more pressure for me to be gregarious, social, cute and fun than for me to be a great musician. I think that's sexism.

LOU: That's the classic... It annoys me so much whenever I read anything about your records — the way people are actually surprised that you're singing the things that you're singing. They think you're somehow stepping outside of your role as a woman. I'm like, "What fucking role?!" When I got your record I reacted pretty strongly to it. I really enjoyed it, like, "This is a rare kind of thing." And then when I started to read what people thought, it annoyed me so much.

LIZ: I brought so few values to it — and they brought so much.

LOU: Exactly. And for people to think that the sensitivity in *my* songs is somehow a gender role reversal is just ridiculous. That's just my upbringing.

LIZ: But maybe the kind of man you are hasn't been seen in a public sense for a while. You know how centuries have their trends as to who's the voice that's listened to? Who do we want to look through the eyes of now? I mean, I think there are gender roles. I did it all over my own album — "Look at this, I fuckin' gender flipped!" — without knowing it. I'm about as girlie as they get on some levels. I think of myself in a multi-ethnic, multi-economic category, but I'm perceived as a very specific item.

LOU: And I've sung certain songs from a feminine perspective — just trying to understand power. Power between men and women — that has a lot to do with a lot of the songs I've written. I've had to actively think: what would it be like to be in that position? I've tried to really get into the situation and understand it.

LIZ: That's what my whole first album was, for me. That's the whole *Exile* thing: to appropriate "What the fuck is wrong with you?"

SEX IN THE REAL WORLD

LIZ: My dad's chief of infectious disease at Northwestern, and what he does is work with AIDS clinics. I think AIDS has been around probably about five to ten years longer than you think, and I think to a large extent the fear of it is just the swings of paranoia in our culture. As far as I can see, it's like people dying from any disease. It's pretty much like any pathology of disease.

I don't buy that whole idea that there was this change in sexual politics because of AIDS. It could have been anything, and I think whatever it was would have affected our sexuality too. I think anything could have been inserted in the place of AIDS. And it pisses me off. [*laughing*] I don't know. It's my issue. I just think it made everybody scared in this really evil way. It didn't make people scared in a constructive way. I think it was just a catalyst for the paranoia of our time.

liz phair & lou barlow

LOU: It didn't make people scared enough to actually stop...

LIZ: To stop doing it. It just made people like, "I'm looking out for myself and you are a threat to me in a gross way — in a way that I can look down upon." Like a status thing. I thought people who wouldn't really get the disease spent a lot of time thinking about it. People who are still becoming really infected and developing symptoms and living with it — they're kind of passé now and we're just mulling over how we feel about them. I think the fear of AIDS is a scapegoat; that it's our generation's scapegoat. I think we were born aimlessly neurotic; too many choices and not enough direction.

THE LO-FI THEORY, TAKE 1

LIZ: I like that four-track sound, man. I'm going back, I'm fucking going back!

LOU: I write songs using a four-track.

LIZ: Yeah, exactly. It's a sketch pad.

LOU: Yeah, totally. The thing with my four-track stuff is, I'll just sketch it out so hard and in so much detail that I don't want to take it to a studio, 'cause it'll ruin all the tracings and all of the layerings and the texture of the sound. But then, I record in the studio all the time with Sebadoh. If you have a band — guitar, bass and drums — I think it's best to at least try to experiment with the studio, 'cause there's got to be a good way to get a good studio sound. As long as you can hear the voice, and the voice has some texture to it. Liz, the way you sing has that total four-track feel. It really registers with me.

LIZ: That's the thing about live stuff. With that kind of volume and wattage attached, you can't have the kind of intimacy you want. On a four-track you can pound the drums, throw it all on a track, do anything you want at the intensity you want, and be like Chet Baker, you know?

LOU: And it'll have so much of a presence over the top of everything else.

LIZ: Just floating like a little Cheshire cat.

LOU: That's exactly it. It gives it personality. I found that I had to learn how to sing my songs in a stronger voice.

LIZ: That's really what it is. It's learning how to sing. I was going to take singing lessons. You've gotta become a performer. It's not even related to the studio situation. Like, Branford Marsalis loathes my music because of the lack of musicianship, but at the same time I've been in loads of music classes, so there's a certain amount of *conceptual* musicianship. So what's the difference? It's the lo-fi thing; indie rock humbled us.

The idea that there are God-given musicians, and it flows freely from their souls — that's not what we are. We're privileged, trained, white kids, so we just get down on our knees and we're like, "I will not pretend to perform. I will just do my best to be the same way, like a soul, straight." Lo-fi feels like it's giving a clean offering. Do you know what I mean?

LOU: I think so.

LIZ: 'Cause we'd think someone was bogus who had a lot of glitz to them; like it was so clearly contrived. But we're probably very contrived on some level too. We know what we're doing, but we respect more than anything our ability to just freely come up with something. So we go lo-fi to be humbled before the gods or something.

LOU: I go lo-fi because that's all I have.

LIZ: Really?

TELEVISION

LIZ: I watch HBO a lot. I watch a lot of movies. Some TV — *Beavis, Married With Children...*

LOU: I just watch comedy. Comedy and nature documentaries.

LIZ: Oh, the *stoner* channel — absolutely a must. Nature and God in the living room!

LOU: It's between that and comedy. And then CNN, you know, occasionally.

LIZ: CNN? I don't trust them anymore. It's like the *New York Times*.

LOU: I have this belief that people who work real jobs, like out in the actual working world — for them, TV somehow serves this real function, like this meditative function. It's really strange. It's like they *need* to watch TV. My father's like that. He works eight hours, dressed for the job, and he comes home and just turns on the television and just fucking channel surfs the entire time. It seems to me like a lot of people do that.

LIZ: I think you're exactly right. I know exactly what you're talking about. I'm sitting here trying to fathom why that is.

LOU: Just the monotony of having a nine-to-five job. I'm really happy that I escaped from that. There's something really debilitating about working a real job. I always thought that watching TV was pretty similar to sitting out in nature and just listening to the breeze blow. I never believed that one was better than the other.

NOSTALGIA

LIZ: How old are you?

LOU: 28.

LIZ: I'm 27. So we're roughly the same generation. Your babysitters would be my babysitters, right? So '70s rock. It's like you're stuck. I think there's something that happens to people as they reach adulthood. They spend a lot of time trying to figure out what first hit them about rock'n'roll. It's like the first time you took a drug. You want that first time back. You want that first deviance from the world as you know it.

LOU: Right.

LIZ: And so you're pretty much destined to rehash that over and over again. It's scary.

LOU: And that's Urge Overkill!

LO-FI, TAKE 2

LOU: I'm super defensive about this, 'cause I just spent the last three weeks in Europe and every fuckin' day it was like, "Why are you lo-fi and why do you think you're a loser?" It's exactly like you were saying — you're just this middle-class kid, you know, whatever. I just don't understand that lo-fi...

LIZ: OK, Veruca Salt goes into the studio and do their vocal takes billions and billions of times until it is perfect and it's not patched together. It's that professionalism.

LOU: So, it's lo-fi *not* to do that stuff?

LIZ: Yeah, it's lo-fi not to do that stuff.

LOU: Well I do all that stuff all the time.

LIZ: But not the way everyone else does. You do it in your own flaky, retarded way.

LOU: Yeah.

LIZ: I think I sound more mainstream working retarded than I do when I'm being professional. And that's the disparity, because you think you're selling out completely with these lo-fi productions, you're using all the cheeseball moves, and then radio won't play it because the sonic quality is not that of a tapestry that can meld into the secretarial pool.

LOU: Yeah, but I do all of the recording techniques to totally emphasize the voice and the lyrics and the emotional impact of the song, which to me is being as commercial as I could possibly be. I feel like I have always been completely commercial, but I can never tell anyone that at all.

POP IN A BOX

LIZ: Idiosyncrasies are what keep you unsold. Like Cindy Crawford has one little mole, but the rest is great. But she has one defect. You have to hone it down till you just have a few acceptable defects. I think that's commodification. You get to pick your three worst flaws and you can exploit them, but everything else has got to be goddamn perfect. And then you win the lottery. Wouldn't you like to win the lottery? The music lottery?

LOU: Just become a huge, huge star?

LIZ: Really quickly, under a different name. And then go up to Canada. I've always said I wouldn't mind being off on my own.

LOU: Being off on your own? What do you mean?

LIZ: The freedom you have once you become a commodity in the extreme.

LOU: So when are you *not* a product? And *who* is not a product? There's no way I could properly answer those questions. Either way, people'd grumble. So what am I going to say? — "There's nothing wrong with being a product." Or, "OK, there *is* something wrong with being a product."

LIZ: The thing about being a product is that, partially, it gives you power to be who you want to be. But obstructively, you forget why you wanted to be powerful in the first place. You have a big, booming voice, but you have less to say, 'cause you're spending all of your time worrying about your bigger, booming voice. At some level, that's why you played your songs for a friend to begin with. You were hoping that somebody would see the true you, and that this would mean something. That the true you was not just your mother's illusion. There was something you could offer that was your own creation. You could offer something that was poetic. Commodification blurs that line really fast, because the world of business and the world of vision are too much alike.

LOU: It took a really long time before I was able to do that. The whole act of playing my own music was such a huge step that I waited a really long time. I was listening to it, just myself, and I was like, "I know I have something to give." And then you start giving and it starts perpetuating itself.

LIZ: But then your audience is like little baby birds going: "More, more, more!" There's probably something essential and archetypal about what you give in songs that people want, but if you hear all those different voices — "Lou, when you did this it was fantastic!" "Lou, when you did this it blew my mind!" "I can't believe how much it touched me when you said this!" — it's all these different mouths to feed...

LOU: Do you still keep making music when you reach that point where you're like, "This is the most absurd thing?"

LIZ: Remember how you said you were absorptive instead of reflective? You tend to be someone who took everything in, sat quietly and watched everyone doing what they did? You've absorbed it all — now what you're hearing from people is so harrowing to absorb that you can't do it anymore. So commodification is the process of being eaten alive, more or less. There was just one or two people you were saving up all your songs for. Then suddenly there are like 30,000, and you're dimly aware of it.

LOU: But you're still concentrating on those one or two people anyway.

LO-FI, TAKE 3

LOU: I figure I could never walk into a studio and sit down and work on vocals and lyrics that meant that much to me. I have to be totally alone. I think in order to find your own identity and sound in a world like this — a world that is constantly bombarding you with the idea that you are not original and there's nothing you can do to be original — the best thing you can do is somehow cut apart all the rock myths and offer your own rearrangement of them. What four-track and lo-fi meant for me was crafting the way I was going to speak and the words that I wanted to say. And it's something that will just keep evolving. It's not something that I'm attached to. It's simply a recording technique.

LIZ: I'll betcha. You pay me $50 if in five years you don't change your mind.

LOU: About what?

LIZ: About recording — that it's just a technique. I bet it means something more to you. Betcha.

LOU: Hmm. More than a technique. But it's a technique that I would probably always come back to, 'cause it means a lot to me.

LIZ: But you just said it didn't mean anything.

LOU: No, I'm just saying — what I'm trying to say is, um, you're right. OK. But I'm trying to devalue the whole lo-fi thing. I just hate that it *means* anything. I hate that there's music that's described by the way it's recorded. That, to me, is just a total violation.

LIZ: I totally know what you mean. The radio will only take certain kinds of arrangements as legit.

LOU: But that's not *my* problem.

LIZ: But it *is* your problem. It's *completely* your problem.

LOU: No, it's not, because I've been able to do so much already. I'm already a complete success. I've already satisfied all of my artistic goals. All that's left are just vanities. Otherwise it's like, "Wow, I've been able to make music!"

INTEGRITY

LOU: So you'd definitely be into being a huge star?

LIZ: But I've always craved my privacy. I think I'm at a great point now. I think this is the point at which I can indulge my ego in feelings of famousness, feelings of fabulousness, without really having to take the knocks for walking down to that shitty beer garden and having everybody know who I am. No one has told me where I can't go. And no one has told me I'm only this good. They've said I could be the fucking best. And people still don't know who I am. When I get really crowded in, it makes me miserable. I cry. I feel horrible. I feel like I have rotten self-esteem. Like I'm really ugly, really stupid and self-centered. It's a drag. So I think being megafamous would truly be a painful transition.

LOU: I still don't have to worry too much about that. It's just a total oddity for me. This is the first time I've been able to shamelessly throw myself into the media loop. Before, there was too much of this white boy, punk rock guilt factor. Now I don't give a shit. There's so many things in the world that are so much more mediocre than what I'm doing, so why not toss what I have out and see how many people take it? There's not a question of integrity involved.

LIZ: I could explain it in concrete socio-economic terms, in terms of how my family mistrusts my motivation, how I mistrust everyone I know, or how I no longer have a sense of identity. I don't know what I am anymore. All that stuff really takes a toll on your ability to live.

LOU: There's so much I'm not willing to lose. The one thing that I fear is becoming alienated from people you know, like your friends and people you love.

LIZ: Just like a Vietnam vet. Joan Rivers once referred to people who were not in the entertainment business as "civilians." You know what I mean? Let's face it, I'm well on my way to being a star. I was on the cover of *Rolling Stone*. But I don't talk about all this with my friends. I want desperately to have people to talk about it with. And you just can't. It's one of the loneliest jobs at some level, because to all the people I love, I just live this entire existence like I don't do what I do. I just go along with the people I'm close to as though it was the same old me. But clearly things are totally weird.

LOU: And you don't talk about music? You don't talk about where you have to go and shit like that?

LIZ: Where I have to go or what it was like to pose for *Sassy* — we really don't talk about it.

LOU: Really?

LIZ: Really.

September 1994

pavement

INDIE EVER AFTER

BY **JASON FINE**

OUT PAST THE STRIP MALLS, donut shops and Chinese fast-food joints that line Stockton's Miracle Mile, along a narrow county road that cuts through a jigsaw puzzle of dusty, sun-scorched farmland, Pavement headquarters is tucked away in a quiet residential enclave just east of the city limits. Band founders Scott Kannenberg and Steve Malkmus grew up here, in a neighborhood shaded by giant oak and eucalyptus trees, where kids leave their bikes unlocked in the driveways and American flags fly above manicured front lawns. Malkmus's house burned down a few years ago and his parents moved to Idaho, but Mr. and Mrs. Kannenberg still live here, along with Scott's younger sister Kelly, who runs Pavement's mail order business out of a back room, and Alabama, the family's five-year-old golden retriever.

Rumbling through the old neighborhood in Kannenberg's blue 1982 Saab, Malkmus slouches low in the back seat and points out personal landmarks along the way. Over here is where he got arrested for walking across people's roofs in the middle of the night; over there is an irrigation ditch where you can catch the biggest crawdads in Stockton. Up the road a ways, the flat brown landscape is suddenly broken by a whitewashed stucco wall separating the farmland from a sprawling new housing development. Both Kannenberg and Malkmus groan as we roll past row after row of identical pastel-colored ranch homes and giant multicolored flags welcoming potential home buyers to "The California Dream...Made Affordable!" A little further ahead, Kannenberg slows down to admire a place where the subdivision ends and a creaky old green farmhouse stands alone, a solitary reminder of Stockton's rural past.

"The people who live here have been fighting off these big

developers for years," Malkmus explains. "The developers tried to get the guy to sell, but he refused. So they just built up around him.

"I was so proud of them for not selling out," he adds. "They're like our very own Bikini Kill or something..."

"Or Fugazi," Kannenberg cuts in.

"Yeah," says Malkmus, grinning. "The Fugazi of Stockton land development."

PAVEMENT LOOKS AT THE WORLD through an indie rock lens. From the intentionally lo-fi approach of its records to the tongue-in-cheek parallel Malkmus and Kannenberg draw between one farmer's stand against land developers and the struggle of independent-minded punk bands, the group's identity is rooted in an oppositional sensibility that arose among bands, fanzines, college radio and small independent labels in the post-punk mid-'80s. Embracing low budgets, loud guitars and an anti-corporate ethos which demanded that music be treated as something more than "product," indie rockers transformed punk's loose-knit DIY principles into a formalized subculture that often seemed to view signing a major label deal as the ultimate sell-out and obscurity as an achievement in itself.

But at a time when the underground has become mired in an orthodoxy as rigid as the mainstream pop market it defines itself against, Pavement makes indie rock fun again. Not simply because the band turned down major label deals to stick with feisty Matador (though that label is affiliated with Atlantic, Pavement's latest album, *Crooked Rain, Crooked Rain*, is not a joint-label release). And not just because guitarist Kannenberg has refused to appear in *Rolling Stone*, a magazine he reviles for "ignoring all the best music of my generation." Rather, Pavement is fun because Pavement is *truly* independent: Steve Malkmus and Scott Kannenberg don't play by anyone's rules but their own.

Often portrayed as smug, contemptuous slackers hiding behind fake names and cryptic lyrics, slagging both Smashing Pumpkins and Stone Temple Pilots in the song "Range Life," and greeting MTV VJ Lewis Largent with slack-jawed glares during an interview on *120 Minutes*, the band has in fact stepped out of the murky indie underworld with rare poise and humor. Particularly on

pavement

Crooked Rain, Pavement's casual, brilliant guitar rock transcends indie convention and challenges notions of what (if anything) "alternative" really means, investing punk's corporate-backed Second Coming with more guts and vision than any other American band.

IT'S A WARM, WINDLESS summer day in Stockton, and after lunch at a downtown Mexican diner, Malkmus and Kannenberg, accompanied by Kannenberg's girlfriend Chrissy, shove off on a tour of the town. Although Pavement has never actually performed here, the band's two 28-year-old leaders have deep roots in this agricultural hub located at the tip of the Sacramento River Delta in California's vast Central Valley. Malkmus and Kannenberg played on the Tokay High School soccer team together in nearby Lodi. They worked in local record stores and movie theaters, and spent their free time smoking pot, collecting punk and new wave records and making up songs for their short-lived first band, Bag of Bones. These days, when Pavement isn't touring, Malkmus splits his time between New York and Memphis, and Kannenberg lives with Chrissy 100 miles from Stockton, in San Francisco. But Stockton remains Pavement's home base, the place it receives its fan mail and deposits its royalty checks, and the place where Malkmus and Kannenberg find their sense of perspective.

"People always think there's so much pressure on us now that we're selling some records and getting played on MTV and stuff, but we don't really feel it," says Kannenberg, browsing through a dusty row of used guitar amps at a downtown pawn shop. "I guess if we had movie star girlfriends and hung around in Hollywood or something, maybe we would feel the pressure. But it's not like that. I mean, we're from Stockton, where there's no scene, no bands — where there's nothing. And I guess that's part of the charm."

While most aspiring rockers would kill for the kind of critical acclaim and commercial success that's greeted Pavement, Malkmus and Kannenberg strategize ways to avoid entering the rock star realm. It's not that they lack ambition, as has often been written, just that they view rock'n'roll as more of an absurd aberration than a full-time job. "When we started, every record was like this little project we did on vacation," says Kannenberg, "and that's kind of how we want it to stay. Traveling around and playing is a lot of fun, and I'm glad we're getting a chance to do it, but that's not all there is. We don't ever want to let this run our lives."

Dressed in a blue T-shirt and jeans, Kannenberg is clean-shaven, square-shouldered and solid, with an easygoing smile and a stoner's laugh. Malkmus, the band's singer, is ganglier and more ruffled, wearing an orange thrift-store sweater and crooked baseball cap. Clutching a tape recorder in one hand and a can of Coke in the other, he delivers a rambling tour monologue that's equal parts sarcasm and earnest nostalgia, unearthing memories around every corner and putting together pieces of the Pavement puzzle.

"I have a sad story to tell about the first punk rock show I ever wanted to go to," he announces as we drive north from downtown into a battered industrial zone that was once home to several part-time punk clubs. "It was the Dead Kennedys, and I had just gotten my driver's license the day before. I wanted to drive there really bad but my parents said, 'No, you can't take the car. It's in a bad area and it's too late.' I really wanted to go and I threw a temper tantrum. I got so angry that they wouldn't even let me go with anyone else 'cause I was acting like such a brat."

Malkmus got his punk rock initiation a year later, though, when his own band Straw Dog opened for Black Flag at another local venue. "I was backstage before the show and all those guys, they looked so scary, I was afraid of them," he says. "Like Greg Ginn was mixing up this stuff in a glass. It was probably just protein powder or some healthy drink, but I thought it was like heroin or something — some kind of drug. And before they played, Henry Rollins was back there with this pool ball, this white cue ball, just squeezing it to get pumped up for the show." He pauses, looking out the car window at a graffiti-covered box car sitting on rusty train tracks.

"I mean, squeezing a cue ball!" he continues. "You're not going to get anywhere! I guess that was his point. It's like smashing your head against a brick wall. That's what I thought punk was, you know. That's when I knew that maybe I'm just not punk enough."

BEYOND THE JUNKYARDS and abandoned factories, around the corner from a massive gated compound that houses Stockton's glimmering Christian Life Center, Kannenberg pulls into a '60s-era subdivision and parks across the street from a nondescript, one-story house at 9318 Waco Way. This is the former home of local drummer Gary Young, who operated a small recording studio called Louder Than You Think out of his garage. This is also where on one dull afternoon in the summer of 1988, Pavement cut its first record.

At the time, Malkmus was visiting his folks between semesters at the University of Virginia, from which he graduated with a B.A. in history in 1989. Kannenberg had moved back home after dropping out of Arizona State. They had remembered Young from his days with the Stockton hardcore band Fall of Christianity, and decided to book some recording time.

"We were just hanging around, you know, getting stoned and watching TV at Steve's parents' house, and we'd started making up these songs," Kannenberg says, standing the driveway while Chrissy snaps photos. "Steve had just started being a DJ at UVA and I think he just got the idea that, well, there's all these bands, we can do it too. It was a completely naive thing."

The duo's ragged, out-of-tune guitars and screeching vocals didn't much impress Young, who spent most of his studio time recording demos for riff-heavy local metal clones. "The thing is," Young remembers, speaking from his current home in nearby Linden, "they didn't know anything. When they walked in the door they were two kids with two guitars. They had what I considered to be trash noise. I didn't realize that there was a market for this at that point in time, so I just said this is noisy trash, what's the deal?"

Young ended up drumming on some of the tracks Malkmus and Kannenberg laid down and thought he'd seen the last of Pavement. But while Malkmus ditched fall semester at UVA for a trip to Europe, Kannenberg pressed the record and sent it out to fanzines and record companies. By the time Malkmus came home, Pavement's first 7-inch, *Slay Tracks*, had been released through Dutch East India and was getting write-ups in 'zines across the country. Returning to Young's garage during the following Christmas and spring vacations, the duo tossed off two more mini-albums, *Demolition Plot J-7* and *Perfect Sound Forever*, as well as assorted fanzine-distributed singles. (Drag City ultimately compiled all three albums, plus early singles, as the CD *Westing By Musket And Sextant*.) Though the music was still raw and unfocused, employing only two guitars and Young's spare, rubbery drumming, there were also fragile melodies and crisp, inventive guitar lines reaching out of the harsh soundscape, signs of the band's sonic vision evolving with each new song.

By the time its first full-length album, *Slanted And Enchanted*, finally came out in 1992, Pavement was riding a major buzz. Songs hinted at myriad influences — the Velvet Underground, the Fall, Wire, the Pixies, Sonic Youth — but also had an edgy, spacious sound all its own, full of clipped, ringing guitars, choppy rhythms and melodies close to perfection but always on the brink of falling apart.

Live shows were similarly precarious. Up until *Slanted*, Pavement had never performed outside of the studio. In fact, bass guitar didn't even become a regular part of the band's lineup until *Crooked Rain, Crooked Rain*. So to greet a sudden wealth of opportunities to play live, Malkmus and Kannenberg quickly pieced together a band — with Young on drums, Mark Ibold on bass, and percussionist/chanter Bob Nastanovich — and hit the road after only a half-dozen rehearsals.

Before the group's sold-out San Francisco debut, Gary Young stood outside the Kennel Club greeting people with gregarious handshakes and requests that they buy him beer. Onstage, he stumbled around and forgot the names of tune after tune, often forcing his bandmates to start and re-start songs until he finally got it right. Young's drunken antics became legendary as the band crisscrossed the U.S. and Europe, but they also made for chronically unpredictable performances. Following a particularly grueling European tour last summer, the 42-year-old drummer was replaced by Steve West, a high school buddy of Nastanovich.

If West has provided a more stable if less entertaining presence, Pavement's haphazard approach has remained much the same. With Kannenberg studying urban planning at Sacramento State, Malkmus and Ibold living in New York, and Nastanovich in Louisville, little rehearsal went into the making of *Crooked Rain, Crooked Rain*. Recorded for $10,000 in a makeshift New York apartment-studio, the album contains the same tossed-off, unvarnished feel as *Slanted And Enchanted* but is sharper and more cohesive throughout. Breezing from jagged, sarcastic pop tunes, like the single "Cut Your Hair," to a tinkly reworking of "Take Five" by Dave Brubeck (a fellow Stockton native), called "5-4=Unity," and the earthy country jam "Range Life," *Crooked Rain* is like a secret tour of rock'n'roll, full of clever allusions, subtle references and sonic juxtapositions that hint at influences ranging from Creedence Clearwater Revival to the Beatles, Hüsker Dü and again, VU and the Fall.

In his lyrics, written mostly in the studio, Malkmus drops the arty ambiguity of past efforts for songs that dig into the tension, ambivalence, disgust and absurdity of making a career as a rock musician. "Songs mean a lot/When songs are bought/And so are you," he deadpans in "Cut Your Hair," and the lines succinctly describe the challenge facing Pavement and other bands trying to hang on to their indie values in the mainstream rock marketplace.

By early fall, *Crooked Rain* had sold 150,000 copies, spawned a hit video on "Alternative Nation" with "Cut Your Hair," and even earned Pavement a spot next to Drew Barrymore on Jay Leno last summer. But if the band is flirting with fame in the U.S. and abroad, in Stockton they may as well not exist. While another native son, retro-crooner Chris Isaak, is widely regarded as a local treasure, no one around here seems know who Pavement is. When I mention the band's name to a teenager working the counter at a Taco Bell, his only reaction is a dull shrug. Even at the record store where Kannenberg used to work, not a single Pavement album sits on the shelves. Maybe that's why the guitarist seems surprised to find several copies of *Crooked Rain* on display at the nearby Tower.

"It's here," Kannenberg announces, holding up a copy. Then he notices the price tag: "$15.98," he says. "What a rip-off."

IF MALKMUS IS PAVEMENT'S eccentric spirit, Kannenberg is its indie conscience. He's the one who seems most uneasy with the band's escalating commercial success, and the one most inflexible in his indie ideology. Kannenberg is also the one who refused to be interviewed or photographed for a July 14 *Rolling Stone* piece on the band. The rest of the group went along with the story, but as Malkmus explains in his own roundabout way, the episode highlights tough issues facing Pavement. "I have a problem with appearing in that magazine too," Malkmus says. "They really gave a skewed, unfair history of rock in the '80s. But to me it was more of a slippery slope kind of thing. I mean, what's the difference between saying no to *Rolling Stone* but still being on MTV? MTV makes you bend down more — it's like, 'Make us a video, make sure it's hot, spend a lot of money on it, and maybe we'll play it. And then we'll take the credit for it and we'll play it as much as we want whenever we want.'

"To me, MTV is way worse," he continues. "Even to sit down and talk with an MTV VJ, it's so insidious. They'll lead you on, just like that Lewis Largent tried to do with me, asking those dumb questions. So what do you do? When you're on there you can protest it by just ignoring him and trying to be civil. Or you can just be rude for no reason; spit on Lewis Largent or something. A lot of kids'll think that's real cool — 'You spit on Lewis Largent. Oh, that's real punk.' But there's no point to that. Besides, you might give him a disease."

Late afternoon sunshine beats through the car windows as we drive past the vineyards and apricot orchards that line I-99 on the way to Tokay High. Pulling into the school's parking lot, past a group of Asian teens sitting on the hood of a car, Malkmus points to a grassy area across the street where he says kids used to smoke pot between classes. "They hired a narc because so many kids were showing up stoned," he says. "But it turned out the narc was also the dealer. So it worked out pretty good."

Wandering through the empty halls of their alma mater, the two peek into the gym and point out a squat stucco building called the Newcomb Media Center where, Malkmus says sarcastically, "we spent many hours plotting, reading the magazines, and dreaming that one day we'd be as big as Toto." They show me the assembly hall where Gary Young's band, the Fall of Christianity, was set to play during lunch one time; the show was broken up because a bunch of kids blocked the entrance in protest and began chanting, "Jesus lives! Jesus lives!"

"Everything was always in very black-and-white terms here. It was like, rednecks versus punks," says Malkmus. "In fact, that's kind of how our song 'Fillmore Jive' was inspired: by this high school where everything was just so easily separated."

As athletes, stoners and part-time punks, Malkmus and Kannenberg say they didn't fit into any of the neatly defined Tokay cliques. "We kind of hung out with this group of punkers from another high school," says Kannenberg, "but we didn't dress the part or anything. We were just kind of normal, I guess. But we were still outcasts."

"It's funny," he continues, stopping to sit on a bench in the quad. "Today, the people who listen to alternative music are the people who were like the rednecks then; the people who would tease us and stuff. The people who listen to Pavement are *those* people. It's kind of weird."

September 1994

beck
FOLK FUTURIST

BY **MARK KEMP**

Why do people like Beck? You know he's a loser definitely. How do you fans like a song about Beck being a loser? He isn't the only loser around. All of you are that are supporting a retarded rocker.
— Mike, Prodigy computer bulletin board, 2:12 a.m., 3/16/94

BECK HANSEN IS STANDING next to a tropical mural inside the Super Giant Wash in L.A.'s Highland Park neighborhood, neatly folding his faded-green, Farrah Fawcett T-shirt. "I have *two* Farrahs," the 23-year-old avant-hip-hop-folkie superstar announces, as he tosses the shirt aside and plucks a pair of blue Dickies workpants from the dryer. "And I have a Burt Reynolds and, uh... let's see, a pretty cool Sesame Street." Beck's voice is unusually deep for his delicate, five-foot-nine frame. His doe-like features are soft and fair like those of a 12-year-old, and his fine, brownish-blond hair is a greasy, stringy bird's nest. When he speaks, Beck sounds as earnest as a preacher.

Beck is not a preacher. He's a musical sponge, the ultimate product of a generation of young adults raised in broken homes, shuttled back and forth from one family member to another, and nurtured by the almighty TV. Today Beck doesn't even have a TV. Yet television — specifically MTV — has made him practically a household name. By the end of March, his oddball hit, "Loser," had rocketed into the Top 20. That's not normal for a song recorded on an eight-track machine at a friend's house in six hours.

But will Beck be able to weather the storm of hype surrounding "Loser," and walk away a lasting folkie figurehead for the kitchen-sink generation? Or is he doomed, despite his best intentions, to be another one-hit wonder? No matter how clever and observant Beck is, to the pop world at large, "Loser" is a novelty song. Aside from a few indie purists, and the kids who debate about him on computer bulletin boards, hardly anyone knows about the other Beck projects, such as the obscure Fingerprint 10-inch, *A Western Harvest Field By Moonlight*, or his various indie cassettes and singles. Moreover, while his major label debut, *Mellow Gold* (DGC), is a strong first album with plenty of promise, it ultimately finds Beck a not-quite-fully-realized artist who could use a little time to grow.

Fortunately, Beck is asking those questions too. "At first I thought it was a joke," he says of the hubbub surrounding "Loser." "So I just ignored it for a while. But when the commercial stations started playing it, and the thing started getting on the charts, I figured it must be for real. It was so freaky. I spent about seven months trying to decide if I wanted to have any part of it or if I should just ignore it."

He couldn't ignore it, because the major labels wouldn't stop knocking at his door. But when Beck finally answered, he had a list of conditions: he would get to do whatever he wanted to do musically, including continuing to put out weird records on indie labels like K, Bong Load and Flipside. "I figured if people wanted me to come and play my songs for them, I'll come and play 'em. But they have to know that it's not all going to be like 'Loser.'"

I just wanted to tell all the teeny-boppers who like "Loser" that you won't like Mellow Gold. *It's mostly folk music with a little punk stuff. Did anyone see the new video for "Pay No Mind" on 120 Minutes? I hope they don't turn it into a "poser clip" like they did "Loser." — Donna, Prodigy computer bulletin board, 12:30 p.m., 3/23/94*

FROM HIS T-SHIRT COLLECTION — which also includes an Orange Crush, a Reese's Peanut Butter Cup, and a vintage green Mountain Dew — to the *Star Wars* storm-trooper mask he sports on the back cover of *Mellow Gold*, to his references to mini-malls, Dixie cups and K-tel, Beck is an amalgam of late-20th century multi-media fallout. In his music, he spits it all out in tangled, Dylanesque lyrical puzzles, hip-hop sound collages, bleeps, blurps, distortion and old-timey folk melodies. If Dylan had his finger on the pulse of his inquisitive generation back in 1966 when he declared, "Everybody must get stoned," Beck seems every bit as in tune with his own cynical peers when in "Loser" he commands, "Get crazy with the Cheese Whiz."

Take away the noise and beat-box backing tracks, the voice modulators and wacky non-sequiturs, and Beck Hansen is a fairly traditional folk musician. At 17, the fan of Pussy Galore and Sonic Youth made a musical discovery that changed his life. "I was at my friend's house and I saw this album with a close-up of an old man's wrinkled face on it; he was sweating profusely and sort of had a sleepy look in his eyes. It was Mississippi John Hurt. I guess it had been issued in the '60s, because the lettering was all psychedelic and stuff. I thought, 'Wow, this is going to be crazy.' But when I took it home and put it on the record player, it was this droning, deep, slow, warm world that just let you come in and be there with him. All the music I'd ever heard before that was just big beats and drums pumping and everything. It never really gave you any room to step in, look around and breathe the fresh air."

BORN IN LOS ANGELES, Beck spent his pre-teens moving back and forth between his paternal grandparents, who lived outside of Kansas City, and his single mom, an office worker who lived in the rough, Pico-Vermont area of Los Angeles. Beck's mom and dad had split up when he was young, and he never had much contact with his dad, who remarried and started a new family. When he mentions this, there's only a trace of resentment in his voice. One way he dealt with his feelings was to immerse himself in *Star Wars* culture at around age seven; he estimates he saw the movies more than 50 times.

Beck's grandfather, a Presbyterian minister, tried to encourage him to become a Christian. By 12, Beck decided he'd rather stay with his mom full time. Like many creative teenagers, he felt alienated from the kids his age and wound up hanging out with an older crowd. Beck became fed up with school and quit after junior high. "I just didn't have the patience for it," he says. "It was just so mind-bogglingly tedious and hollow. Of course, I didn't go to a very good school. I know some people who went to good schools and probably benefited from it."

He worked a series of dead-end jobs — including driving a forklift at a warehouse in South-Central, and moving furniture — to help his mom. But after discovering Mississippi John Hurt, and later Woody Guthrie, Beck started getting antsy. "I was just constantly romantically envisioning this Woody Guthrie-type America — just traveling around and singing. So one day I saw this commercial on TV about a Greyhound bus ticket to anywhere in the U.S. for like $40. I got the ticket and took off to New York. It was a long hot trip."

Arriving in New York in 1989, he caught the tail end of the short-lived "anti-folk" scene, and hooked up with its spearheads, Roger Manning, Kirk Kelley and Lach (who ran the legendary Chameleon club on Sixth Street below Ave. A). The story goes that most of the anti-folkies, perhaps bitter over their own inability to rise above the fringe, wouldn't give the young troubadour the time of day. And yet Beck, in an uncharacteristic moment of complete sincerity, recalls his two years in New York wistfully as a pivotal time in his musical life.

"It was so creative," he says. "There was so much stuff happening, it was inspiring. To me it looked like everybody was going places. Of course, it never really happened. I dunno," he reflects, "maybe for me it was just my age — I was like 18 or something — but it just felt so great. It was such a special time. Suddenly I was turned on to the whole world. Being 18 really is such a turning point. And being in New York at that time made it so much better. You could write your own music, get drunk, and not really care about anything."

It was then that Beck started getting serious about writing songs. "I would go to the Chameleon for the open-mike night and play Woody Guthrie or Mississippi John Hurt songs — which was my whole *world* at the time; I didn't even want to *know* about anything else. But Lach wouldn't book me for a whole night unless I wrote my own songs. So I said, 'OK.' And I went and got a pen and paper and wrote five songs about stuff like pizza, or waking up after having been chain-sawed in half by a maniac — stuff like that. He finally gave me a Friday night."

After a series of bad financial situations — like getting ripped off by a crack addict in a phony apartment deal — Beck returned to L.A. in 1991. "I got totally depressed because there was no folk scene here. I tried to find one, and there's just nothing. Not like in New York. I was depressed for like a year, 'cause I just felt like there was such a community there. Here, I just felt sort of lost. I was this freak playing solo acoustic guitar."

He discovered the Onyx cafe in Los Feliz, the Gaslight, Al's Bar, Raji's and a string of supportive bands such as Ethyl Meatplow and Possum Dixon, who would let him warm up for them. His mother had even opened up a poetry hot spot, the Troy cafe. One evening at the hip indie nightspot Jabberjaw, he met Tom Rothrock, who was starting a label called Bong Load. The two exchanged phone numbers, and three months later got together one afternoon to do some recording. That was the day "Loser" was born.

"Tom had called up and said, 'Hey, I know this guy who does hip-hop beats and stuff. I said, 'Oh yeah, well sometimes I rap between songs and get people from the audience to do the beat-box thing into the mike.' So we went to this guy's house and I played him a few of my folk songs. He seemed pretty all-around unimpressed. Then I started playing this slide guitar part and he started taping it. He put a drum track to it and it was, you know, the 'Loser' riff. I started writing these lyrics to the verse part. When he played it back, I thought, 'Man, I'm the worst rapper in the world — I'm just a loser.' So I started singing, 'I'm a loser baby, so why don't you kill me.' I'm always kinda putting myself down like that."

The casual birth of "Loser" reflects Beck's breezy worldview. He didn't give the recording another thought until a year later, when Rothrock called again and said he was thinking about putting "Loser" out as a single. He pressed a few copies, sent them out to a few alternative radio stations, and — boom — the song became an instant smash. First the tiny, L.A. college station KXLU started playing it, followed by the NPR flagship KCRW, and then the commercial "alternative" station KROQ. By that time, nearly every major label A&R rep in town was scrambling to sign the wunderkind. Geffen won the bidding war partly because they offered him the most freedom — but also because it's the label of Beck's guitar-noise heroes, Sonic Youth.

beck

Beck is cool. If you think he's a loser, well we all know who the f-in' loser is. (It's not him!) Besides, he's good-lookin' — Sarah, Prodigy computer bulletin board, 5 p.m., 3/16/94

Ohmygod, isn't he!!!!!!! — Lisa, Prodigy computer bulletin board, 6:24 p.m., 3/16/94

AS WE WAIT for another load of laundry to dry, Beck and I walk into the dim light of the parking lot and sit on the hood of his faded gray Volvo with two bumper stickers on the back that together read, "Dream On!" "Karaoke Queen." It's a typical hazy L.A. March night — kind of cool, kind of scary. Two kids on Rollerblades whiz by and giggle.

"I think the biggest misconception of me is that all this hype is something I planned or something," Beck says. "I've had no part in it, I'm really surprised about it, and I think it's completely ridiculous when people put me on the cover of magazines. It seems really funny, you know. Sometimes I go out of my way *not* to get into that position, but I keep ending up there.

"Like when we made the video for 'Loser' — we were *fucking around*. We weren't making anything slick — it was deliberately crude. You know? It wasn't like one of these perfect new-wave color soft-focus extravaganzas. We were just fucking around. And now they're playing it all the time. It's the same thing with the song — that song was written and recorded in six hours. No plans went into it."

His face turns slightly frightened. "It's just totally ridiculous. It's like waking up on an airplane that's going down, and you don't know if you should get in a parachute and jump or... wait until they serve the drinks."

March 1994

green day
THE MONEY SHOT

BY GINA ARNOLD

OCTOBER 1993, MIDWAY THROUGH Green Day's set at the 2,500-seat Warfield Theater. Not only is this the biggest venue the trio has ever played, but it is only the third time in the group's five-year existence that they've performed in San Francisco. It's not as though they live so far away. Berkeley, the band's hometown, is only about five miles east across the Bay Bridge.

Green Day is not well-known to the majority of the crowd, but the band's tight, poppy punk rock is winning them over. The kids — it's a rare all-ages show at the Warfield — crush the stage and pogo to what the Ramones might sound like today if they were shorter, cuter, more earnest, more energetic, and a hell of a lot younger. After a rousing version of "Don't Leave Me" from the band's LP *39/Smooth*, during which singer Billie Joe and bassist Mike Dirnt trade supercharged antics across the stage, the band stops for a breather.

"Hey," says Billie Joe, clad in a fetching white ladies' slip, sans underpants, "I thought they only let old hippies play this joint."

The crowd cheers. "This," he continues, "is a song off our upcoming album."

This time one member of the crowd jeers. "Green Day sucks!" yells a lone voice at the front. "Sell outs!"

"Takes one to know one!" ripostes Dirnt, gleefully. "Ah, hah-hah…" adds Billie Joe, "this is about you, buddy." And then the band rips into "Chump."

DO YOU REMEMBER 1985?

Ronald Reagan was President. Madonna wasn't a monster. The Berlin Wall was still standing; Yugoslavia was at peace. In 1985 there was no *Simpsons*. No *Roseanne*. No Guns N' Roses. No

Sharon Stone. The Replacements, Sonic Youth and Hüsker Dü were still on independent labels.

It was a different era entirely.

Since those days, new countries have been invented and countless children have been born. A lot of bands from those days still haven't broken up, but more have been formed than you can count. And yet — though one acknowledges the futility of judging, say, new Supreme Court rulings, the Bible, gun laws, or current U.S. AIDS policies on the standards of a bygone era — many fans of independent rock persist in upholding standards of those innocent times on behalf of a host of young bands whose goals, priorities and, most importantly, temptations are entirely different.

Accustomed as many of us have been over the past decade to think of major labels as the Corporate Ogre, things are not the same as they were nine years ago when Warner Bros. signed Hüsker Dü. Things are not even the same as they were five years ago when Slash signed a punk/pop band called Sweet Baby. At the time, Sweet Baby had contributed one track to *Turnaround*, a compilation on the Lookout! label documenting the work of a tiny group of bands which congregated around a punk rock collective located at 924 Gilman Street in Berkeley.

In 1990, Sweet Baby, championed by then-Slash producer and A&R person Matt Wallace, was given an estimated $10,000 to make its self-titled record. There was no advertising budget for the record, because Slash felt advertising would ruin the band's punk rock credibility. They didn't release the record on CD (it was vinyl and cassette only). They sent the band on a little tour, which fell apart halfway through due to a series of gigs booked on nights when the clubs were generally closed. After returns, Sweet Baby's record sold approximately 2,000 copies.

That same year, Green Day, another Gilman Street band, recorded its first 7-inch for Lookout! Three years later, Warner Bros. signed the trio and purportedly gave it $300,000 (not including money for video and tour support) for its major label debut. A few weeks before the release of the record, *Dookie*, Warner bought Billboard's back page for $15,000. The week the album came out, the marquee outside of Tower Records in San Diego screamed: "Green Day record finally in stock!" The very next week, February

19, 1994, *Dookie* entered the album charts at number 127 and sold 9,000 copies.

Karl Marx once said, "History repeats itself: the first time as tragedy, the second time as farce." Sweet Baby's history may well have been tragedy, but it remains to be seen whether Green Day's shot will turn out to be a joke.

"THE ONE THING THAT GIVES MUSIC its potency," says Sub Pop's Bruce Pavitt, "is its context. You have to look at the artists' community at large, where they're coming from, who they were speaking to in the first place. Look at San Francisco in the '60s: Haight-Ashbury, Owsley, Ginsberg. That was what made the Grateful Dead and the Jefferson Airplane more than just bands; what made them resonant and important. A better example is Dischord in D.C.: teenagers making records, and their whole anti-drug philosophy, putting huge X's on their hands to mark their solidarity with people underage. The context is the whole story."

What Green Day has that many other bands on the market today lack is context. Green Day's roots are real, embedded as they are on the corner of 8th Avenue and Gilman Street, four blocks shy of Highway 80 in Berkeley. That's where a collective of teenage punk rockers, led by *Maximumrocknroll* founder Tim Yohannan, started the all-ages punk clubhouse 924 Gilman in 1988.

The club, an old cane shop decorated with grafitti and a couple of basketball hoops, is run on a strict percentage basis by volunteers. The stage cuts off one corner of the room; the tiny "bar" area, papered with notices for upcoming riot grrrl meetings, band-member-wanted posters and fliers of old shows, serves only Hansen's soda and a variety of candy. But the club has, since its start, flourished in the hearts and minds of Berkeley teens, providing a safe haven — a community — for runaways, misfits and putative punk rockers. Waiflike girls in junk-store dresses, guys in dumpers and dyed hair. Jawbreaker, Samiam, Blatz, Fifteen. A romantic world, where, according to Green Day's Billie Joe, "you'd have this total connection."

The atmosphere was one of complete support. "It was even kind of neat when the van's transmission blew out and stuff," Billie Joe says. "It was cool that we were in the hole, because all we cared about was that we were really tight as a band and we got to play a lot of basements and rec halls and squats for beer, and kids would get together in their kitchens and talk about Gilman Street and Lookout!"

As with many a revolutionary concept, Gilman Street's first year was its headiest. In its earliest incarnation, it flourished with the help of a host of bands, including Isocracy, Sweet Baby, Crimpshrine, the Lookouts and Operation Ivy, the latter being the cornerstone band of Gilman Street legend. And legend is the right word: in underground circles fueled by articles in *Maximumrocknroll* and *Flipside*, the club has served as a model to punk rock communities ever since. Sweet Baby's Dallas Denery recalls playing similar clubs around the country on the band's one tour: "The kids would always say, 'Is this anything like Gilman Street?' And we'd always tell them, 'Hell, this is better!'"

Operation Ivy was Lookout! Records' breakout band, and thus the one which funded early pressings of Green Day's records back in 1989. If you think initial sales of Green Day's *Dookie* seem phenomenal, consider that even though Operation Ivy lasted less than two years and toured just once, the group has sold almost twice as many records as Green Day — all by word-of-mouth, with no advertising and only a smattering of college radio airplay. Soon after Operation Ivy broke up in 1989, Lookout! label head Lawrence Livermore signed Green Day.

At the time, the members were only 17 years old. Beginning in 1989, Livermore helped the band release a 7-inch called "1,000 Hours," and then sent them on tour. After five years, two records, seven U.S. circuits, three European tours, and 70,000 copies of *39/Smooth* and *Kerplunk*, the major labels were after Green Day, despite the band's distinct lack of mainstream profile.

In early spring, 1993, attorney Elliott Cahn, a former member of Sha Na Na and more recently the lawyer for bands like Testament, Mudhoney and the Melvins, started playing Green Day's demo tape to A&R people. Each one bit hard. Cahn was in a position to dictate his terms, which were relatively modest ($300,000 is, after all, $75,000 less than Nirvana got three years earlier from Geffen, and considerably less than bands like American Music Club, Helmet and Rocket From the Crypt have received since Nirvana's success). That Cahn and Green Day got what they asked for is not even an issue. What is surprising to East Bay onlookers is that Green Day wanted to be on a major label at all.

Green Day's deal with Lookout! stipulated that they receive 60 percent net gross of the profits from their records sales, which adds up to somewhere between $150,00 and $200,000. "They are, without a doubt, the only band I've ever met who had a good experience on an independent label," claims one industry onlooker who was interested in signing them.

Nevertheless, Green Day decided to go major, thus setting themselves up to be scapegoats of the indie world. It's the final proof that Nirvana forever changed the pop music world, which is much different from the one that had dealt previously, wickedly, with Sweet Baby and so many other long-forgotten bands.

AND SO THE LIMOUSINES rolled up Ashby Avenue, one containing Interscope's Tom Whalley, who, according to Billie Joe, "seemed nervous about our neighborhood and kept looking at his really expensive watch." The Sony and Geffen people came too — invited, like everyone else, to hear Green Day play in a postage stamp-sized practice room in the basement of their rundown house.

In the end, it came down to Sony and Warner (Interscope had axed itself with the limo performance, and Geffen's Gary Gersh was already rumored to be jumping ship for the presidency at Capitol). Sony, whose 24-year-old A&R guy Benji Gordon (responsible for Soul Asylum's success) was actually on the Green Day tip well before Cahn came into the picture, came close to nailing the deal shut. But in the end, Green Day went with 30-year-old Rob Cavallo of Warner Bros., who had signed the Muffs and Goo Goo Dolls. Cavallo, whose father managed Lovin' Spoonful, Little Feat, and Earth, Wind & Fire, came to Green Day's house carrying a guitar case, jammed on some Beatles tunes with them, smoked some pot with them, and took them and their girlfriends out for Indian food on Shattuck Avenue. He signed them even before he'd seen them play live.

In some ways Cavallo, a graduate of USC, is an unlikely choice for Green Day to have choosen as mentor, but Billie Joe and his friends somehow found common ground with him. "He's from L.A. and stuff, but he's married and thinking about having kids," comments Billie Joe. "That made him seem like more of a genuine person, whereas a lot of those fuckers are just like hipsters. Some of them just seemed to want to get laid, to tell you the truth."

In addition to signing Green Day, Cavallo produced them, a fact which some industry insiders decry as a conflict of interest. One source claims Cavallo told a producer's agent not to let Green Day meet any other producers, so that they wouldn't know they had other options. However, Green Day was enthusiastic about the Muffs album, which Cavallo also produced. For his part, Cavallo says, "I did mention to them before I signed them that I would be thrilled to produce, but it wasn't part of the deal. It just signified how interested in the project I was. I considered it a gift to spend time in the studio with them."

Still, there are reasons Warner Bros. may not have been an ideal choice for a punk band such as Green Day. The label's track record for alternative acts has been poor up until now. "They never push the right buttons and there's too many managers there," says one industry onlooker. "Even sure things like Paul Westerberg do bad there. It's a really comfy, happy, jolly place to work, but they have nothing in the charts."

Cavallo and Green Day took to the studio last summer, and at first the band managed to keep a fairly low profile despite the big-label deal. They deflected resentment from their close friends by continuing to be just regular guys. They continued to play gigs at Gilman Street and Berkeley Square (since drummer Tré had just turned 21, it was now easier than ever to play out). They also arranged to give Lookout! excellent terms for the back catalog. And they insisted that the recording be done in a studio they could bike to — which turned out to be Fantasy. None of this saved them from getting shit from their audience, however: at a gig mid-summer at the Phoenix Theater in Petaluma (which, along with the city of Benecia, is a teenage, Green Day stronghold), there was a picket line outside made up of punks who passed out literature urging fans to boycott the group's upcoming record.

In part, the problems were due to the tight Gilman Street world they came from, but it was also partly the result of inevitable jealousy among other bands. Mostly, perhaps, it was a holdover from attitudes formed around the results of decade-old deals.

The members of Green Day remain a bit unsure about their decision. "Sometimes," says Billie Joe, bemusedly, "people ask, 'Why did you do it?' And I'm still like" — he shakes his head, eyes open wider and wider — "I don't know! I just don't know!"

The story of Green Day's success is nothing new, according to Cavallo. It reflects nothing more sinister than the usual way major record companies work. It is the logical end to a tale of talent. "If I got the demo tape five years ago, I think it would have interested us," he says. "Let's face it, this record is not the most radio-friendly in the world, but the songs themselves would have interested us, plain and simple."

IT'S EVENING ON GILMAN STREET, and Lawrence Livermore is thinking about getting out. "It's sad," he says, "because this thing we've been involved with is going away from me. But I can't get bent out of shape about it. For years we specialized in East Bay bands, but the chemistry has changed radically. Now, as soon as a band gets 200 people to show, they want tour support, a bigger recording budget... They're like, 'If Green Day can do it we can.' Which is totally forgetting the five years of hard work Green Day logged."

Brian Zero is a member of the Gilman Street band Siren and ring leader of the anti-Green Day movement that picketed the Petaluma concert last summer. His objection to Green Day, he says, is not personal or musical, but philosophical. His points are exactly the same ones that were used ten, 15, even 25 years ago. He is against "big record companies coming and in and marketing our music... polluting the strength and integrity of the independent scene."

Zero's zealousness is naive, and not much different from that of a hippie preaching peace and love well into the '90s. But his idealism is nonetheless vitally important to the health of independent music. He believes, for example, in an underground resurgence of sorts; that an independent network will once again rise up against the corporate structure.

"The thing is," he adds sadly, "this society is so cultureless. It has no identity of its own. The punk scene not only helped make me a person, but it gave me a community. It's not Utopian, but it is my tribe. And I think that sense of identity is being completely decimated by the major labels. This is kind of an ironic comparison, but it's like indigenous peoples working with Hollywood and then seeing this totally phony result on screen. People aren't receiving what it's all about, they're just receiving a product."

As it stands now, Green Day (the product) is either Warner Bros.' idea of a slacker generation anti-hero (what Cavallo calls "meaningful aggressive punk pop") or, according to Billie Joe, "songs about yet another generation falling down the chutes; songs for people who have the same ideas as I do; songs that will maybe help some of them get up off their asses and see another world."

Co-option or conversion? You be the judge. If, as *Village Voice* rock critic Robert Christgau once said, the compulsion to great refusals is a mark of virtue, oppression, neurosis, or all three, then Green Day's Great Big Yes may mean that they are liberated, sane, and utterly immoral. In the final analysis, the tension between major labels and independents is — as it has been since the times of Muddy Waters and Elvis Presley — a simple class issue: black vs. white, worker vs. management. Billie Joe is the youngest of six children whose father, a jazz drummer, died when he was ten. His mother supported the kids on her salary as a waitress. Mike Dirnt also comes from a single-parent home and, at times, has supported his mother. The fact that kids from this background would choose the security of a major label future over the more romantic and Marxist life of selling records out of the proverbial back of a van, is hardly surprising.

"I am exploiting myself," Billie Joe says stubbornly. "One thing that really bugs me is all the rich, snobby kids who claim all this punk rockness coming out and saying you can't make money and stuff. How can they say that to me? They already have money. They live punky now, but in 20 years their parents will keel over and they'll get everything.

"I've been really fortunate to be part of the punk rock scene," he continues, "'cause I see my friends back in Pinole stuck in a rut. An alternative lifestyle is a lot more fulfilling, sometimes just because you don't have money. But my situation was that I could care less about which way I go — indie or major — as long as I can keep playing music."

March 1994

hole

GOOD SISTER BAD SISTER

BY **LORRAINE ALI**

THREE MEMBERS OF HOLE are left waiting again. Eric, the tall one, cracks a nervous, almost apologetic smile. Kristen glances at the clock. Patti offers her guests some more tea, its aroma wafting through the living room on a gentle breeze. A bowl of shortbread on the table by the couch is nearly gone. You can hear the patter of rain against the window. And then, two hours after everyone has converged at Patti's apartment in the hip Capitol Hill section of Seattle, the stomp of feet in the stairwell breaks the tension.

"Patti! Patti!" a raspy voice calls out, and the front door swings open. Courtney Love rushes in, dumps her turquoise leather jacket and plastic Barbie backpack on the floor, and announces in a huff, "Sorry I'm late. I've been shopping."

IT'S NOT HARD TO IMAGINE Courtney Love standing in a Chanel boutique snapping her fingers at a quivering saleswoman as Madonna did in her pseudo-cinema vérité *Truth Or Dare*. The 28-year-old singer, guitarist, punk rock star and wife of Nirvana's Kurt Cobain has mega-attitude and the cash to back it up. But it's more likely she's been tearing through local thrift shops today, looking for a shredded velveteen dress or another ratty sweater. Too raw to play the bitchy diva and too outspoken to blend in, Love is a shake-and-bake of trash culture and *Vogue* airs. She even bought a Lexus the other day but took it back, she says, "'cause it was too embarrassing. Our old Volvo with one bald tire will have to do."

Love's bandmates watch, apparently unaffected, as the frazzled peroxide blonde blows through the flat like a storm. Bassist Kristen Pfaff (pronounced "paff") plays with the holes in her ripped black tights. Guitarist Eric Erlandson flips through a book. And drummer Patti Schemel, an ultimate tomboy, pulls her skate-rat tennis shoes back on and asks again, "More tea?"

Love would like to push Hole's music to the fore today; after all, *Live Through This*, the band's second album, three years in the waiting, is scheduled for an April release. Yet Love's dominant nature betrays her and she winds up focusing on her own complicated life. Amidst the many colliding facets of her personality — feminist, victim, attacker, protector — her musicianship gets lost in the shuffle. Which is precisely why, at least for now, she wants to be respected for that more than anything else. It doesn't matter that Hole's 1991 debut album, *Pretty On the Inside*, stood on its own, powerfully and brutally exposing the furious songwriter beneath torrents of noise and feedback. The music was soon buried under the media storm surrounding Love's marriage to Kurt Cobain. Then came the accusations of drug abuse during her pregnancy, the birth of her baby, Frances Bean, and Love's legal fight to be deemed a fit mother.

"I thought about getting a boob job, but I don't know," Love free associates, as she plops onto the couch with a plate of crackers and dip. "When some asshole yells, 'Show us your tits,' I want to do it. But they're kind of saggy, so it wouldn't have that 'fuck you' impact." She lights the first in a chain of Dunhill cigarettes, and then unleashes a flurry of unedited ideas, jumping erratically from subject to subject, spitting out flashes of brilliant clarity in a sea of raw thought. She crunches, then puffs, then seems embarrassed when a rare moment of silence catches her off guard. That's easy enough to fix — she picks a fight with Erlandson, who co-founded the band with Love four years ago.

"What do you mean you knew the guitars were wimpy!" she grills the guitarist, referring to the mix of the new album. When he tries to explain — "Well, I..." — Love bowls him over: "Then why didn't you *say* anything?! Why do I always have to be the bitch?!"

Live Through This, produced by Sean Slade and Paul Q. Kolderie, veers far from *Pretty On the Inside*. It's more melodic than its predecessor, which was marked by Sonic Youth-like dissonance (Sonic's bassist, Kim Gordon, produced that album) together with Love's wrenching, guttural howls. Ironically, the melodicism on *Live Through This* is what renders the new album even more powerful. Though you can still hear the rage and discontent in Love's voice and lyrics, the emotions are housed in more solid structures this time.

The earlier Courtney Love screamed out symbolically shocking lines like, "Slut-kiss girl won't you promise her smack?/Is she pretty on the inside?/Is she pretty from the back?" behind shards of angry-sounding feedback and distortion. Today, tormented lines such as, "I am the girl you know/Can't look you in the eye/I am the girl you know/So sick I cannot try... I am the girl you know/I lie and lie and lie," come with a ripened, almost bittersweet sense of acceptance, the distortion replaced by ringing, mellower guitars.

Yet Hole has hardly lost its edge. Songs like "Violet" blow up in chaotic bursts of feedback, while "She Walks Over Me" has an almost hardcore foundation. And Love's vocals are as rippingly angry as ever, only now she lures you in with moments of melancholy rather than constantly rubbing you raw. Love claims the words aren't based on her personal life, yet amidst the chaos of "I Think That I Would Die," you can hear her shriek, "I want my baby."

"I understand why Polly Harvey did *Rid of Me*, but I have no interest in doing that," she says. "It's something I did a long time ago. The last thing I want is the public saying, 'She's having a nervous breakdown in front of our eyes; let's go watch the freak show.' Fuck you! I'm here to write classic rock now. If you want someone to be *bad* for you, there are plenty of girls with charisma who are *bad*, who shoot drugs intravenously and sleep with lots of people, who will play the part of Ophelia. I'm just not gonna do it. I'm just not."

"A lot of women in bands like to call it that 'cathartic thing,'" offers Schemel. Love doesn't miss a beat: "Fuck that! I go to a therapist."

"We're all neurotic, so we *need* to be cathartic," adds Pfaff, sarcastically. And Courtney fires back again: "I would rather keep my guts to myself, thanks."

Love's bright red lips and big blue-green eyes stand out against her powdered pale skin and blanched hair. Chipped red polish dots her nubby nails, which she bites in between cigarettes. Her matching toenails are exposed under silver '70s cocktail party shoes that clomp rather than click when she traipses across the hardwood floor for another glass of lemonade. Tight black jeans, a pink, junior-sized, ruffled sweater and cutesy kitty T-shirt make up the rest of her outfit. She looks like a teenage runaway, circa 1975.

IN FACT, IT WAS THE RUNAWAYS ALBUM *Queens of Noise* that lured the prepubescent Love away from her Bay City Rollers-style tartan jumpsuits and into the world of bad-ass rock'n'roll fashion. "They looked like the foxy stoner chicks at my school," she says of the godmothers of all-girl punk bands, "but they were way cooler and badder. They were standing in front of a 7-Eleven — Lita and Joan — looking like, 'Ah, photo sessions, god I hate them!' That's when I became fascinated with becoming a J.D. — a juvenile delinquent."

Born on July 9, 1965 in San Francisco, Courtney is the oldest of five half-brothers and half-sisters, all of whom, she claims, "have masters degrees and went to college from the day they were born." Her mother, Linda Carroll, is a psychologist who was recently in the news because of her client, Katherine Anne Power, a fugitive '60s radical who turned herself in 23 years after a notorious 1970 bank robbery murder. Her stepfather is a teacher and renowned fly fisherman. "You know how in most family homes there'll be pictures of the kids at the head of the stairs?" Love asks. "There's not a picture of me — and it's fine, it's OK. I mean, she didn't have an abortion."

Love's youth was a whirlwind of communes, boarding schools, juvenile halls and even foster homes. When she was very young, her mom and real father, who were hippies, moved to Eugene, Oregon, where they divorced soon thereafter. The family then moved to New Zealand, where Love's mom lived in a commune and Courtney attended boarding school for two and a half years. At ten, she was hauled off to a free school in England; two years later, she was sent back to Eugene alone to live with her mom's therapist. "He was like her private guru," she says.

Love recalls her high school in Eugene as full of Led Zeppelin heads. "I couldn't listen to Zeppelin," she says. "It scared me. It sounded so far away and sexual and evil. It was too ominous and dark. I liked pretty things. Fleetwood Mac's *Rumors* is still one of my favorite albums." In the early '80s, her mother and stepfather moved the family again, this time to Portland. There, Courtney got to fulfill her fantasy of becoming a J.D. — she was busted for shoplifting and ripping up a sheet in a local store. She violated her two-year parole by running away from home, and spent the next four years in foster homes and juvenile care facilities around

Portland. By 1983, Love had taken a job in a drag-queen disco and begun hanging out with older groupies on her off nights. "I was intrigued with it," she says, "but I wasn't pretty enough for that stuff. I had no style or tits."

The next year, Courtney met Kat Bjelland, now of Babes In Toyland, and the two formed a new wave band. From then until the late '80s, she was constantly on the go, moving back and forth between San Francisco, Portland, Minneapolis, Seattle and New York, and playing with everyone from L7's Jennifer Finch to early lineups of Babes In Toyland and Faith No More. In 1987, she wound up in the movies, appearing in Alex Cox's weird western *Straight To Hell*, alongside Elvis Costello and the Pogues' Shane McGowan. Around the same time, her meager trust fund had run out while she was living in Alaska, and Love wound up working as a stripper all the way down the west coast, ending up at Jumbo's Clown Room in L.A.

Love pulls a compact out of her cluttered purse, applies more lipstick, and winces. She thinks she's ugly and she says it often. Even after losing more than 50 pounds and undergoing a $2,000 nose job, she remains unsatisfied. "There are many, many a time when I wish I was a guy and wasn't compelled to keep bleaching my hair," she says. "Every time the roots grow out I swear I'm gonna let it be brown. It's just an affectation I have. I already changed my face so I would take better photographs and sell records and not be considered the way Frightwig was considered — 'Oh, they're fat, they're ugly, no wonder they're screaming.' I want my anger to be valid, and the only way to do that is to be fairly attractive."

She feels the same way about her comments. "I stopped being sarcastic because it looks terrible in print if you're a woman," she continues. "I think it's because I'm supposed to be dumber. My theory is that I'm supposed to be what people would prefer me to be — the bad girl, druggie, Nancy Spungen-type. That doesn't go well with literacy or college or intellect or humor. What goes well with that is rock'n'roll, that sort of date-Billy Idol type of shit. A faux spirit they'd like to hoist on me. I'm not really that bad, I'm just not supposed to be smart."

So there's also Love-the-intellectual. Moments ago, she had

casually dropped a hardback copy of *Caligula* onto the table so that it was in full view of everyone present. Then she proceeded to drop a litany of literary references, from Thomas Pynchon to Katherine Dunn. Whether or not she's read the stuff is irrelevant; it seems she mainly wants to be associated with these things as part of a calculated image which she constantly flubs by exposing her real self. Despite her best intentions, Love's vulnerability and humanness shine like beacons: she ends up gossiping about one person, saying sweet things about another, discussing the pros and cons of prenuptial agreements, and then talking about having gas pains.

"Most of the mail we get says stuff like, 'Everyone hates you, but I love you,'" she reveals. "If I had ten dollars for everyone who said that, we'd all be rich. It's a sort of love-to-hate-you sort of thing, almost affectionate."

IT'S DAMP, COLD AND DRIZZLING outside the Seattle Coliseum where Nirvana is scheduled to play in about an hour. Love picks up her pace, taking big strides across the VIP parking lot with Erlandson and Schemel close behind. She snaps at the probing security guards: "Yes I have a fucking pass!" and "I'm here to see my husband, do you mind?" You can almost hear their balls drop in her wake.

In the coliseum dressing room, members of Nirvana and the Fastbacks trade stories about Eddie Vedder's latest stupid stunt, as Courtney goes into backstage overdrive. She's hardly trackable, running about as if on a mission — and rarely standing anywhere near Cobain. When the couple finally does come together, it's turbulent: they mumble some words at each other, then yank away, and then, suddenly, handfuls of corn chips are flying about them. Just as quickly, they've gone their separate ways again.

People expect a show from Love, whether she's onstage or backstage. She once punched K Records owner Calvin Johnson in the face, has been spotted brawling with women in public, and was hauled away by the cops last year for rumbling with Cobain at home. Still, Love can't understand everyone's violent expectations of her. "Sometimes I'll go places and people want me to cause trouble," she says. "I went to Fugazi and everyone was just expecting me to make trouble. Even Ian MacKaye was sitting there, 'Are you gonna make trouble tonight?' *Make trouble tonight?* I've met the guy three times and every time it's been completely pleasant and fine. What do you mean, trouble?"

She also has to contend with her image as a controlling force over Cobain. "People think I'm the bitch who's ruining Nirvana or something," she says, rolling her eyes and snorting. Yet when Nirvana hits the stage before 15,000 screaming teens, Courtney darts about the parameters as if conducting the show. As the band churns into "Rape Me," you can hear her ripping vocal influence in Cobain's own howl.

"I think Kurt has a better singing voice than I do, but I know I'm a better lyricist," she says. "It's just the way it is. I'm not saying that Hole will ever sell as many records as them, because the truth of the matter is, girls don't sell as much as guys, no matter what. If I'd have made *Nevermind* — every song the same — and put it out at the same time, and made the same video, it wouldn't have sold 500,000 [*Nevermind* sold more than four million copies]. That's just the way the market is. Girls don't buy records by girls."

IN 1989, WHEN LOVE PLACED AN AD in L.A.'s classifieds newspaper *The Recycler*, Erlandson responded to it. "It said something like: 'People wanted to form band with influences Big Black, Sonic Youth, Stooges,'" he recalls. "She called me back at three in the morning and talked my ear off for two hours. I met her and thought, 'This is not gonna work.' She didn't know how to play and she had a really crazy lifestyle. I didn't think she would get her shit together, 'cause so many people in Hollywood don't." But Courtney was persistent. "She called again and we got her neighbor to play bass," Erlandson continues. "Then we saw something happening."

Erlandson had been looking for a group since he moved away from his hometown of San Pedro. There, he'd played in various Doors-style garage bands. Erlandson grew up the second youngest of seven in a strict Catholic family; his father was dean of Liberal Arts at the nearby Loyola Marymount College. When local bands the Minutemen and Black Flag (Eric delivered newspapers to Flag guitarist Greg Ginn's house) became punk legends, he decided that he wanted to play in a band, too.

Erlandson and Love started rehearsing together and went through a series of rhythm sections before solidifying with bassist

Jill Emery and drummer Caroline Rue. In March 1991, the quartet put out a single on Sub Pop, "Dick Nail"/"Burn Black," before signing with Caroline and releasing *Pretty On the Inside* the following month. Five months later, Love started dating Kurt Cobain during a Hole/Nirvana tour. The relationship sent Love's life (not to mention Hole) into a whirlwind. On February 2, 1992, Love married Cobain while pregnant with his child. Four months into the pregnancy, she put her group on hold. Meanwhile, a major label bidding war had ensued for Hole, and after turning down Madonna's Maverick and Rick Rubin's Def American, the band landed a reported million-dollar deal with Nirvana's label, Geffen. At the same, Emery and Rue quit the band over the usual "musical differences."

As Love's life became more convoluted with every sale of a Nirvana record, Erlandson had begun looking for new Hole members. In San Francisco, he met up with Schemel, a native of Marysville, Washington, a farming area about an hour north of Seattle. Schemel had always dreamed of playing in a band. "I wanted to be drummer from the first time I saw Buddy Rich play as a kid," she says. Pfaff, originally from Buffalo, New York, hooked up with Hole in 1993, just after quitting her Minneapolis-based band, Janitor Joe. The 26-year-old classically trained pianist, who studied English and Women's Studies at Boston College, never even played rock until she was 22.

It wasn't easy to re-ignite Hole's career after the whirlwind of attention that focused on Love and Cobain's relationship in late 1992. About a month before Love delivered her child, Frances Bean, on August 18, 1992, the August issue of *Vanity Fair* hit the stands with Love's explosive admission that she'd been using heroin during her pregnancy. (Love claims she was quoted out of context, though *Vanity Fair* stands by its story.) "That article really took its toll on our band," she says, "but it took a lot of my spirit, too.

"Physiologically, when you've had a child, you have this loving, angelic creature that you're part of," she continues. "And there's nothing like somebody trying to interfere with that process. It was horrible. I'd hear this wise mother voice in my head saying, 'Don't give her [writer Lynn Hirschberg] so much power. This happened to you for a reason. It happened to you because you can take it. It happened to you because you don't have a weak character. You're not like your father. You're not like your mother.' But then there's the weak part of me that's like, 'Oh my God! My pediatrician looks at me like I'm crazy. My lawyer doesn't believe me. God, a fucking illiterate social worker is in my house questioning my right to be a mother.' These aren't real happy things."

Frances Bean turned out to be a healthy seven-pound infant. "It was almost obscene how fast I had her," Love says, almost nonchalantly. "I was like, 'You have one head, *I know* you do.' And then she came right out. I'm really thankful — she's my friend." Love had to undergo a series of court hearings and drug tests in order to keep the baby.

As Courtney describes that particularly difficult time, Patti and Eric are beginning to fade. After all, Love is now entering her third hour of non-stop chatter. She says the *Vanity Fair* article brought up some family issues that forced her to take a serious look at her life. She saw similarities between her father and the woman depicted in the article. "My dad is scary and I want him to stay out of our lives," she says.

"Everything that's bad about me, everything that Lynn Hirschberg saw in me — which must have been there to some degree for her to see it — my father's ten times that," Love continues, adding that she sometimes sees herself as a megalomaniac, dishonest and overweight. On the upside, the article brought Love and her mother together. "That was the only time I ever had my mother be really supportive; she understood. I think it's a real bad idea to breed with people that you're gonna later be repulsed by physically, mentally or spiritually. Even if I end up hating Kurt, I'd never be repulsed by him. He's so graceful and beautiful. Even if he can be a big, piggy grump sometimes, and cruel, he'll never repulse me. Repulsion is a real problem I have. I try to fight it off. I get real repulsed with everybody — not that *I'm* so great. In fact, I'm really repulsive too.

"I don't think anybody's entirely good," she continues, and then pauses before adding, "But I do wish I ruled the world. I think it'd be a better place."

IN THE EARLY '90S, Hole was lumped in with the so-called "foxcore" movement, a joke term coined by Sonic Youth's Thurston Moore and used to lump together bands such as L7 and Babes In Toyland. It was basically just another way of ghettoizing girls with guitars. Now Hole is often mentioned as a precursor to the riot grrrl movement. But Love never felt a part of either contrived group. "To be a riot grrrl, it's like you either have to physically make yourself very unattractive or else you have to act as though you haven't had a menstrual period yet," she says. "The other thing is their attitude about merit: 'We don't have to subscribe to the male-measured idea of good, so therefore you have to like us even if we suck.' Fuck that. We didn't fucking work this hard to get as good as we are at what we do. Neither did P.J. Harvey."

"I saw this little riot grrrl in *Spin* who was holding a little magazine called *Princess*," she continues. "She's 15, but everything in her little riot grrrl world — like Hello Kitty products — is telling her to act like she's seven. That's not feminism, it's cultural anorexia."

Love believes she knows a little bit about feminism and incorporates it into Hole's world. But she doesn't make it an obvious, overshadowing issue. Because she married Kurt Cobain, she says, "I was forced to fight this uphill, retarded, moronic battle that who I fuck is me. It's a lesson, and I think it was handed to me for a reason. I was trained my whole life by feminists to handle something like this, and I am enough of a feminist that I can articulate and separate myself from it. So maybe it's my duty to serve as some sort of unevolved fuckin' martyr, so it won't happen to the next person that gets involved with a powerful man."

Courtney Love smiles. "Somebody said something great to me about all this once. They said, 'You know, as much shit as you are taking for your marriage and stuff, you've really affected the role of the rock star's girlfriend. You really fucked it up!' And the fact that I personally am the first woman to break a guitar onstage in Great Britain, that's enough. I mean, you can't have everything, right?"

January 1994

the breeders

SISTER ACT

BY **GINA ARNOLD**

KIM DEAL IS STANDING IN HER PAJAMAS in front of a chi-chi clothing shop on the Sausalito quay. It's seven o'clock on a cool March evening and she's been distracted by an outfit in the window — an enormous white polyester jump suit with foot-wide lapels, perfectly creased legs, two-inch cuffs, and fake turquoise and gold rhinestone studs around the collar and belt. She wants to wear it to an upcoming photo shoot she's doing for an *Interview* magazine spread on "Guitar Heroes."

"You guys don't like it, do you?" Deal asks as her fellow Breeders stand with their mouths gaping. "Tell me seriously, do you think it's too much? What do you *really* think?"

It's a clear-cut "Glamour Don't." The thing isn't even *pseudo* Elvis — it's *Married To the Mob*-meets-Naomi Judd. But Deal's not about to give up. "That's what's so cool about it," she pleads. "Don't you think so? Wouldn't it be funny if I wore it?"

THE BREEDERS BEGAN as a side project while Kim Deal was still playing bass in the now-defunct Pixies. They made a splash in 1990 with their debut album, *Pod*, which also featured bassist Josephine Wiggs of the Perfect Disaster, ex-Throwing Muses guitarist Tanya Donelly and drummer Britt Walford. With a new album in the works, and new members — Deal's identical twin, Kelley, has replaced Donelly, and drummer Jim Macpherson has replaced Walford — the Breeders are now poised to pre-empt the acclaim Deal's erstwhile band received.

The four members are hanging out in this pricy Marin County yachting town across the Golden Gate Bridge from San Francisco, working on their second album for 4AD at a legendary studio called the Plant. Back in the '70s, Journey and the Jefferson

Starship recorded here, but today it's frequented by the likes of Pearl Jam and Tad. While in town, the Breeders are staying on a houseboat in the harbor. In true rock star fashion, Deal has sat on the roof of the boat and watched the sun come up four mornings in a row. "And you know what?" she blurts out. "*I hate* the sunrise. It sucks! It's stupid! No more, OK?"

It's nighttime now, and the group has gathered on the roof again, this time just to talk about music. As the water laps the side of the boat and fog rolls over Mt. Tamalpais, Deal tells why she chose to produce the new record herself. "I have opinions," she says succinctly, "that's all." She swears it's not a matter of wild ambition. "We only took a certain amount of money, and that's so we wouldn't have to wear lipstick in a video. If we took $500,000, we'd have to pay back $500,000. To do that, you have to do an MTV video, have a hit single, and wear lipstick. You have to look into the camera and do a hard sell. If you *don't* take that much money, all you have to do is sell a pretty good amount of records and not do anything weird. It seems so fucking obvious."

It may be obvious to Deal, but she was a Pixie for six years. That's long enough to understand the arc a band travels from indie darling to corporate product; to become accustomed to the ways of recording studios, major labels and the rock'n'roll lifestyle; and long enough to develop expertise and confidence, to gain some control and power over a music career.

"One thing I've noticed about Kim," says her sister Kelley, in a milder tone, "is she's adamant about everybody doing everything as a band. Like there was an idea about doing a press tour; one was for me and Josephine to do Europe, and Jim and Kim to do America. Kim was adamant that *everybody* do it. She's making sure it's not the Kim Deal Project."

In a careful tone, Kim adds, "I think that being in two bands gives you some perspective. Just being older helps too. Being older and wiser. And being girls — we don't have that ego thing." Does she mean women have less ego than men? Could that be why, traditionally, so few girls have chosen to play rock'n'roll? Kelley picks up the ball. "Women," she explains patiently, "don't *need* to get onstage just to get laid."

the breeders

An onshore breeze keeps things cool as the conversation heats up. Kim Deal has begun pacing about the deck. "I've got another theory," she says. "Throughout time, women have had jobs entertaining men by prostitution, strip joints, etc. So when there's an opportunity for a woman to get in front of a large group of men in their teens and early twenties, and expose all of her vulnerable points, and entertain them, it feels more like prostitution than a form of art."

So does Kim Deal feel like a prostitute? "Well," she says, as a huge cloud of cigarette smoke billows from her mouth, "there are flashes when I'm going, 'Is everybody just staring at my boobs or something?' But that only comes in flashes. Normally it just seems really sonically cool and, like, 'Wow, everything is just totally justified by our sonic ability to take people places.'

"In some queer way..." she continues, but then trails off, either unable or unwilling to continue the thought. "It's always weird when people go, 'You're a girl. Why do you play music?' Why is it supposed to be so hard? I think girls have to like it enough to make it worth it. What are they doing — waiting for some phone call that goes, 'OK, your gear is here, all you have to do is show up, look halfway decent and play'? You've gotta fuckin' buy your shit, you've gotta ask for it for birthday presents and Christmas presents, and you've gotta collect your amps and equipment yourself.

"It was important enough for us to continue, and shit, it wasn't that hard. When you see all those bad, guy bands, you know that you aren't crazy. Gimme a break!"

Kelley emphasizes another factor in the Deals' fate: "We were sisters and had each other. So it was a little easier. If you have someone there — a comrade — you can bond and have more strength or something."

Kim exhales another cloud. "I don't know," she concedes, "a lot of it just has to do with women not feeling like carrying a fucking big heavy amp up the steps. It's one thing to sit here and think in a really poetic and vague way about why women don't get in bands, but the practical side of being in a band is: you've got to carry your amps. There are a lot of women who are really lazy and, even though they may be physical, they're not physical in that way. They won't play fast songs, they don't have the energy to do it, and it doesn't really appeal to them; it doesn't seem like a fun thing to do. So anyone who wants to listen to fast, aggressive music has to listen to guys. A lot of girls, in a smart way, just go, 'Why bother?'

"It's a waste," she adds, "because if anybody can produce a good rock song, girls can."

KIM DEAL NEVER BOUGHT THE JUMP SUIT, but she did spend two hours having enormous, inch-long fake nails — the kind that would make playing guitar impossible — applied to her fingers before the photo shoot. For all that, however, she is not crusading in some ironic way for women's rights. Deal doesn't have a set agenda; her personality is more complex than that. Besides, she just thought the jump suit and long nails might be funny.

Yet this is a woman who recorded her first two albums with the Pixies under the moniker "Mrs. John Murphy," a seemingly defeatist gesture (Murphy is her former husband) that may actually be the most subversive thing she's ever done. When it comes to women's issues, Deal is the ultimate example of one who walks the walk without feeling the need to talk the talk. Unlike other women in rock, she is supremely *un*-angry at the status quo. But if actions really do speak louder than words, Kim Deal is screaming bloody revolution.

For instance, one of her new songs, "Go Man Go," is about a beauty queen who bombs the final pageant rather than let someone else usurp her title. "No Aloha" is a conceptually complicated song which Deal describes as "the big slut scene." She explains: "It's like, if I wasn't a slut, I would have to face womanhood and motherhood. So the last line is, 'Saw it on a wall: motherhood means mental freeze.'" It's the kind of free-spirited thinking that explains why she prefers to take less money from her record company while putting it in terms of not having to wear lipstick. "I just don't want to do it," she says. "I don't want to wear shoulder pads either. My mother used to go, 'Kim, wear shoulder pads.' It was like, 'No, mom — and I'm not going to wear lipstick either.' That doesn't make me a rebel, it makes me normal."

In San Francisco and in the age of girl-style revolution, that's perhaps a given. But it wasn't in Dayton, Ohio, where the Deal sisters grew up and still live today. "In Dayton, the only way you could listen to cool things was if you had a friend who had a friend who lived on the coast and would send you tapes," she says. "Luckily, Kelley had a friend who was arty. I remember getting Captain Sensible, Undertones, Elvis Costello, some rockabilly, Buzzcocks, Gang of Four, the Specials... stuff like that. But in Dayton, if you didn't do a decent cover of Night Ranger, you didn't have anything going on."

"And if you were a girl," adds Kelley, "you fucking played keyboards or sang and shook your ass."

"Ohio was fucking Loverboy, Night Ranger, .38 Special," Kim continues. "Girls were groupies. In Ohio, if you're a girl and you want to be involved in music, you go see your boyfriend's band. Period."

Dayton, Ohio's vacuous rock scene didn't stop Kim and Kelley Deal from pursuing their dreams, though. In the early '80s, the two performed together as a duo, playing blues songs and covers of Hank Williams and early Stones. Kelley sang and Kim played guitar. One time, at a disco, they wore twin outfits and did "Car Wash"; another time, they opened for an aging John Kay of Steppenwolf; most often, Kim claims, they played at truck stops. "We could get away with playing out live if we did old blues songs or country songs," she says. "So we did Delaney & Bonnie, Blind Faith — we could do all that bad cover band stuff. We just really, really liked music."

IN 1986, KIM MARRIED John Murphy and the couple left Dayton for Boston. That same year, she answered an ad in the paper from a band seeking someone into "Peter, Paul & Mary and Hüsker Dü." The ad was placed by the Pixies, and Kim got the gig. What few people know, however, is that Kelley nearly did too. "Me and Charles [Thompson, better known as Black Francis] split the airfare to fly Kelley to Boston to audition, because she played drums in high school. She played a set and we asked her to join. But she said no, flew home and continued on her job, and that was that."

"I just didn't like the Pixies as much as I like the Breeders," Kelley says. "I mean, I thought they were great, but I just wasn't going to..."

"...quit her life for it," Kim cuts in. "Whereas you would for us."

"Not at that time," Kelley corrects. "But after *Pod* I thought, 'Oh, this is what Kim's going to do — *I* want to do this too! I want to belong to that club, 'cause it's so cool. So...'" She trails off at the thought of one small hitch: the problem with Kelley becoming a guitarist for the Breeders was that she didn't know how to play.

It wouldn't have been that big a deal — after all, a zillion punk guitarists of the late '70s and early '80s couldn't play — had Kim not brought her on as *lead* guitarist. Kim had bought Kelley a Fender Strat for Christmas of 1991, but while the Pixies toured the U.S. opening for U2, Kelley was too busy to practice, working a full-time computer job. "Also," says Kim, "Kelley is the laziest person in the world. But she finally learned the *Pod* songs, and she played on *Safari*," the Breeders' 1992 EP.

"Well," Kim pauses, and puts on a smile wide as Montana, "she *sang.*"

Meanwhile, Tanya Donelly was busy forming her latest band, Belly, which left the Breeders' guitar slot open. In March of 1992, the Breeders made a video for "Safari," and during the filming, Kim says, Kelley finally learned how to make a barre chord. "If you watch the video, you can see the light bulb go on over her head and in her whole face — it's like, 'Oh, oh, that's how you do it!'"

At the time, Josephine Wiggs wasn't aware of how little Kelley Deal knew. "You know how it is," Wiggs says. "Just about every person you meet can play guitar. So when Kim says, 'Oh yeah, Kelley's going to be the guitarist in the Breeders,' I thought, 'No big deal.' Then I came over to America to rehearse for our dates opening for Nirvana in Europe..."

"...and it suddenly dawns on her that Kelley *cannot* play guitar," says Kim. She turns to Wiggs. "So, Josephine, when you finally realized she really couldn't play, were you about ready to leave? Were you about ready to take a flight back to England? What were you thinking?"

After a long, dramatic pause, Wiggs responds in measured tones: "I just thought we'd kind of bitten off more than we could chew."

"But didn't it all turn out OK?"

Wiggs pauses again. "I'm still waiting to see, really."

the breeders

JOSEPHINE WIGGS STANDS in direct contrast to the Deal sisters. Her demeanor is so elegant that even before she speaks it's obvious she's not an American. She has an M.A. in philosophy from the University of Sussex and, unlike Kim, wears so much lipstick (a shade called brickbat) that one afternoon, as she furiously applied more, Kelley suggested she get her lips tattooed.

Wiggs has played cello since she was six years old, and bass for nearly a decade. In addition to three albums with the Perfect Disaster, her band since 1988, she did an album called *Nude Nudes* (Playtime) as a part of the duo Honeytongue, along with John Mattock of Spiritualized. On that record, Wiggs played all the instruments except drums.

She joined the Breeders in 1989, during the recording of *Pod*, while on a brief hiatus from the Perfect Disaster. Wiggs had met Kim Deal twice: once when her band opened for the Pixies in London, and another time in Frankfurt a year later, when she hung out with Deal for a few hours after a bar gig. A few months later, 4AD owner Ivo Watts approached her about playing bass on Tanya Donelly and Deal's side project. When Steve Albini arrived in Edinburgh to produce the record, he reportedly asked Deal how the two had hooked up. "I met her," she said, "and I thought she was cool."

These days, Wiggs has a somewhat tricky job: she lives and plays with a pair of inseparable identical twins. Yet somehow she exudes an amazing calmness and stability, useful traits around the high-strung Deal sisters. "The thing is," she says diplomatically, "in any band there's only enough room for a certain number of egos. There's always this aspiration to democracy, but in the end that's a fantasy. If there's disagreement, somebody always has to back down. The best you can hope for is a benevolent dictatorship, and we're lucky we have one."

When the Breeders opened for Nirvana in July of 1992, Kelley Deal had been playing guitar for little more than a month. "I learned the songs during rehearsals," she recalls. But sometimes the band still has to cover for her. "What I think is so cool," says Jim Macpherson, who has remained relatively silent most of the evening, "is that, during the show, if Kelley happens to be a little late, Kim just sings all the lead guitar parts into the mike."

The result is quite entertaining. During an October performance, Kelley was mostly on target, yet she was straining, biting her lip, looking at her fingers, and perpetually smoking and giving off that oh-so-effective Deal smile. The audience started rooting for her. Each time Kim would say, "My sister will start this song," or when Kelley would step forward to the mike, a delicious sense of tension, which normally comes from rage or noise or some other hackneyed rock'n'roll pose, would fill the room. It was the emotional equivalent of Nirvana smashing their instruments to bits — defiance of authority at its most audacious and bizarre.

And it worked. One time in Chicago, Wiggs recalls, Kelley completely demolished a solo. Afterwards, Wiggs cracked to the audience, "We're trying to earn enough money for Kelley to finish her course of guitar lessons." The joke was met with a round of boos.

Says Kelley, "It will be a year in May that I've played guitar and…"

"…now you can play, right?," Kim finishes. "If we go downstairs and get a guitar, can you play 'Limehouse' — right now, on beat?"

"Right now?" Kelley asks, timidly. "I think so, yeah."

"No way!" Kim shouts. "No she cannot!" But she pauses mid-protest to defend her sister. "I just thought this would be irreverent and fun. All those people who take rock so seriously… It was like, 'I'll just go get a guitar player who can't even fucking play! But it's not just a shtick, it isn't a joke. Kelley is really very musical. There's no real problem with her playing. There's a lot of people who can play really well, but they're not musical, they're just competent. And who wants fucking competence?"

Wiggs agrees: "It is way cooler. I'd have been really bummed if we'd chosen somebody who was just a really good guitarist, who would be really dull. It's so much more exciting to think each night, 'Is Kelley going to play the part in the right place tonight? And when she does it right, it's like, whoa! It's the greatest thing."

WHEN KELLEY DEAL TOOK THE STAGE in Dublin last June, opening for Nirvana, she wasn't the only one living out a heart-tugging, made-for-TV movie — Jim Macpherson was working on his own script. Until June, he played drums in a Dayton, Ohio, band called the Raging Mantras.

Kim explains how he became a Breeder: "We did some demos in Dayton in January, but we needed a drummer. One night, we went out to see a band, and Jim was playing drums. We automatically thought he'd be great. I liked the way he just smacked the drums. I thought it was nice."

The Deals had never seen the Raging Mantras before that night, but Macpherson had seen the Pixies — and was a huge fan. A week after the gig, Deal called and asked him to do some demos with her at a studio in Dayton. "She gave me five days to learn all the Breeders songs, and I did, Macpherson says. "I learned them and I learned them and I learned them. I knew there was maybe a little opportunity there, because she asked me to learn all the songs. I also knew Josephine was coming over to rehearse and I'm like, 'Holy shit! I'm not stupid!' So I learned those songs backwards, forwards, upside down."

"Which was a strange coincidence," Wiggs cracks, "because Kelley learned them backwards too."

Macpherson suddenly found himself headed to Ireland to perform at the Glastonbury Festival, which draws some 50,000 people, and open for Nirvana. Not surprisingly, he and Kelley were scared shitless. "Their knees were knocking, they were nauseated, they were throwing up," says Kim. "I was, too, you know. I was like, 'Is the band going to be able to play through it?'"

IT'S NEARLY SUNRISE and Kim Deal is destined to see the sun come up for the fifth day in a row. The Breeders still haven't thought of a title for the new record. They've considered *Pink Noise*, after a Moog setting, or *Gagging For the Arrow*, after a line in the song "Roi," or possibly *Hag*, after a song on the album inspired by some graffiti that showed up on the side of the band's Ryder rental truck parked outside the studio.

"We thought, 'Oh, god, some youthful three-chord pop band that's got a lot of muscle and energy, who look really cute, just wrote 'hags' on our van.' It made me think, 'We're so old and dirty and worn out.' I had a total self-esteem crisis. Then, you know what? We found out there's a girl band practicing there and they're called the Hags. They wrote it everywhere: on the bathroom stalls, all over the place.

"Isn't that a great name?" she asks. "The Hags. That's what we are, too." She puts on another big-Deal grin: "Riot Hags," she says, and exhales another cloud of smoke. Everyone breaks into laughter.

"Damn!" Deal says, tapping her ashes and eyeballing the Bay Area sky. She reaches for her guitar. "I am the sun," she sings, "I am the new year, I am the way... home." She stops, changes key and sings another: "You're just like a woman, you coastal cut-throat, you dirty switch."

"That's about Josephine," she cracks, as the sky turns from black to dull gray.

March 1993

screaming trees

HARD'N'HEAVY

BY **JASON FINE**

FOUR SONGS INTO THE SCREAMING TREES set at the University of Rhode Island, singer Mark Lanegan wants a drink. "Anybody got some refreshments out there?" he asks, squinting at the crowd through a bank of hot yellow stage lights. "Old gramps is parched."

Using his mike stand as a walking stick, Lanegan stumbles forward a few feet and leans toward the rim of the stage, hoping for someone to pass him a beer or, better yet, a bottle. But if any of the clean-cut, flannel-clad collegians in the audience tonight are drinking, they're not sharing, and Lanegan's outstretched hand is left dangling empty above the crowd.

"Fuck it," he mutters to himself, and then tears into the next song with a coarse, stuttering howl.

FOR LANEGAN, it's another night on the job, another 70 minutes of singing to a swirling, faceless crowd — another reason to get drunk. The only problem is it's Sunday, and as Lanegan and four members of the road crew were heartily polishing off the last gallon bottle of vodka on the tour bus last night, no one anticipated that you can't buy over-the-counter liquor in Rhode Island on the Sabbath. But while his bandmates chose to face the gig sober, Lanegan found a friend with a car who was willing to taxi him to the nearest cocktail lounge five miles away. There, along with the driver, a roadie and assorted hangers-on, he spent several hours before the show hitting vodka-cranberrys two at a time, searching for the inspiration to perform.

"Without booze," says Lanegan, in his dry, scratchy baritone, on the way to the bar, "things can get ugly."

After a couple of days on the road with the Screaming Trees it quickly becomes clear that alcohol is key to fighting off the tedium of a tour that's lasted six months and had the band zigzagging twice across the U.S. and Europe. The members say things have gotten particularly tiresome in the past two weeks, with the band stuck playing a string of gigs at East Coast colleges like this one. "I'm trying to mellow out," 25-year-old bassist Van Conner says during a five-hour downtime between soundcheck and the show. "But I just sit here and I'm so fucking bored that I'd like to be drunk. At least then I wouldn't know I was bored."

Even if they were less than motivated going into tonight's show, the Screaming Trees burn from the first song. The set, drawn almost entirely from the band's current album, *Sweet Oblivion*, includes mostly mid-tempo rockers and earthy ballads that recall '60s heroes like Cream and Creedence Clearwater Revival more than the grungy post-punk bands the Trees are most often associated with. Using congas and other percussion instruments on several tunes, drummer Barrett Martin and bassist Van Conner lock into a fluid, aggressive groove, while Gary Lee Conner's windmilling psychedelic guitar licks explode like buckshot all over the mix. Barreling sweatily across the stage in a kind of half-horizontal slam dance, it's no small feat that the giant guitarist keeps his balance, let alone avoids ramming into the rangy six-foot-three Lanegan or his own equally large, bass-playing brother.

For years the Screaming Trees were written off as a rock'n'roll freak show; even in the band's adopted home of Seattle, soundman Rod Doak says the Trees were long treated like "some weird guys from the woods." Judging from the ecstatic response of the sold-out Rhode Island crowd, however, yesterday's misfits are today's teen heroes. During "Butterfly" and "Dollar Bill," two sentimental ballads that show off Lanegan's deep, pained vocals, the entire audience sways back and forth, with many members singing along to every word.

In fact, it looks as if the show is going to come off without a hitch, until some over-zealous student security guards begin manhandling stagedivers and crowd-surfers during the encore. In the middle of the last song, "Ivy," one guy jumps off the shoulders of some friends, rises a good two feet in the air and lands on the edge of the stage. The guards, instead of simply nudging him back into

screaming trees

the crowd, hold him down and drag him across the stage by his wrists and feet. Lanegan, watching from behind his mike stand, charges the security guards and shoves one out of the way so the kid can break free.

It's a heroic move, but doesn't please school authorities, who immediately stop the show. By the time Lanegan scrambles back to his microphone, the stage lights blink off and the P.A. is cut. With only the sound of Martin's unamplified drums flailing on, Lanegan looks briefly up at the crowd, shakes his head and walks off.

"SO WE GOT SHUT DOWN," Lanegan mumbles a half-hour later, rolling his head forward as he laughs. "Well, fuck it." He, Martin and a couple of female fans are back at the bar they'd visited earlier, in nearby Kingston. It's a dingy place decorated with bowling trophies and beer posters. The half-dozen old-timers quietly watching minor league baseball on a small TV don't look too thrilled when the giggly young women start pumping quarters into the jukebox and yelling out their selections.

Lanegan, an intensely guarded person who can be surly when he wants to, tonight talks easily about his days playing quarterback for the Ellensburg High football team, his musical hero Roky Erickson, and the ups-and-downs of life on the road. The 28-year-old singer seems uncertain about the Trees' new prosperity; he's happy to be finally making a living playing music, but he's also grappling with the price of success. Particularly now, at the height of a media frenzy surrounding the "Seattle scene," times are strange for a band that has long bucked rock'n'roll trends.

"I've been ridiculed by people on this tour for wearing a flannel shirt," says Lanegan, dressed tonight in a black leather jacket and a black ski cap with 'White Trash' scrawled across the front. "But, fuck it, I'm not going to stop wearing something I've worn for 27 years just 'cause it's not cool anymore; 'cause someone's going to say we're part of some fashion thing...

"All this Seattle shit," he goes on. "We made three records while still living in Ellensburg and played Seattle only as much as any other major city. It wasn't like we were out pressing the flesh every day. We still don't. It's never been our thing to shamelessly self-promote, get out and be seen and all that; shake a lot of hands, sign a lot of shit. It's just not us. We're private people. We'd rather sit down and have a beer with somebody than be placed on a pedestal."

He pauses and grins. "Some people play that game really well," he adds. "We stumble a lot."

A few minutes before one a.m. and the Screaming Trees tour bus pulls up out front. As a parade of long-haired, tattooed crew members and drunk musicians from opening bands Pond and the Poster Children file in, the dark suburban lounge begins to look more like an MTV video set. Though last call was made ten minutes ago, and the few remaining regulars are slowly staggering out, it doesn't take much to convince the bartender to pour another round. In fact, within minutes he's shut the shades and locked the door from the inside, and we all find ourselves guests at a private after-hours party.

Draft beer and whiskey shots flow up and down the bar as several people sing along to Elvis Costello's "Alison" and an endless string of '70s hits coming from the jukebox. At one point, a pair of old Neil Young tunes is followed with a heartless ballad by America. It's striking how both groups mine such similar heartland turf, yet achieve such different results.

"What a Neil Young rip-off," Lanegan says quietly, amidst all the clamor. "No fuckin' soul."

THE ROAD TO RESPECTABILITY has been a long, bumpy one for the Screaming Trees. Even in Ellensburg, a college town (population: 13,000) in rural Eastern Washington, the band's ability to play every song off Black Flag's *Slip It In* did not win any talent contests.

"We couldn't even get a gig in Ellensburg," says guitarist Gary Lee Conner, the band's oldest member at 30. "People thought we were complete shit. One time we were maybe going to get this gig opening for this other band, like the hip band in Ellensburg — a band I tried out for but they wouldn't let me in. And we were going to maybe get to play with them, but one of the guys, Joe Kingston, I remember, he said, 'What do you think, are people going to laugh at them?'

"It was like '*Fuck you*, man!'," Conner says, wagging his middle

screaming trees

finger in the air. "Now we can just totally tell those guys to fuck off."

It's the day after that long night, and Conner is sitting on a bench overlooking the grassy plaza and stately colonial buildings of the University of Rhode Island. He grins as he looks back on the band's meager beginnings. "We didn't really even know, like, how you got to be a band, how to write your own songs," he says. "But I started messing around, trying to write some stuff on a four-track I had. I played it for Lanegan one day and he said, 'Jeez, we could actually try and do some of these songs.'"

At the time, a local musician, Steve Fisk, had opened a fledgling studio and indie label in Ellensburg called Velvetone. In the summer of 1985, the Screaming Trees recorded a six-song demo there called *Other Worlds* (issued in 1988 on SST), followed a few months later by the full-length album *Clairvoyance*. At a Black Flag show in Olympia, the band gave a copy of the *Other Worlds* cassette to Flag guitarist and SST co-founder Greg Ginn. He liked it, and a few months later phoned the Conner family's video store and offered the Screaming Trees a contract.

"That was probably the coolest thing that ever happened to me," says Conner. "It was a total dream come true to be on a label with all those great bands. It's funny, because at the same time we were also getting an offer from [the former Restless subsidiary] Pink Dust. If we took that, we probably wouldn't even be sitting here right now. I'd probably still be working at the video store."

Between 1987 and 1990, the Screaming Trees recorded three albums for SST, an EP collaboration with Beat Happening for Homestead, an album for Sub Pop, and various solo projects. Van Conner quit the band in 1988 to stay home with his wife and newborn son Ulysses. He rejoined seven months later to record *Buzz Factory*.

The Trees' last album for SST and best recording to date, *Buzz Factory* is a raw blast of fuzzy guitar psychedelia, full of killer hooks, harmonies and dark, penetrating vocals. Though it sold a respectable 15,000 copies and established the Screaming Trees as a national college radio favorite, the band was plagued by infighting, lack of funds and several threatened break-ups.

"I think everybody has quit the band and rejoined at least once," says soundman Doak, a childhood friend of Lanegan who estimates this is his 12th tour with the Trees. "They got to a point where they were just about ready to break up; they'd gone as far as they could, as far as any band could make it without taking it to another level. [Ex-manager] Susan Silver was trying to get a deal with a major label but no one was interested. I remember someone from Atlantic once said, 'Well, if you get rid of one of the fat guys we'll sign you.' They were just like, forget this."

In 1990, the Trees signed to Epic. The following year's *Uncle Anesthesia*, despite some solid songs, suffered from poor production and the chaos surrounding drummer Mark Pickerell's exodus from the band. Thinking the next album could be their last, the three remaining Trees sat down in the summer of '91 and collaborated on songs together for the first time in years. They hired ex-Skin Yard drummer Barrett Martin to replace Pickerell (who now runs a record store in Ellensburg), and that fall began recording *Sweet Oblivion* with producer Don Fleming.

"Before I joined I'd heard these stories about the dueling brothers," says 26-year-old Martin, a native of Olympia, Washington. "Jack [Endino, Skin Yard's guitarist, and the producer of *Buzz Factory*] had warned me about these two huge guys, but really everything was pretty mellow. I was surprised."

"We just found that after all those years it was a lot easier now to work together," shrugs Lanegan. "I guess it's a matter of learning to respect each other. We all seem to get along real well now. It's been a long time. It's been hours since we had a fist fight."

With *Sweet Oblivion* fast on its way to selling gold and the hype surrounding the band's Northwest pedigree feeding the fire, the Screaming Trees are on the verge of a major commercial breakthrough. Success has been a long time coming, though, and like so many other likeminded bands that have been swept up in the latest major label feeding frenzy, all four members seem adamant about sticking to their punk rock values in the corporate rock world.

"Sometimes you feel like such an idiot doing this for a living," says Van Conner. "We learned from [Firehose bassist] Mike Watt and a lot of those early punk guys about this idealistic thing: that even if you're not singing about politics, you're going out, playing to people and making them part of the whole thing rather than becoming a rock star. It's getting really hard now, though, because

screaming trees

the more records you sell the more impossible it is to do that.

"It used to be you'd hang out with people before the show, talk, have a beer," he continues. "But now people are kind of freaked out, like 'Hey, rock stars!' We don't want it to be like that."

TWO DAYS AFTER the Rhode Island concert, 60 or 70 college-age fans gather around a makeshift stage at a record store in Boston, anxiously waiting for the Screaming Trees. *Sweet Oblivion* is playing softly over the sound system, posters are taped to the walls, and store employees are wearing Screaming Trees tour T-shirts. Local "modern rock" station WAAF is broadcasting from a mobile studio parked in front of the building, and two Epic label executives are milling about, nervously trying to ensure that things run smoothly.

Meanwhile, the Screaming Trees are sitting around a small dressing room table backstage, picking at warm cold cuts and trying to figure a way out. "My voice is fucked," says Lanegan. "If I sing now, I won't be able to do the show tonight."

"I hate doing these things," adds Van Conner, unscrewing the cap from a fresh bottle of Jim Beam and pouring a healthy slug into a plastic cup half-filled with Diet Coke. "Who's idea was this, anyway?"

"Let's just do one song and split," Martin suggests.

"I wouldn't feel bad at all about walking out of here right now," says Lanegan. "Just tell those people to kiss my ass."

For all their complaining, once the Trees make it onstage they seem to enjoy themselves. Though Lanegan's voice sounds raspy and tired, his bandmates pick up the slack, working through "Winter Song," "Dollar Bill" and a funky version of "Nearly Lost You" that turns into a free-form conga-and-guitar jam.

Afterwards, the band sits at a long table, shakes a few hands and autographs a stack of promotional items. It's time for me to leave, but on my way out I stop and turn around for one last look. I see four large, unshaven men slumped in a row, looking tired and a bit cranky, sipping bourbon-and-cokes from red plastic cups. Seven teenage boys linger nearby, anxiously clutching posters, CDs and T-shirts, and talking amongst themselves. They look eager to approach their heroes, but also a little scared.

May 1993

melvins

PUNK ROCK HIGH LIFE

BY **LORRAINE ALI**

EVERY CULTURAL MOVEMENT has its unsung pioneers. Take Buzz Osbourne of the Melvins. Nirvana's Chris Novoselic calls him "the punk rock guru of Aberdeen." You might ask, "So what?" — or "Where the hell is Aberdeen?" — but if Osbourne hadn't transformed a few clueless stoners of that small Washington logging town into leaders of the current loser's revolution, Nirvana would still be slopping out backyard-party covers of "Rock & Roll" and sucking bongs to the "heavy, hardcore" sound of the Scorpions.

"Yeah, I infected Kurt and Chris," Osbourne brags, as he gingerly picks at his breakfast — a Mr. Goodbar and an Orange Crush — and brushes a few stray, frizzy locks out of his dark, glassy eyes. "They got into punk rock because of me." Osbourne also de-FM-ized Matt Lukin, the Melvins' original bass player, who left in 1988 to form Mudhoney. In the mid-'80s, Osbourne was well-known around Aberdeen for his notorious cassette compilations of obscure punk and hardcore songs — all of which featured a few staples by Flipper, Black Flag and "always, always 'TV Eye' by the Stooges" — that he would distribute to his music-hungry friends. Ask anyone who comes from Aberdeen and they'll tell you it was Buzz Osbourne, not Kurt Cobain, who put the Pacific Northwest at the forefront of cool.

Today, the Melvins are in Southern California, preparing for a performance later this evening at Bogart's in Long Beach. The sprawling suburbatropolis, some 25 miles south of L.A., is just one stop on the group's three-week tour. At previous shows, they've combined their familiar grinding, sludgy songs, cultivated over a ten-year period, with the cleaner, more accessible material on their Kurt Cobain-produced, self-titled major label debut for Atlantic. "My dad thinks the career might work now, whereas before the

Atlantic deal he didn't," says Osbourne. "But he still talks about the opportunities opening up at Boeing. Sorry, dad, I'm not going to be a welder."

THE MERCURY IS AT 92, and drummer Dale Crover has been standing outside his motel room for half an hour, waiting in the barren parking lot for Osbourne and bassist Lori Black to emerge from their room. The motel, a Best Western, features such luxuries as plastic, shell-shaped Jacuzzis and beds with fuzzy pink headboards and built-in stereos.

There's little movement on the motel's balcony until Osbourne finally ventures into the daylight wearing a down vest over a long-sleeved shirt, baggy purple pants and red hightops. Lori Black trips out of the room behind him in a daze, her dyed-black hair hanging limp, her thin frame appearing boyishly curveless through the gloomy black lace of her long dress. Large sunglasses cover most of her fragile face.

As the two approach, Black mumbles something unintelligible. Osbourne feels obliged to explain: "Due to epilepsy, Lori takes medication that makes her kind of out of it." Dubious as that may seem, Osbourne should know; after all, Black, daughter of former child actress Shirley Temple Black, is also his girlfriend.

Half an hour or so later, the Melvins have decided to eat at a trendy, '50s-style café called Johnny Rockets. As they settle in, Osbourne drops a quarter in the jukebox and "Chantilly Lace" blares out of it, more distorted than Sebadoh on a plastic Close'n'Play. "I was always into heavy music, or at least what I considered heavy music," he explains. "Ted Nugent, Aerosmith, Kiss. Then I got into the Sex Pistols in '78 or '79 — I guess out of curiosity." Black interrupts, slurring, "'Cause you're smart and original." When a perky, preppy waitress approaches, Black screams out her order for a chocolate malt and peanut butter and jelly sandwich, mispronouncing the words like a child.

"Buzz has always been a freak," she continues, her warble dipping from low mumbles to loud blurts. The waitress looks mortified. "He was *born* a freak. Buzz is an original person, and if you're an original person and you live in Aberdeen, you get killed." She punctuates the statement with a loud blurt: "Aberdeen doesn't like it."

Osbourne rolls over her monologues with care and patience. "I didn't know anybody else who was into that kind of stuff," he says. "I just sort of happened on it. Then I got into the Clash and the Damned, then into the L.A. hardcore scene, like Black Flag, the Germs, Circle Jerks, the Chiefs, Middle Class, Weirdos, Fear..."

Black cuts back in: "You *made* Kurt. They were all jocks. I saw the yearbook." Crover, who until now has been quietly biting his lower lip, attempts a smile. "I thought Iron Maiden was punk rock," he says. "I was a stoner, and they played fast."

DALE CROVER DROPPED OUT of high school his junior year to tour with the Melvins. Though he can't recall the name of the group's first single, he knows it was on "some K compilation." Osbourne and he had worked together at a pizza place when the Melvins landed on the C/Z compilation *Deep Six*, which also featured Soundgarden, Green River (which split into Mudhoney and Pearl Jam) and Malfunkshun. (A&M plans to reissue this tidbit of grunge history in the near future.) Crover's mom funded much of the Melvins' subsequent recording, which turned out to be the 1985 7-inch EP *The Melvins*, also on C/Z. (He says he still owes her for it.) The group's first full-length, *Gluey Porch Treatments*, came out on Alchemy in 1987, and was the Melvins' last project before defecting from Aberdeen.

The Melvins had been a band since the early '80s, but didn't perform a paying gig until 1985, when they were handed $20 to play at the Tropicana in nearby Olympia, home of K Records and Evergreen State College. In Aberdeen, they had only played local parties, most of which turned out to be disasters; Dead Kennedys covers don't go over well in rooms packed with drooling goons demanding "Freebird." Crover recalls a situation in Montesano in which the Melvins shared the bill with a metal band called Sabre. "They were hot," he says, with heavy sarcasm. "We got all liquored up and didn't know what we were doing." He pauses, reconsidering his last statement; with an utterly straight face, he adds, "That was the only time we ever played when we were wasted. Never done it before or again. Can't do it."

Osbourne backs him up: "We don't do drugs at all. I don't even drink a beer — not for years." Before he can continue, Black pops up like a rag doll on cue. "Never," she slurs. "Hardly ever. In fact, that's what I thought was so great about this band." Her head drops back down, and Crover just stares at his plate of fries.

In 1988, Osbourne moved to San Francisco. Crover followed him to the Bay Area, where they landed jobs at a Mrs. Field's Cookies. "I quit when a new manager came in and asked us to count the cookies every hour," he says. With no dough to roll, the two hooked up with Black, who had played bass in a band called Clown Alley. Over the next couple of years the Melvins put out *Ozma*, *Bullhead* and *Melvins* on the Berkeley-based Boner Records. Last year, when Black took a brief hiatus from the band, the Melvins each did solo records (with short-term bassist Joe Preston) and released them simultaneously, as Kiss did back in 1978, complete with Kiss-like logos and information on how to join the "Melvins Army." Of the three, Osbourne's was the most arty and experimental, especially when pitted against the Melvins' normal tangle of bone-crushing power chords and feedback goo. "It's the first thing my dad ever liked that I played," he says.

"ABERDEEN IS THE 'Redneck Sports Town of Unemployment,'" Osbourne pronounces, as if reading from a stone plaque in the town square. Crover agrees. "You grow up with Billy Joe Gunracks all around you, but" — here's the consolation — "it's also full of second-hand stores. Which is great" — he puts on a sarcastic face — "if you're into 'grunge' fashion. It's like..."

Black's face is turning yellow. She squirms. "I gotta get up," she says desperately, as the refrain of the Archies' "Sugar Sugar" trumpets from the jukebox. She numbly scoots out of the booth and to the bathroom, her peanut butter and jelly still untouched.

Osbourne doesn't miss a beat. "Even people living there now," he continues, in a hopeless attempt to keep the focus, "don't know anything about punk rock. All they know is Nirvana. They have no idea we started anything." His face becomes downright resentful. "None of the people I went to high school with give me credit for anything. They still think I'm a total loser." His pace is beginning to wane, and Crover picks up the slack. "There was actually music that came out of there before, like Metal Church" — Osbourne interjects with a big "Yuck!" — "and also a guy that played in the

Doobie Brothers. The look there is fleece Levi jackets, moustaches and chewing tobacco — even the girls."

Osbourne's face is turning a slight shade of green. He's beginning to fidget. The chipper waitress attempts a smile as she brings some extra napkins. But Osbourne slowly backs away from the table. "Don't feel very good," he mumbles. "Can't eat this now. It's from being on tour. I've had the flu." He gets up. "Be right back," he says as Crover sits alone, trying to explain. "When you're on tour with no sleep for weeks, what do you expect?" he offers sheepishly. "I'm the only one who hasn't gotten sick."

NO MATTER HOW YOU LOOK AT IT, the Melvins is a geeky name. It doesn't offer a clue to the group's heavy, dirgy, smacked-out brand of hardcore; it rings more like some Devo goon's idea of clever. "I know it's kind of a dumb name," Osbourne had explained earlier in the afternoon, when he was feeling better, "but part of the reason we wanted it was so people wouldn't categorize us or put us in a league with other bands."

When the Melvins recorded their *Eggnog* EP in 1986, some people accused them of selling out by signing to Boner. Crover laughs. "Yeah, we sold out to Boner. They gave us $2,000 to record. Wonder what they'll think of *this* album? It's going to be the *big* sellout." He does, however, seem fairly concerned. "Just because Kurt's producing it means we're going to get away with it. I don't care. Working with him was great, 'cause we've known him for so long and he knows our music so well. Even though he's never produced before, he has a lot of good ideas — usually at four in the morning."

Black exits the bathroom and walks straight past the table on automatic pilot, Osbourne following close behind her. Crover keeps talking. "I got to do some really cool stuff with the drums," he says, as Osbourne seats and comforts Black at a table outside. When he returns, Osbourne himself has begun to nod. But he makes an attempt to rejoin the discussion. In a slow, measured tone, he explains, "We made a conscious effort to write stuff the general public will like, but won't gut our band. Won't be a complete turnaround. Hard to do. Just 'cause we're on Atlantic. They'll scream sellout."

"Yeah," says Crover, more upbeat, "but people said the same about Nirvana — 'Ah, *Bleach* was such a better record than *Nevermind*.' I don't agree. I think *Nevermind* makes *Bleach* sound like a shit record." Osbourne concurs: "The reason *Nevermind* sold a lot is 'cause it's a good record."

As Nirvana hit number one, and Soundgarden took a headlining spot on Lollapalooza, the Melvins remained on a tiny indie label and continued working lame jobs. It must have been frustrating. But Osbourne won't admit it. "The reason things didn't move as fast for us is because those bands are a lot more accessible than us," he mutters. "Our stuff is harder for the general public to listen to. Doesn't bother me. I kind of expect it. I don't think we're like those bands. We don't sound anything like Nirvana." He pauses, then adds, "They might sound like us."

It was Nirvana who introduced the Melvins to the bigger rock world. Cobain mentions the band as often as Lenny Kravitz pilfers Curtis Mayfield riffs. Otherwise, what would Atlantic want with the Melvins? "Atlantic is sick of looking stupid," Osbourne offers. "They're like, 'It's going to make us look a little more with it.' Genesis just isn't cutting it for them anymore."

Indeed, the number of Melvins tattoos that have shown up on people recently, and the dedication the fans have toward the band, indicates something of a grass-roots movement. Could they be the Grateful Dead of anti-straightedge hardcore? "I'd like to think our audience isn't that dumb," says Osbourne, "but give us a few years. I'm starting to get gray, pushing 30." Adds Crover, "There's also a computer Melvins Hotline. It hooks you up with other people you can talk to." Moreover, the Melvins Army thing is for real. For five bucks, Melvinites receive a membership card, a plastic T-shirt transfer and a Melvins newsletter.

BUZZ OSBOURNE HAS BEEN REFERRED TO lately as the "granddaddy of grunge." He puts on a shaky, old man's voice: "There's a feather in my cap, get me to my wheelchair please. I drink Geritol before every show." But does the Granddaddy of Grunge feel any brotherhood towards the flannel-clad MTV icons? "Hell no!" he says, coming nearly 100-percent back to life. "That stuff sounds like AM radio crap to me. There's nothing alternative about that.

They're alternative for people who don't really want to hear anything alternative. Pearl Jam are not like us. I know what they're into and it has nothing to do with us. They're into Mötley Crüe and Queensryche and Aerosmith. They're into all this 'feeeeeling' music — what a crock. I hate those bands. I remember when the bass player had a Mötley Crüe haircut."

He's on a roll, and feeling completely isolated. "I would say we have *no* brother bands out there," he says. "We're an alternative band trying to be a *real* alternative." He rubs his nose sleepily and begins to wander again; then, in a tone that lies somewhere between nihilism and optimism, he adds, "The world doesn't need no more bands like us, but it definitely needs us."

March 1993

mike watt
FOREVER FLANNEL

BY **JASON FINE**

TWENTY-FIVE MILES SOUTH of downtown Los Angeles lies San Pedro, a city in flux. Boasting the world's largest man-made harbor and the busiest port in the U.S., it was once a salty, rough-edged blue collar town populated by sailors, stevedores, fishermen and shipyard workers. But today Pedro is slowly becoming gentrified, looking more like the ritzy beachfront enclaves that crowd L.A.'s coastline to the northwest. On cliffs overlooking the jutting Palos Verdes Peninsula, Mediterranean-style villas dwarf the wood-frame bungalows and courtyard apartments that once housed Italian and Portuguese immigrants. Alongside seedy sailor bars, greasy diners and nautical supply stores now sit sparkling new business parks, boutiques and streets lined with freshly planted palm trees. It gives the area an upscale ambiance that prompts longtime resident Mike Watt to refer to the city these days as "Marina Del Pedro."

Watt, the bass player of Firehose, has lived in San Pedro for a quarter of a century; when he was ten, his father transferred from Newport News, Virginia, to San Pedro's Terminal Island naval station. For the past 15 years, Watt has made his home in a small, dank, second-story apartment near the water that his wife — bassist Kira Roessler, Watt's partner in the duo Dos — calls "a one-room hell-hole." Bullet holes from stray gunfire dot one wall, and more can be found on the side of Watt's white Ford Econoline van parked on the street outside. But the hazards of the neighborhood don't vex Watt nearly as much as the idea that his town is turning into a yuppie playground.

"This is originally a fishing town, a beautiful land," he laments, sitting in his cramped living room in a swivel chair that squeaks every time he shifts his weight. "But a lot of the Italian, Slav fisherman — man, they grew old and their kids put 'em in the retirement homes. The kids moved out and put up an eight-unit on the property. It's fucked up, 'cause the streets are still skinny, there's no work here, so now the people who live here have to commute. It turns our thing into a big bedroom. It's a bad thing, really irresponsible."

He leans forward and narrows his eyes, his voice dropping to a scratchy whisper, as if he's about to share a secret. "They've got plans for this place," he says. "I'm telling you, they've got plans for this place."

MIKE WATT IDENTIFIES with the old San Pedro. When he and his best friend D. Boon formed the Minutemen here in 1979, Watt spray-painted "Pedro" on his bass as an homage to the band's blue collar roots. (The reference was usually misinterpreted; as Watt told the *Boston Phoenix* recently, "Everyone thought my name was Pedro.") While the majority of L.A. punk bands were wailing nihilistic songs about hating their parents, teachers and suburban lives, the Minutemen's working class background was central to its sound. Rejecting instrumental solos as "too bourgeois" and fuzzboxes as "too right wing," the trio's sharp, abbreviated songs — often dealing with politics and the toll of thankless day jobs — provided the basis for a musical philosophy Watt still adheres to rigorously.

"To me, it's still like 15 years ago," he says, unapologetically. "I have tried not to change it. In fact, I'm kinda reactionary that way. I want to keep things the way they used to be because it made me do what I do. If I went to another thing, a satisfied kind of thing, a kind of 'by the rules' way of playing, I'd turn to shit. Worthless. Garbage. I mean, we have certain traditions, too. Punk rock wasn't just a stepping-stone thing, it's a way of doing it."

On the wall just inside the front door hangs a tuba, a gift from Flea of the Red Hot Chilli Peppers; a postcard from Sonic Youth's Thurston Moore hangs on another wall along with a black-and-white promo glossy of Madonna with a personalized autograph to Watt. Hovering in the air like smog is the overwhelming stench of cat piss.

Watt shakes his head, musing on how much punk rock has changed since his buddy D. Boon died in an auto accident back in 1985. Like San Pedro, he says, punk is being gentrified, bought

mike watt

cheap by the major labels and renovated for a new generation of CD buyers. Record companies that ignored the music for a decade are now scrambling after any band that looks or sounds like Nirvana; they've repackaged punk as "alternative rock" for the masses.

Even Firehose, the band Watt put together in 1986 with Minutemen drummer George Hurley and guitarist/singer Ed Crawford (a young, diehard Minutemen fan from Ohio), has benefitted from punk's new respectability. With three albums on SST and two now for Sony's Columbia imprint, the group's quirky, bass-driven sound is reaching a wider audience than D. Boon would have ever imagined. But Watt, who tours five months out of every year in his nondescript van, still loads his own equipment and dresses in the flannel shirt, baggy jeans and black Converse low-tops he's worn since high school. And he is adamant about his no-frills approach.

"I run my Sony thing just like SST," says Watt. In his self-described spiels, Watt proudly announces that he is "not a deficit dude," accepting neither recording advances nor tour support from his label. He says the way he runs his business has even touched some of the record executives at Sony. "I'm like a folk hero to them — this going on for 15 years. I've done like 20, 21 tours, and you just don't exist if you don't do it that way. I remember seeing ads in the *Recycler* [an L.A.-area shopper containing thousands of classifieds] saying, 'Need bassist, singer, drummer; have deal.' We're not from that school. That's the other way to do it.

"We go out there in the van, and these record company guys see the shelf unit and the safe welded to the floor... they've never seen this. They're used to signing $10,000-a-week checks to keep the bands on the road. I don't take any money; my tours make money. The records are promotion for the gigs; the gigs aren't promotion for the records. But them, being up in their tower — it's weird for them. Punk rock is like an eye-opener. For them, punk rock was like a style 15 years ago, kind of noisy. They never understood it as a way of doing things."

Like an old sailor spilling memories in a dark Pedro bar, Watt is a spokesman for a bygone age, a reminder of a time when punk wasn't a pose, but a way of life. This morning, his publicist left a message on his answering machine reminding him that *Spin* wants to interview him about his "econo" approach to touring. Recently, a *Details* fashion supplement ran an interview with Watt in which he expounded on his philosophy of the flannel.

"I wish I hadn't done that," he says. "I have to be more careful. Especially something as special to me as the flannel shirt. To cheapen it like it's some kind of fashion accessory scares me. I got it from John Fogerty as a kid. I thought he had a real special look. Through high school it was a great look in this town — Levi's and flannels. If you didn't wear it, people gave you trouble. Now it's come around, it's a funky thing. I know about all this grunge. It'll blow over in a year. They'll be into rockabilly hot pants or something, but now it's really gross. I know it's just reality, but it's really hurting me."

THESE ARE STRANGE DAYS for Watt, whose hometown, cherished shirts and even the music he helped pioneer have become trendy commodities. But if he gets weary of talking too much about the changing face of San Pedro, the challenges Firehose faces and the struggles of hanging onto his ideals, Watt breaks into an easy smile when the conversation turns to Dos. A part-time project for Watt and Roessler (who once plucked the bass with Black Flag), Dos is a duet for two basses. It may be an unconventional idea for a band, but unlike many of the cold, academic-sounding (yet similarly unconventional) groups you'll find alongside Dos in the "experimental" bins of record shops, the music of Dos is rooted in real, fleshy chunks of ideas which bind Mike and Kira's lives.

"There's no sitting back, there's nowhere to hide in Dos," he says. "It's kind of scary, it's more like the Minutemen, there's no rock'n'roll to go back on. But it's really made us both go for it, distilling it, editing it, getting to the point, to the bare nada. Some people say, 'Yeah, if you just had a drummer.' But we want to make it kind of tough. It's like a total extension of punk rock for me and Kira. To make a band of bass — it's a victory."

Onstage recently at Cafe Largo, a candle-lit pub in Los Angeles' Fairfax district, Dos' hour-long set buzzed and hummed sweetly, filling the room with a glowing sonic intensity. Trading burning riffs and delicate melodies, woozy plucking and thundering rhythmic figures, the music felt like a private conversation — sometimes joyful, other times brooding or melancholy, but always sharing passion and understanding. In warmly rendered cover versions of Billie Holiday's "Don't Explain," Ernest Tubb's "Imagine That" (popularized by Patsy Cline), and a charged version of Bessie Smith's "Down In the Dumps," Kira's dreamy, understated vocals had the audience hanging onto every note.

"I'm not a singer," she insists. "Not really. But I get my inspiration from Bessie, Billie and all those women blues singers. Them and Madonna — that woman's a real firecracker."

LIKE WATT, KIRA ROESSLER is quirky and engaging in conversation. Telling stories about the early days of punk, when as a teenager she worked at Hollywood's legendary underground club the Masque, it's clear she shares her husband's passion for punk rock ideals. "I was in the room when the Go-Go's said, 'Let's make a band,'" she recalls. "I just said, 'Oh god.' I couldn't believe it. None of them knew how to play. That was the cool thing — you could sit around and say 'let's make a band,' and do it."

Roessler was still with Black Flag in '84 and '85 when she and Watt began jamming together, recording tunes as background music for bedtime stories she would read to her nephews. After graduating from UCLA with a degree in engineering, she moved to Connecticut for a one-year internship at Yale. During that period, she and Watt would work out new songs in the ultimate DIY manner, sending tapes back and forth through the mail. When D. Boon was killed in December of 1985, Watt's anguish left him questioning whether he should even go on as a musician. But he and Roessler continued, and used some of the songs he'd written for the next Minutemen album on Dos' 1986 debut for New Alliance (other songs appeared on the first Firehose album).

"After D. Boon died I was very scared," Watt says. "I didn't have any confidence. Still, if I lose my nerve, it's really bad. With D. Boon it was so easy. I'd just look over and laugh. He was so funny. He was intense to watch." Watt pauses, drifting off in memories. He recently visited Boon's father, who gave him one of the late guitarist's old axes. The guitar strap, Watt says, "still had his scent on it." Watt and others plan to do a D. Boon tribute album within the coming year; the proceeds will go to Boon's father. "As long as I had him," Watt continues, "I didn't give a shit. It was like me and D. Boon against the world. With Kira, it's more like, 'Oh, man, I hope I'm not letting you down.'"

Roessler admits that Watt can be intimidating. "I admire Mike a lot for holding Firehose together," she says. "And the Minutemen would still be together if D. Boon was alive. Mike has that ability to keep things going; it's sheer obsession, he will not let go. It's cool, but it also makes him somewhat less than flexible. It's difficult to shift his gears, to impact that flow. With Dos, sometimes, it gets into a little bit of a power struggle. But part of what makes it good is competition. Even though he makes a living at music and I don't, I have to try and stand my ground."

Lately, Watt and Roessler have been spending their weekends in the studio recording a new album. It will feature a handful of originals and covers, including the Bessie Smith and Ernest Tubb songs as well as the Minutemen's "Do You Want New Wave Or Do You Want the Truth?" They expect to release the record in late spring. For Roessler, who designs computer systems for an L.A. firm, Dos is a hobby. And though she'd like to have more free time to devote to the group, she shudders at the idea of making music a job.

"When we started Dos, we didn't really think people could get into it," she says. "We thought some bass players might like it, but it was mostly for ourselves. It still is. I can't worry about people digging what I'm doing. I love it when they do, but I can't make my livelihood depend on it. It's too much of a crapshoot. And I'm too practical for that."

At Cafe Largo, most of the audience was enthusiastic, but restrained. People clapped politely, as if watching an avant-garde jazz performance instead of the latest manifestation of punk rock. Sitting on bar stools in the back of the pub, though, a row of college-age guys made all the noise they could muster. Dressed in backward baseball caps and flannels, they stomped their feet between songs, frequently yelled out Watt's name, and even hung out after the show to help load Dos' equipment into the van.

That part of the scene was reminiscent of another show last summer, when Firehose opened for Primus at the Greek Theatre in

Berkeley. During the encore, when Watt came onstage to jam with Primus bassist Les Claypool, the crowd erupted. All around, scruffy, flannel-clad teens took to the aisles, air-bassing to Watt and Claypool's thundering riffs.

"It's so weird about bass," Watt says. "I mean, back in the days of Cal Jam — in those days, bass is where you put the lame guy. To be a hero to kids is really funny. It's like walking into the Forum to see the Lakers play and saying, 'Who did these floors? What technique!' Most people want to see Magic put it in the hole or something. So it's kinda weird."

He gazes off, trying on a couple of new words for size. "Hero," he says. "Bass hero." Then he shakes his head: "I dunno. I'm Watt. I'm still a thug from Pedro."

March 1993

the jesus & mary chain

SOB STORY

BY **DAVID SHIRLEY**

IT'S THE FIRST OF AUGUST and the raunchy Lollapalooza festival has barreled its way into New York City. We're told that the guiding principles of the tour include voter registration, AIDS awareness, environmental concerns and, above all, a plea for musical diversity and cultural exchange. Yet with the dominance of white, male, hard rock attractions on the bill, you'd be hard-pressed to find a sadder example of a medium bashing its message to bits. It's a sore spot for Jim Reid of Glasgow's Jesus & Mary Chain, one of only two non-American bands on the roadshow.

"The idea behind the whole tour is to get people to listen to different kinds of music," he complains. "But there's just too much of one kind this year. And it's not really just the music. There's too much of this macho attitude out there, too much of a chest-beating kind of thing. Even with Ice Cube on the program, the audience is mostly male and certainly 99 percent white." He pauses, looking blankly into space. "If you've got a mostly white, male, middle-class audience listening to only one kind of music, what's being achieved?"

Indeed, the Lolla list reads like a who's who of wrestling stars: Pearl Jam, Soundgarden, Ministry and headliners the Red Hot Chili Peppers, all complemented on a side stage by the Jim Rose Circus Sideshow, featuring such "consciousness raising" acts as the Amazing Mr. Lifto, who dangles weights from his penis. Ice Cube adds some color, but certainly doesn't challenge the muscle-flexing flavor of the day. Lost somewhere in the sweltering haze are Lush and the Mary Chain, their music as different from the other bands' as their U.K. origins.

jesus & mary chain

Lush has two arguable advantages: they open the show and feature the only female performers of the event. For those reasons, the group earns modest tolerance from the crowds. No such luck for the Mary Chain. Following Pearl Jam and posing the only remaining obstacle to the non-stop fare of high-powered rock to follow, the group faces one hostile and/or indifferent audience after another. Stripped of their elaborate light show and removed from the smaller, indoor venues which make their sustained feedback and dark, ambient guitar riffs roar, the Mary Chain sounds slight and unimposing. Performing in daylight — during which they discovered that sunglasses have a practical value — they are even robbed of their aloofness. And William Reid's occasional drunken tantrums — during a show in Raleigh, North Carolina, he smashed his mike stand in disgust over some technical problems — seem harmless alongside the manic fury of Ministry's Al Jourgensen.

THE DAY AFTER LOLLAPALOOZA'S New York show, lead singer Jim Reid is having a late, hungover breakfast in the restaurant of his mid-Manhattan hotel. Guitarist William Reid is in bed with the "flu." Although the brothers suffered plenty of rough spots during the two weeks leading up to their New York performances, yesterday's show at nearby Jones Beach has been the worst yet. And Jim Reid is showing it. Minus his trademark sunglasses, his eyes are bloodshot and sunken, his skin beginning to break out under three days' growth of beard.

Shy and soft-spoken, both Reid brothers are often regarded as withdrawn and uncooperative. "The really difficult thing for us about what we do is that people expect you to have just one mood," Jim explains, uncomfortably. "You can't ever just feel like not talking to anyone or not doing a show." On this particular morning, however, he's patient, gracious and honest. "Yesterday's show was just terrible, a real nightmare," he groans, and then looks away, cradling his hands around a three-dollar cup of coffee.

"After the first few songs I wanted to leave the stage. It was just awful."

The Jesus & Mary Chain had been scheduled to do last year's Lollapalooza tour alongside a more diverse group of bands, including the Butthole Surfers, Siouxsie & the Banshees, Ice-T and others. "It sounded like a good idea at the time, but we were working on *Honey's Dead*" — their latest album, on Def American. "So when they asked us again this year, we accepted, thinking we were going to be a little more involved than we actually have been in putting things together."

A few days later, with a couple of less-nightmarish performances under their belt, older brother William seems less distressed. "The week at Jones Beach was one of our worst gigs ever," he says, echoing his brother. "There was just no atmosphere there, and no Jesus & Mary Chain fans in the audience. But really," he insists, "some places have been brilliant. Obviously we don't have as many fans as Pearl Jam or the Red Hot Chili Peppers, but plenty of our fans have turned out."

He catches himself. "To be honest with you, the whole thing has been much, much too hard. I'd like for there to have been a softer approach."

There's a certain poetic justice in having the Reid brothers tossed unmercifully into a throng of bewildered, unsympathetic hard rock fans and a line-up of ferociously aggressive bands. Since the release of *Psychocandy*, the band's celebrated debut in 1985, a remarkable number of like-minded, and often crudely derivative musicians have thrashed their way into the clubs and onto the college charts, spreading the Mary Chain's rather limited esthetic of sweet melodies, brooding lyrics, carefully modulated feedback and roaring, layered guitars. Even for those who love the sound, it's sometimes too much of a good thing.

The overwhelming critical and commercial success of the Mary Chain's early work made things easier for the Rides, My Bloody Valentines and Lushes of the world, maybe even gaining a few fans for unacknowledged antecedents like Sonic Youth. The Reids are understandably proud of their impact on so many younger bands and listeners, but they're also careful not to overestimate its significance. "After *Psychocandy*, a particular kind of music was easier to make than it was before," Jim maintains. "I'm not saying that those bands wouldn't have come along without us, but we certainly made it a lot easier for them."

Things weren't always so easy for the brothers Reid, though. Prior to their present incarnations, William and Jim were listless, wayward sons of Protestant, working class parents from the small, nondescript Scottish town of East Kilbride. Today a contented Londoner, Jim, the younger Reid, still groans when describing his hometown's "thousands of square-shaped houses, row on row, and all exactly the same. There's nothing to do there, nothing to see" — he pauses to make the most damning observation of all — "and nothing but *Rambo* movies at the local movie house."

SURPRISINGLY, THE BUDDING ICONOCLASTS maintained a low profile all through their school years. Too timid and withdrawn to risk any overt signs of rebellion, they spent most of their time alone or together, quietly cultivating the stubborn, brooding sensibilities and wildly eclectic musical tastes for which they would later find a voice.

"I don't really know where our approach to music came from in the first place," Jim reflects. "We would be sitting around listening to Burt Bacharach at the same time we were listening to Einstürzende Neubauten, and wondering why those two types of music hadn't really come together before. Probably the closest thing to what we were looking for up till that point had been the Velvet Underground, where you could get really catchy, sweet melodies and intelligent lyrics with this really big, dark racket going on behind it. But we wanted something more than that," he insists emphatically, still visibly irritated by endless VU comparisons. "We were interested in the idea of taking that approach several stages further than where it had been in the past. We just wanted to make the most extreme, but well-crafted songs that had ever been recorded." Reid seldom makes eye contact, but he pauses now to make sure he has my attention. "I think we did that!"

After finishing high school, the Reid brothers did everything they could to avoid work, preferring to hang with their punk-clad friends during the dreary East Kilbride days and work on song ideas in their bedroom at night. Gradually, their ideas began to take shape and the brothers began trying out their material with different groups of local musicians, each ensemble sporting a different name. "Most of the names were crap, to be honest," Jim remembers. "They were just there because we had to write something on the demo tapes that we were always sending out to clubs."

The still-nameless duo got its first real break during the summer of 1984. "We'd given one of our tapes to a club and the agent at the club wasn't interested in the band at all. But he kept the tape anyway because it had a Syd Barrett compilation on the other side. Then he gave it to Bobby Gillespie of Primal Scream because Bobby really liked Syd Barrett. But Bobby listened to the other side, too, and he really loved our stuff. So he called us up excited and said, 'I can get you a gig!'" Jim laughs, rembering how Gillespie's initial enthusiasm caught them off guard. "Shortly after that, Bobby became our drummer."

The tape featured rough demos for "Upside Down," an incoherent mess of a song destined to become the band's first single, as well as "Never Understand" and "In a Hole," two of the highlights of *Psychocandy*.

Gillespie was true to his word and quick about it. He introduced the Reid brothers to Alan McGee, owner of Creation Records and manager of a new club called the Living Room. McGee was equally taken with the demo, hiring the two on the spot without having seen them perform.

The rest is a bit embarrassing, but propitious musical history. With little time to rehearse, William and Jim recruited their old chum Douglas Hart to play bass for the gig, along with Gillespie on drums. Things began to fall apart even before the four had managed to set up for the show. "We did a sound check," Jim chuckles, "and it was just amazing how completely untogether we were. We practically split up over it right there on the spot; William and I were screaming at each other across the stage. This was supposed to be our big break, and here we were, practically clubbing each other to death."

And McGee? Jim shakes his head incredulously. "He was watching all of us from the side and comes back to us and says, 'Yeah, this is great! Let's do about five albums together!' William and I were just stunned; like, 'Sure, OK, we'll do it.'"

As funny as it sounds today, the story recalls the band's early, less-than-humorous reputation of being indifferent and often completely oblivious to fans. Even worse, William would sometimes burst into violent tantrums, pounding his mike stand to bits or hurling things at the audience.

But the Mary Chain never did like performing live or touring. "We don't write while we're on tour," says William, for whom songwriting is an ongoing process of self-realization. "I'm always writing songs; even if I didn't do it for a living, I'd still write songs. It's the most important part of my life. Everything else is just work. So when you're out there performing live and you're not doing what is really important to you, you gotta ask yourself, 'Why am I doing this?'"

Still, the Reids maintain that their whole "stupid hooligan" image was vastly overblown. Most of the commotion, they insist, resulted from the band's early inexperience and technical ineptitude, along with a couple of serious cases of drug-and-alcohol-medicated stage fright. Jim's version is that some of the tales were pure mythology. "The backs-to-the-audience thing never really happened. Sometimes William would stand in front of his amp to get feedback or whatever, and occasionally Douglas was like that, too. But that was really all it was."

Still, it would be hard to exaggerate the extent, or the impact, of alcohol and drugs on the band's performances. "Seven or eight years ago," Jim admits, "I would get completely wracked on stage and throw a bottle at somebody. That was always happening. I'm not exactly proud of it, you know. It's just something that happens when you get absolutely shit-faced."

These days the Reids have axed the drugs but not the drink. "Do we still drink?" he smiles. "Compared to other people, yeah, I guess we still drink a lot. It just makes it easier to get through the show, to be honest with you."

AS FOR TECHNICAL INEPTITUDE, through a combination of hard work and attrition — paring back to two members in the studio — the band has slowly developed. Gillespie eventually found his way back to Primal Scream, and Hart, who had basically stepped in as a last minute favor, was gently let go. "Douglas was more of a friend than a musician," Jim says, laughing fondly. "He couldn't play bass to save his life. After a while it seemed a bit ridiculous to be taking the time to show someone else how to do it when we could do it better — and we couldn't even play that well ourselves at that point."

But the brothers did know what they wanted. "They were our songs," he continues. "So it got to where we just didn't ask anyone else for help. Even on *Psychocandy*, it was mostly me and William. Half the tracks were layed down live with the four of us, and the rest were me and William fumbling around to see what we could do."

"Jim doesn't really know the names of the chords," says William, of the duo's trial-and-error approach to songwriting. "He'll point to the chord he wants me to play. I'm just a couple of steps ahead of him; I can actually name the chords and play a few more. But that's about it. It's more intuitive for us."

Listening to the rough edges of the band's early singles — "Upside Down" (Creation, 1984) and "Never Understand" and "You Trip Me Up" (Blanco y Negro, 1985) — the Reid's account of their early, naive working method seems plausible enough. *Psychocandy* is another matter entirely: the recording is a small gem. With its carefully balanced feedback and its meticulously layered guitars, it's the perfect mixture of sweetness and rage — and seemingly the very antithesis of the learn-as-you-go punk esthetic. Technically, the band's subsequent releases, *Darklands* and *Automatic*, were even more accomplished. But on both of those albums, much of the sweetness got lost in muted rage and the band lost its appeal to many of those who had hailed *Psychocandy* as the album of the decade.

Just prior to *Psychocandy*'s release, Jim had dreamed aloud to reporter Chris Heath about his then-future album's significance: "It's got to stand up for years. I hope it's going to be one of those LP's like the first Velvet Underground LP which always sells, everybody's got it and it's always in the shops. I'm trying to think of something like 20 years from now."

Only seven years later, the Reid brothers sometimes wish a few more people had left the record on the shelf or off the air. "The whole thing — all the attention given to *Psychocandy* — used to annoy the shit out of me, basically," Jim admits.

Time and widespread praise for *Honey's Dead*, however, have made the Reid's more content with the legacy of their early success. "Nowadays'" Jim continues, "you just have to laugh, really, because now there are all these other bands who are getting compared to us — you know, Mary Chain sound-alikes. So you just figure that we must have our own unique sound or nobody could be compared to us. But I really don't care what people say about it, to be honest with you."

The Reid brothers are reluctant to discuss just exactly it is that holds the Mary Chain sound together. "I don't really like to analyze it that much," demurs Jim. "Whatever it is, it's a good thing that we do, and if you examine it too much, it could blow it for us. If you look at anything too closely, it starts losing its mystique." Mystique or not, that layered, ambient Mary Chain sound came straight from a studio. "When we first signed," laughs William, "we didn't even know what a producer did. But we told them that we weren't recording unless we had total control and the time to do what we wanted."

Oddly, one thing the recording process won't allow for is alcohol. William explains why two men notorious for their drunken stage performances are teetotalers in the studio. "Recording is much too much a technical thing; it's tough enough as it is. If you've been drinking, you don't know what the fuck you are doing."

Honey's Dead is clearly an attempt by the Reids to distance themselves from the critical and commercial constraints of their early success. With the addition of Curve's percussionist Monty on eight of the tracks, the recording has a much livelier, more danceable feel than any of the band's earlier releases. On songs like "Frequency" (a stripped-down reprise of the single "Reverence") and "Tumbleweed," those traces of Modern Lovers and Ramones that haunt the margins of the earlier records are brought more to the front. And other numbers, like "Sundown" and "Almost Gold," are unambiguosly lovely, even upbeat — so lovely and upbeat, in fact, that the Reids are bewildered with the band's ongoing image as an "alternative" act.

"If the music is good enough," Jim pleads, "it should be heard by as many people as possible. I'm proud of what we do and I want more people to hear it." Something like "Almost Gold," he continues, shaking his head, "I don't see any reason why five million people shouldn't be snapping their fingers to that." But the main reason for the band's lack of mainstream recognition isn't the music at all, but the Reid brothers' bad boy, "new Sex Pistols" image. Apart from their reputation for riotous and riot-provoking performances, the band has a proud history of public confrontation and blasphemy (the B-side to one of their earliest singles, "You Trip Me Up," was outrageously titled "Jesus Suck"). "If something annoys us," Jim boasts, "we tend to talk about it rather than just let it go. We'll hold an interview and say, 'Why not?'"

Honey's Dead fits right into that scenario. The ironically titled "Reverence," the album's first single, raised a stink when it was released in England last winter. With its morbid, in-your-face megalomania ("I wanna die just like Jesus Christ/I wanna die on a bed of spikes…/I wanna die like JFK/ I wanna die on a sunny day"), the song entered the British charts at number 10 and was promptly banned by *Top of the Pops*. This time, however, the official rejection by the British music establishment and the media attention it generated were a godsend for the Reids, whose work had been subjected to more subtle restrictions in the past. "We've had singles in Britain for the past five years," Jim says, "but nobody plays them. Really, it was a good thing for us. When 'Reverence' was banned it gave us a chance to explain to people what had been happening to us all along — that those other records were banned, too. It's just there is no official thing, which is worse. Because at least with 'Reverence' people were actually talking about our record not getting played, as opposed to just completely ignoring it and not caring.

"We're aware of the fact that we're going to piss people off," Jim argues, "but that's not the reason for doing it. We do it because, 'Why shouldn't we?' It would be tacky to suggest that we just do it for attention," he bristles. "That's never been what we're about."

ONE THING THAT HAS BECOME PAINFULLY CLEAR to the Reids during the past few months is that they absolutely despise life on the road. In the past they've restricted their promotional tours to three weeks in Britain, a month in Europe and a few extra weeks in the U.S. This year, they've chosen to throw abandon to the wind, combining a much lengthier European tour, the special four-week "Roller Coaster" tour of England (with Blur, My Bloody Valentine and Dinosaur Jr.), a trip to Japan and finally nine sweltering weeks of Lollapalooza.

"This present tour was supposed to be a kind of back-to-the-start for us," explains William, who seems less confrontational about the subject. "We're playing to audiences that don't know our music and that might not be into what we're doing. But you've got to stand there and face them. We thought it would be a challenge."

"Being on tour is probably more difficult for us than any other band," insists Jim, for whom the major issue seems to be discomfort with trying to please the crowds. "We're just not showbiz types of people. All we care about is making the music — just making the music. And sometimes we're not in the mood for anything else.

"If you're onstage and you don't want to be there," he goes on, "and you've got an audience that doesn't want you on — that's one of the worst feelings imaginable."

AFTER MONTHS OF TOURING — and their less-than-flattering juxtaposition with younger, more aggressive performers at Lollapalooza — the Reids are wondering what an older, gentler Jesus & Mary Chain might sound like. Jim just turned 30, and William, whom Jim describes as "vain about age," is already 32. "I really don't want to get into any undignified scene," William insists. But Jim says, "I can see myself still making records at 50, but I can't see myself going on the road forever. It's the equivalent of some aging movie actress who paints herself with makeup and has about 18 face lifts. She just can't face getting old. I don't think there's anything wrong with getting old, but when you do get older, I think you should adjust and not pretend it's not happening." He grimaces. "Someone like Mick Jagger, trying like he does to keep up with the likes of Prince, to still be regarded the same way by the same audience — I think that's pathetic."

What aging rock star is *not* pathetic? "Van Morrison," says Jim. "He's accepted the change and he's adjusted and he's growing old gracefully. I mean, if he were still doing 'Gloria' that would be ridiculous. But instead he's become a fairly dignified musician. That's what I'd like to do."

September 1992

thurston moore & mike d

STARPOWER

EAVESDROPPING BY **MARK KEMP**

THE SCENE: A TRENDY RESTAURANT in L.A. called the Hollywood Canteen. Thurston Moore of Sonic Youth is sitting in a corner booth, slouched over a plate of pasta, wearing a punk rock T-shirt and a backward baseball cap. He's flanked by a couple of pudgy major label dudes gesturing and talking excitedly to him about ad copy for his band's new DGC album, *Dirty*. At the other end of the table is Beastie Boy Mike Diamond (better known as Mike D), also in an oversized T-shirt with his cap on backward. Fortunately for Mike D, the ad copy for the Beasties' latest release, *Check Your Head*, has already been written.

Earlier in the day, Moore and Diamond were looser and more animated, sitting in the sun room of Diamond's two story, Spanish-style stucco home, located on a hillside in L.A.'s Silverlake neighborhood. Moore had flown in from New York for the day on the glitzy MGM grand airlines; with a few hours to kill he decided to visit his old friend from the New York hardcore scene of the early '80s.

No one on that scene with a shred of sanity could have forecast the Sonic/Beastie career path of the last ten years. The Beasties' first record, *Polly Wog Stew* (Rat Cage, 1982), came out the same year as Sonic Youth's first, self-titled EP on the obscure art label Neutral. The former featured snotty hardcore songs like "Egg Raid On Mojo" and "Transit Cop"; the latter was total noise and poetic posturing. By mid-decade, the two groups had gone in completely different directions. The Beastie Boys' hip-hop leanings had been hinted at on the goof-rap indie single, "Cookie Puss"; by 1986, the

Beasties were selling four million copies of *Licensed To Ill*, the first rap album ever to top the charts. At the same time, Sonic Youth was turning the dissonance and feedback of its early records into beautiful noise on *EVOL* (SST).

In the years since, while the Beasties' palefaced punk has emboldened acts like the Red Hot Chili Peppers, they themselves have become more experimental on *Paul's Boutique* and *Check Your Head*. Meanwhile, Sonic Youth has developed into one of the most influential guitar bands of its generation, continuing on *Goo* and *Dirty* to infuse its dissonance with the best elements of pop. Likewise, both groups have re-embraced the sounds of their shared New York roots.

Surrounded by a couple of turntables and endless shelves of LPs and singles, Mike and Thurston talked for nearly three hours about hardcore, artcore, obsession, rock stardom, record collecting and getting shit for free.

What goes around comes around.

THE FREE SHIT PROGRAM

MIKE D: The best part of rock stardom is that period just before people know who you are on any kind of big-time national or international level. It's that period of time where you get, like, free shit. And it's at a time when you really *need* free shit. See, most people don't understand the value of the free-shit program. When we were at the point where nobody'd ever heard of us outside the island of Manhattan, it was great. There was a certain period of years when Sonic Youth was putting out a record every six months and we weren't doing anything, but we were going out to clubs and getting in for free and getting free drinks and shit. That was really cool because it enabled us to live a life that was, like... I don't wanna say fantasy, but it was like a totally untroubled existence. We didn't really need to have much money.

THURSTON: You mean like Springsteen? I think it was Springsten who said, like... uh, what did he say? Oh yeah, he said something like it makes living easier, but it doesn't make life any easier.

MIKE D: No, I'm talking about the *irony* of free shit. Getting free shit when you really need it, before you get to the point where free shit isn't important anymore. I'm talking about the kind of local stardom that has nothing to do with being a rock star on any kind of national level; stardom within a really small world. You're a celebrity in New York, and it's great because you don't have the negative side effects of being a celebrity on any kind of broader scale; you don't have people expecting stuff from you on any kind of big scale yet. You know what I mean? But at the same time, you can take advantage of your situation. You can go out and get into places for free and check out stuff and get free drinks or whatever. Without having to worry about the pay-back side.

And then you move onto the big-time free-shit program. That's where we are now. Like, when you have an album out and you're going on tour and you're actually getting paid to play shows and stuff. But people will still give you free shit, right? But it doesn't matter so much anymore because we're playing shows. [raising his voice] I mean, we don't *need* free shit! We can actually afford to go out and *buy* shit now. I mean, it's still cool — getting shit for free is always cool — but now it's just kind of a minor victory. Whereas back then it was necessary.

THURSTON: That is weird man. The more popular you become as a band...

MIKE D: ...the more free shit you get! Like, now I get a box of free clothes and I don't *need* free clothes! Like, if I want clothes...

THURSTON: ...you can go out and buy the shit.

MIKE D: But when I had no money, and when I had no record and I was a total bum, I really needed free shit. It's totally ironic.

THURSTON: When our records starting becoming more popular and I would go in a record store to buy something, they'd give me a fucking discount. And it's like, I didn't need a fucking discount. I'd be with a friend and he wouldn't get a discount because nobody knew who the fuck he was. But he'd really need the discount. He wouldn't have a pot to piss in. So he'd just sort of bum and say, "Man, you're making money off your records now and they're giving you discounts. What's the deal?" Capitalism is funny that way. Not that I'm against capitalism, but it's... [pauses] you know, you just have to deal with some of the trickier aspects of it.

MIKE D: It's totally weird.

THURSTON: What you have to do is give the shit away. You just give it away to people.

THE BEASTIE BOYS RULE

THURSTON: To me, the Beastie Boys are the weirdest band in the world. Look what's going on: three white Jewish kids from New York being a hip-hop band. And they're good at it. That's not supposed to happen. Why is that happening? It isn't supposed to be. But it's like you guys are good, you're one of the best hip-hop bands around. So people don't really think about it like that; they don't think about how absurd it is. That's weird. Why's it authentic? Well, because it's got soul. But why? I mean, our whole thing with [the experimental EP] *Master Dik* and [the noisy side project] Ciccone Youth was, like, we can't fuck with the soul. I'm not going to pretend I got hip-hop soul, 'cause I don't. So Ciccone Youth was never really like a hip-hop project, it was more sort of "anything goes." We were just in there kicking tape recorders and shit.

MIKE D: But that's not all that different from what we do. When we make records it's really kind of close to that attitude. And it's not really that absurd, dude. I mean, if you look at it more in terms of a geographic thing and not a racial thing, then it makes sense. We grew up on that stuff; we're totally a product of the late '70s and early '80s and growing up in Manhattan. So there's no way we could have arrived at where we are now without having gone through not only the hip-hop side of music, but all of the other kinds of music we were exposed to — like hardcore, PiL, stuff like that.

The thing is, that period in New York is kind of underrated in terms of music history and influence. Even in terms of the existence of free jazz and where it was going at that time. After seeing [the harmolodic guitarist James] Blood Ulmer play with Public Image, I definitely checked out Blood Ulmer a few more times. And then I checked out Art Ensemble at Public Theater. And then [drummer] Ronald Shannon Jackson. There was that kind of fusion crossover shit from No Wave that really influenced how I started hearing things.

THURSTON: You saw Art Ensemble at Public Theater?

MIKE D: But that was only because I became aware of that music at that particular time. I don't even know why, but I think it was a combination of the fact that it was going on in the clubs and the fact that I was reading the *Soho Weekly News*.

THURSTON: Yeah, that period was really important. And the thing is, a lot of it went by so fast, got passed over so fast, and now different things are happening. But a lot of new-style shit that's going on now — you know, shit that's very hardcore and very Nike — is going back and taking the real strong elements of the stuff from that period. It's really important and relevant to what's going on now. In England, they may look at the Beastie Boys doing old school stuff and say, "Why are the Beastie Boys doing old beats now?" But, see, they just don't get it. They're like, "This isn't new," but what they don't understand is that it *is* new. It's not retrogressive, it's not "Stray Cat Shuffle;" this stuff is still fresh. It went by so fast and few people really got it because it was sort of kept to an elite few.

MIKE D: I think about some of the records that came out back then on the hardcore scene and they're really overlooked because the bands never went anywhere.

THURSTON: Right now, there's a big insurgence of young people getting into music that was very, very obscure even back then. And there's a lot of people getting involved in the total improvisation music that was going on back then. And that's really wild. The improv scene then was really small; like, in England there was Derek Bailey and New York had John Zorn. But it was a very, very tiny scene. Now, it's pretty huge. All these styles that were way obscure back then are coming out now and being treated in a big way. So you might as well wear old school Pumas now because they are way fresher than new school Nikes. It's weird, 'cause that's never happened before.

MIKE D: That's true, because it's like you're wearing something that's old, but it's definitely newer than some things that are new.

THURSTON: And do you know what that is, D? That's super-postmodernism. That's my term for it.

thurston moore & mike d

HARDCORE, ARTCORE: THE EARLY YEARS

THURSTON: I knew *you* back then, but you didn't know me. Like, I heard "Cookie Puss," but you never heard [our first album] *Confusion Is Sex*. But that's because you guys were punk rock and we were art fags; we were like SoHo and you guys were like East Village.

MIKE D: Yeah, but now artcore rules. Artcore actually beat out hardcore. You know, Fugazi's artcore. But Sonic Youth was artcore from the beginning.

THURSTON: See, the Beastie Boys were really deceptive, really scary. When "Cookie Puss" came out, I thought it was like a joke. I never thought you guys would start getting seriously into beats and shit. But when *Licensed To Ill* came out, we thought you guys were going disco. We didn't know what the fuck was up with that.

MIKE D: What people don't know is that we were actually about to go new wave.

THURSTON: I remember the first time I heard about the Beastie Boys. It was in *Short News* [an early NYC punk 'zine] of a show you guys did at a hardcore festial in Tompkins Square Park. It went something like, "This band called the Beastie Boys came out and nobody knew who they were and they immediately went spastic and left the stage." I was like, "What the fuck?" And then I went to see you at the Kitchen or something.

MIKE D: No man, that was later. That was after we became artcore.

THURSTON: Oh yeah, 'cause the Kitchen was just an art space, but then they decided to start having all different kinds of music on the same bill. So they would get an art band, a country band, a punk rock band...

MIKE D: ...and it was really cool. The bill would be Ned Sublette, the Beastie Boys and Swans all in one night. And maybe Sonic Youth and, uh...what was that band that I didn't like, Thurston?

THURSTON: Rat At Rat R?

MIKE D: No, no, the one with the violins.

SO YOU DON'T HAVE TO

THURSTON: Oh, oh, the Ordinaires. Yeah, you made fun of 'em afterwards.

MIKE D: Well, the Ordinaires *were* kind of weak — *come on!*

THURSTON: Yeah, you were coming out dissing the Ordinaires, and you were dissing the audience, too. You were saying, "Man, it's hard to play because there's too many people out here with beards; I'm not used to playing to people with beards." You kept saying that over and over, and finally the Ordinaires came out and one of them had a beard.

ENGLAND'S DREAMING

THURSTON: Did you read *England's Dreaming*?

MIKE D: Yeah, I got it, but I gotta start reading it.

THURSTON: Dude, man, you really gotta fucking read that book! It's kind of annoying, but it hits on some really crucial stuff. It's written from an academic viewpoint, covering the whole idea of multi-directionalism coming into focus in the '80s after punk rock became established. You know, it's like punk rock became established then it collapsed in on itself, but at the same time nothing's been the same since. And the only thing that's breaking up this multi-directionalism is politics and a bad economy. People want to cross over culturally — nobody's really scared to get in touch with the ethnicity of their country — but politics and the economy have gotten in the way.

MIKE D: People are always fascinated to some extent with other cultures.

THURSTON: Yeah, and that's the strongest cultural point this country has — its multiplicity. To split it up through totally destructive economic policies is totally fucked up. And it starts in the cities because the concentration of money is now outside of the cities. But anyway, I've been talking politics long enough. That's all they wanted to talk to us about in England. But it's significant musically.

CRIME AND OBSESSION

MIKE D: Obsessions are the best parts of life.

THURSTON: But when you get older you get a more sophisticated perspective on things, which is important. And that's when your obsessions actually become fun, because you have a better perspective on them.

MIKE D: Obsessions are *really* important. Like, music is my obsession, right? And music is probably the most cross-cultural part of my life today. I mean, I'm far less integrated in terms of the people I come into contact with or what I do on a daily basis and stuff, so probably the only extent to which I'm truly versed in any cross-cultural way is through music. I certainly don't consider that I know all there is to know about music, but in terms of just being completely obsessed with discovering different kinds of music, that's the way I am able to open myself up to different cultures and different people.

To me, lately — I mean, I don't know what it is about the world that's making me feel this way — but like lately I've been totally obsessed with aggressive music. There's a beauty I see in that aggressiveness. Whether it's seeing Henry Rollins play or hearing a Sonic Youth record or an Ornette Coleman record or a Miles Davis record, there's just this raw beauty in it. I see it as just anger, you know? And that goes completely across any kind of outward trimmings that any of these different kinds of music may have, or what types of people play it, or even what time frame it came from. When I'm listening to music, those moments are the only times in my life where I can truly transcend where someone comes from or what culture's making it. It's that sort of feeling that runs through every culture and you can hear it in the music. It's just like a raw, beautiful thing.

THURSTON: You can trust music more. It's the most pure form of information.

MIKE D: Yeah, you can check out all different kinds of information from all these different voices of expression. All you have to do is check it out and listen to it to really develop a complete, 100-percent love and fascination with it.

THURSTON: And that's because with music you're getting the emotion of the culture. Politics, on the other hand, is nothing. Politics is like... I mean, it's nothing. Oh sure, it has something to do with culture, but it's not the real emotion of the culture. Politics is just boorish, there's nothing intellectual about it at all. That's why politics tries to destroy the arts — particularly right now, there's like a war going on between politics and the arts, and to me it's like a war between good and evil. I guess politics has to exist because people need policy, but politics really shouldn't be involved in the arts. Without art, all we'd have is psychotic serial killers. That's why serial killers have always been so big in this country.

MIKE D: But there's also that correlation between serial killers and art. You know how some serial killers are good painters or writers?

THURSTON: Yeah, but that's just because they're frustrated genius artists.

MIKE D: Like Charlie Starkweather. I was reading this Charlie Starkweather book where they showed all of these paintings he had done, and I was actually kind of into it. It kind of scared me. Here's this guy who's a total killer, yet somehow this disturbed being inside of him is creating these paintings that I kind of like and am fascinated by. I always thought that the coolest part of *Badlands* is when Martin Sheen, playing Charlie Starkweather, goes and makes his own spoken-word record in that booth. That was just wild.

THE ECONOMICS OF RECORD COLLECTING

THURSTON: D, what's the most you've ever paid for a record?

MIKE D: The most — see it doesn't really count 'cause it's not vinyl — but I bought that Mingus boxed set for like a hundred.

THURSTON: No, no, that doesn't count, that doesn't count; I mean like a collector's record.

MIKE D: It was definitely J.B.'s *Food For Thought*, and that was either 35 or 40 bucks. That's the most I've ever paid for a record. What about you?

THURSTON: I've spent 200 bucks on a record. It was the first pressing of *Call Me Burroughs*, the William Burroughs LP that came out in like '65. It was at a bookstore in Paris called the English Bookstore. It's like this super-obscure beat album. It was released later on ESP and even that goes for a hundred now. That's sick. But, see, I usually trade for records like that. I'll go on tour and buy really obscure jazz records and then trade ten of them for this one really intense thing. But this one I saw somewhere and I called up my sources and said I'd seen this thing for 200 bucks, and they were like, "Pick it up, 'cause you can sell it for five." So I picked it up because I like the artifact aspect of collecting. That's the only reason I started record labels and stuff — to create artifacts. I'm not into getting involved in the record industry at all.

MIKE D: See, I have mixed emotions about stuff like that. Probably the records I have that are worth the most are punk rock records, like that Fred "Sonic" Smith single.

THURSTON: You got "City Slang"? [starts humming the song]

MIKE D: Yeah, lemme find it. [walks over to his singles collections and flips through them] I remember seeing that X-Ray Spex album for like a hunded bucks, and now they've rereleased it. I was so into that record when I was 13, but did I want to buy it for a hundred bucks? Nah.

THURSTON: You have some really rare hip-hop sides, though.

MIKE D: Yeah, but the record collector element hasn't really hit hip-hop culture yet.

THURSTON: I buy that shit because it's, like, mostly gone. Where do you go to get the old singles? You can't find that stuff. Hey, so you have like 100,000 hardcore singles from First Wave?

MIKE D: Definitely.

THURSTON: See, both of us probably have a few grand worth of that shit. If you look in the back of *Flipside* or *Maximumrocknroll*, the first Necros is like 200 bucks. It's sick shit. It's so much sick shit.

WATTS LINE

(The phone rings. It's Mike Watt, the San Pedro-based Firehose bassist and a friend of Thurston since Watt's days with the Minutemen. Mike D puts the phone on speaker mode and the conversation gets heavy.)

MIKE D: Watt, what're you doing, man?

WATT: I'm talking to you from Pedro.

MIKE D: Dude, you comin' over here?

THURSTON: It's time to chow, man, time to go out and get some tuna tacos.

WATT: [surprised] Thurston? Is that Thurston over there?

THURSTON: [loudly] 'Sup, dude!? What's chillin', man? I thought I'd just swing by.

WATT: You're in my town, huh?

THURSTON: Yeah, c'mon over.

WATT: Come on over? To Silverlake?

THURSTON: Yeah, c'mon over.

MIKE D: Hank [Henry Rollins] is playing tonight. Let's all go see him.

WATT: He's playing tonight, huh? Yeah, I'll go.

THURSTON: [flipping through Mike D's record collection] Hey, D, you got two copies of *Frampton Comes Alive*. That's total overkill.

MIKE D: Dude, that's *Frampton Come Alive*! You gotta have two copies. Right, Watt? You gotta have the good parts, don't you?

THURSTON: Yeah, I guess you have to cut the audience cheering on one disc and the squeezebox thing on another.

WATT: Hey, you joke about Frampton, but when I was on the school paper I did a review of that record. Some fucker got a copy of that review later, in the early '80s, and he started showing it to all kinds of punk rockers. I'd reviewed that one and [Kiss'] *Hotter Than Hell* at the same time.

THURSTON: '73 man, it all started in '73. [finds another relic] How 'bout Rick Derringer, *All American Boy?*

WATT: Nah, that wasn't in the review.

THURSTON: I once wrote about John Cale for my college paper and they thought I'd mispelled John Cage, and they "fixed" it for me. So when the paper came out it was John Cage throughout. But I'd written about John Cale, so it made no sense. I quit the school paper after that.

WATT: You've met Cale, though, haven't you? Did you tell 'im that story? [changes the subject before Thurston can answer] So where's Hank playing — Fairfax?

MIKE D: Yeah.

THURSTON: Watt, come over. I'm taking a ten o'clock flight back to New York.

WATT: You going to the show, Thurston?

THURSTON: No, I can't. I just got here a couple of hours ago and I'm leaving tonight.

WATT: I had a feeling you were here. Did you fly all the way over just to spiel?

THURSTON: Yeah.

WATT: Wow!

DEATH TO CLASSIC ROCKERS

THURSTON: Guess what? We were on a plane a few days ago and these people came on and one of them had a guitar case. I looked at it and it was that fucking guy who sued the [rapper] Biz [Markie, for sampling]. What's his name? You know, he does [sings]: "Clair, the moment I met you, I swear..."

MIKE D: Gilbert O'Sullivan.

THURSTON: Yeah, Gilbert O'Sullivan. We were sitting there: me, Kim, Lee and Steve, all in a row. I said, "What the fuck, it's Gilbert O'Sullivan!" And he sits right next to Steve. I was like, "What are we gonna do?"

MIKE D: Yeah, stand up for the Biz.

THURSTON: We were thinking that we'd just go and beat the shit out of him and say, "This is for the Biz." So Steve was sitting next to him and I was like writing on my napkin, "The Biz," and I'm holding it up and Steve's saying like, "No, man, put that down." 'Cause he was afraid the guy would see it and shit.

MIKE D: But what could he do to you?

THURSTON: Nothing, so I was thinking of what I could do. I was thinking of calling up the *New Musical Express* and *Melody Maker* and saying, "Meet us at the airport, we're going to beat up Gilbert O'Sullivan for the Biz." I mean, it was such a great opportunity. Gilbert O'Sullivan created much damage, man, much damage. Sitting next to him, I thought the plane might crash or something.

MIKE D: I would have been scared sitting next to him. Sitting next to him would almost be like sitting next to a Secret Service agent or a narc or something. Here's a man who ultimately, in a way, has ratted out our art.

THURSTON: Oh yeah, it was an evil vibe, man. I mean, it's like the Turtles [who also filed a sampling lawsuit]; after that shit happened with De La Soul I couldn't listen to a Turtles song anymore.

MIKE D: Yeah, you know, they're hassling us too.

THURSTON: Yeah, you did some [former Turtles] Flo & Eddie beats, didn't you?

MIKE D: Right, and we thought we'd done all we were supposed to do about it and that it was cool. But I guess it isn't.

THURSTON: These guys just don't get it.

ONE SAMPLE BEYOND

MIKE D: With us — even so more on *Check Your Head* than on

Paul's Boutique or *Licensed To Ill* — we though it was just the coolest thing to have like Hendrix jam with the Turtles jam with Ron Carter. Ultimately, that's one of the coolest things about sampling. You're just creating all these superstar jam sessions. It's like that Al Kooper/Steven Stills/Mike Bloomfield album, *Super Session*.

THURSTON: We sampled Hendrix on the Ciccone Youth record — really blatantly. Our whole shit was that we wanted to do turntable shit but we didn't have turntables. So this guy in the studio brought out this old BSR turntable that still had the old flicker needle on it. We did all the cutting on that thing. It was like when the Beasties were away, the fuckheads like us played. [Ciccone Youth's *Whitey Album* came out in the three-year gap between Beasties' *Licensed To Ill* and *Paul's Boutique*.]

MIKE D: See that's the thing about rap music. To me, it's weird that people haven't manipulated on a more sonic level. That was what was so amazing about Rick Rubin's first record, [T La Rock's] "It's Yours." The cutting on that record was so loud and so abrasive and so dissonant. It was just basically so fucked up that like [Def Jam co-founder] Russell Simmons never would have made it because he never... well, he would have thought there's just no way that black radio would play something like that because it was too fucked up. So in a way, it took a college student from NYU to be that fascinated that he'd make a record that was fucked up.

THURSTON: It was like punk rock.

MIKE D: That's the thing. Like, when Public Enemy came out with "Bring the Noise" it was so... I mean, for months in New York, you know, sonically, that was all you heard. It was so punk rock. The fact that you could hear that for months in New York somehow was just the most appropriate thing in the world. On our last record, a lot of how we got into using fucked-up Sony mikes and stuff came out of listening to those old fucked-up battle tapes [live hip-hop tapes made on crude recorders in Harlem and the Bronx before hip-hop records started coming out]. Yet, the first generation of rap records were actually more like old R&B records because the people who made them were making them with the idea that they had to sound good so they could get them onto 'BOS or KISS-FM.

THURSTON: Yeah, there was no real lo-fi, punk rock attitude in it at that time — except for maybe those battle tapes, Public Enemy and you guys. That's what we wanted to do with the Ciccone Youth thing. We just wanted to scratch the shit out of records, but with no skills and no production. I'm surprised that the attitude didn't take off more among young, DIY kids. And like the whole Wax Trax thing is such a bummer because that's like getting into real techno beats and shit. It's like this very hardcore stuff, but it's still played conventionally. Nobody ever got into punk rock/hip-hop except for the Beastie Boys.

MIKE D: That Wax Trax stuff is just more speed metal; it's like the whole double kick drum shit. So that automatically turned me off. I mean, some critic from the daily newspaper might think it's cool because they're combining noise with beats, but to me, instead of it being this free and inventive thing, it was just taking something that was still much more conventional.

THURSTON: It's also way too self-conscious — all that goth imagery and all that kind of [in a feigned Nazi voice] *discipline* bullshit. That's just so played out. I don't wanna hear it. I don't wanna see these guys wearing cowboy hats and long hair and *Easy Rider* shades, playing hardcore beats. It's just bullshit. And it also isn't very danceable, it doesn't have the rhythm of hip-hop. It doesn't have the swing. That's the main thing: it doesn't swing. Remember that Schoolly D beat? It was just so hardcore and punk rock.

MIKE D: Yeah, Schoolly D — that was the most punk rock rap record ever. To me, that was a great punk record. Right down to the cover. He just drew his own fucking cover, it was on his own label...

THURSTON: ...and he did it on a little fucking drum machine with lots of reverb. It totally jammed.

MIKE D: Just turntables, drum machine and a mike.

THURSTON: That really excited me. That shit was so fucking down. Our old drummer [Bob Bert] started Bewitched and it was sort of like a cross between Schoolly D and Swell Maps. But they broke up. I remember seeing a picture of you guys at the Ritz and you were wearing...

MIKE D: My Schoolly D T-shirt. Yeah, Schoolly D gave me that T-shirt,

THURSTON: Really?

MIKE D: You know, to me it always seemed weird that more bands haven't come out and taken all these noise aspects, all these punk rock and hip-hop aspects, and just gone for it like that. I wanna see 16-year-olds doing it. I wanna see kids who can rock the computer, but who also can come out with the most amazing, beautiful noise ever. I have this thoughtful, wishful thinking that all of a sudden there's going to be this new generation of kids who are gonna do this thing. Because to me that's the future of music.

July 1992

dinosaur jr.
PALEONTOLOGY

BY **JASON COHEN**

IF YOU GO BY WHAT'S BEEN WRITTEN about Dinosaur Jr.'s J Mascis, his music, history and personality could be summed in the following list: loud, quiet, Neil Young, soap operas, melodic, off-key, Sonic Youth, post-hardcore, couch potato, pedal-hopping, Lou Barlow, suburbs, game shows, still lives with parents, lethargic, "Yeah" and "I don't know." Especially those last three items.

Mascis's laconic personality has been constructed largely from newspaper profiles and the British music press, and although he cultivates that persona, it's not out of any calculating desire to do spin-control on his image. Frankly, J Mascis is not that calculating. He's just reserved.

And while the songs of Dinosaur Jr. partially mirror Mascis's personal alienation, the man has a power that transcends mere disinterest. It's easy to forget — now that Dinosaur Jr. is just another major label "alternative" act — how influential and innovative the band is.

In months past, *Option* has attempted to speak with Mascis but the stories were always scrapped. This time, we decided that if Mascis couldn't speak for himself, others could — so we contacted his family, friends, colleagues and collaborators. What follows are reflections, observations and anecdotes from the folks who know J Mascis best.

The cast of characters includes his father, Dr. Joseph Mascis, Sr., a dentist in Amherst, Massachusetts; his brother Michael, a Boston attorney; former Dinosaur Jr. bassist Lou Barlow, now of Sebadoh; Sean Slade, the producer/engineer at Fort Apache studios who worked on Dinosaur Jr.'s albums *Bug* and *Green Mind*; members of Buffalo Tom, whose first two albums Mascis produced; *Conflict* editor and Matador Records chief Gerard Cosloy, who briefly attended school with Mascis, put Mascis's first band Deep Wound on his *Bands That Could Be God* compilation, and subsequently signed Dinosaur to Homestead; director Allison Anders, who hired Mascis to score her film *Gas, Food, Lodging*; Steve Shelley of Sonic Youth; and various other friends and acquaintances.

I: THE STORY OF J

Dr. Joseph Mascis: It was funny, he was in the hospital ready to come home and with no name yet. We couldn't decide. So finally, when we went to check him out, the nurse said, "Wait a minute, we don't have a name." So I said, "OK, Joe Mascis, Jr." But we called him J. At first people thought it was J-A-Y, but it's just J.

Gerard Cosloy: He and I were friends during the brief period of time I was living in Amherst. We certainly haven't been good friends socially in a long time. J's unusual in that he grew up in that town. I think of that movie *Breaking Away*.

An Amherst acquaintance: He's like a normal guy. His dad's a dentist. He had a suburban mom who had a lot of Harlequin novels. Who gives a fuck? If he wasn't some big fucking star nobody would think he was particularly weird, but since he's sort of quiet he comes off as flippant. All these guys from Amherst are like that; they sort of seem like dicks until you get to know them.

A New York acquaintance: I had this roommate in New York named Jens, and he was in a side band with J called Gobblehoof. J was the drummer or something. Anyhow, Jens had known J from his Amherst days, and it's really funny, everything you read about J fits Jens's personality to a T, 'cause Jens had a hard time expressing himself, too. It seemed to me that all those Amherst guys were like that. When they'd get together it was hilarious. There would be these long stretches of silence, with an occasionally totally aloof comment, like, "Oh, wow," or "What show did *you* go see last night?" or "Hey, man, could you pass the bong?"

Dr. Mascis: You have your doubts, really, the way they dress and that kind of stuff; you figure, 'Oh, boy, what have we got here?' But the only thing he ever had was long hair. Aside from that he never got too wild.

Michael Mascis: He was always very musically talented and just pursued it, spending a lot of time playing music and listening to music — and stealing my albums. He was very much supported by our parents in his decisions. I'd be doing it in a minute if I had his talent.

Dr. Mascis: J's always had that special something. Out of my four children I was always closest to him. He was a good kid, never a problem, a good student, had good study habits; he went to college, all that stuff.

Gerard Cosloy: He was more of a student than I was. There was some paper he wrote that he got a bad grade on that I ended up putting in *Conflict*, some story about a guy that works at the Bonanza and he goes home and kills his mom or something. It was really good. J definitely came across as a really good, really funny writer.

J Mascis (in *Pulse!*): Hardcore was nothing more than sexual tension, your hormones surging through your body. After that you get a chick and that's it, the end of hardcore.

II: THE INARTICULATE SPEECH OF... UM...

DINOSAUR JR. AND MY BLOODY VALENTINE kicked off their U.S. tour together in Houston, and the day after that show I got my first crack at J in Austin. Mascis, Dinosaur bassist Mike Johnson and I went guitar shopping, hitting two music stores. As they quietly scrutinized expensive acoustic guitars and amps, I paced the stores. It was incredibly boring. Mascis bought a pick-up at the second store and then we all ran into drummer Murph, who seems to travel separately from the others. Plans to purchase a new pillow for the van and some haircare products like gel or mousse — "expensive stuff," Mascis said — were thwarted because of the impending sound check.

After the sound check, we sat down for a formal interview. Mascis had a horrible cold and avoided conversation by blowing his nose and clearing his throat frequently. Given my list of questions, the whole thing should have taken about an hour. It was over in 20 minutes. His most interesting comment was, "It doesn't have anything to do with anything."

Allison Anders: His image is surprising to me, because I think reclusive isn't true and inarticulate isn't either. I'm always kind of amazed when you get him going how much he can really talk. He's just so insightful.

Chris Colburn, Buffalo Tom: To me, it's never been that he's acting or anything. With anybody, he doesn't have a a lot to say. The few things he says usually count a lot. There couldn't be a more friendly person.

Sean Slade: J just kind of showed up at the studio. The whole first day, when I asked him a question, he would say, "I don't know." I think he was afraid I'd tell him to turn down the amp. Every time I'd talk to him he'd say "I don't know." The next day I walked into the studio and he was sitting in the lounge with a big bag of groceries and I said, "Hey, what'd you get?" And he said, "I don't know." So I said, "Oh, you're telling me you walked blindfolded through the aisles and picked whatever you could?" Then he laughed.

Lou Barlow: I think he could blow a lot of people away if he really did speak his mind and people asked interesting questions and engaged him. He's very observant. His mind moves. He's a very, very self-conscious person and he really does think a lot, so I think by shying away from interviews he just doesn't really want to deal with it because they're really goofy. I always thought he made a conscious effort to be a rock star, so anything he does is going to be cool, it doesn't matter if he talks a lot or doesn't talk a lot. He's not a slug. When people ask anything of him, that's the best way to get him not to do anything at all.

Allison Anders: In the movie business people are used to the personality thing, so it was hilarious to hear my producers going, "So, J, we're really excited about this project!" and J just standing there with this limp handshake. At one point my producer looked at me and goes, "Is this one of those *faith* things, where I'm supposed to have *faith* that it's going to work out?"

Another acquaintance: The legend is that he apparently used to be a lot nicer, a lot more normal, then Sonic Youth saw his wolfboy streak and told him it was really cool that he was from the suburbs and kind of weird and mopey. Then all of a sudden he started acting like that.

J Mascis (in the *Los Angeles Times*): People have to find something in your character to build a story around. One person in England did it and then another and it just kept going. It's not that I dislike interviews or try to be difficult.

Gerard Cosloy: He doesn't want to come across as being eager or ass-kissing. If he knows people and feels comfortable around them he's probably apt to open up much more. Under certain circumstances he can be outgoing. I'm not surprised at all that he can kind of retreat from [interviews and music biz hype]. I think most people would.

Sean Slade: Basically at heart J's a normal guy. He just likes to hang out with his friends and play rock music. I sympathize with him because he has people coming up to him and bugging him and... you know, he plays music, he's not a politician.

Dr. Mascis: He's really quiet. He won't give you the right time of day if he doesn't have to. But he's very communicative with his friends and peers.

Gerard Cosloy: J is the kind of person who doesn't spend a lot of time saying goodbye. He stayed at my house once and to this day my mother still gives me shit about it. My mom served up some breakfast and I don't think J even acknowledged her "Hello" or her "What are you studying in school?" questions. For the next two hours there was just constant screaming from my mom, "What kind of people act like that?" and "What's wrong with him, what's wrong with his hair?" And my parents have met a lot of fucked up musicians. To this day, if my mom reads the *Boston Globe* and sees an article on Dinosaur, she says, "I can't believe it, how can someone like that be successful?"

Lou Barlow: It makes sense because J writes songs about being totally emotionally constipated, and he is... or he was.

Steve Shelley: I don't think it's an image, it's just the way he is.

dinosaur jr.

III. THE DRUG OF THE NATION

WHEN DIRECTOR ALLISON ANDERS asked Mascis to compose the score for her film, *Gas, Food, Lodging*, she didn't know how appropriate her choice was. Mascis is well-known for his love of things that sparkle on a shiny silver screen. In fact, Mascis is perhaps the quintessential child of the post-modern age: he's a television watcher extraordinaire. Oddly, his other pastime is skiing. One can only guess that's because all good ski lodges have giant satellite dishes and big-screen TVs.

J Mascis (in *Pulse!*): I'm way into *The Love Connection* and *All My Children*. I always wanted to make a cameo appearance on that show. It's the only goal I've got left for myself.

Gerard Cosloy: I don't recall him being a soap opera head then, but he sure seemed to like TV.

Allison Anders: What most people don't know is he's an insane skier, a really avid skier, and "Flying Cloud" [a Dinosaur Jr. song title] was a lodge. But it's true, when he wasn't skiing he was definitely watching those soaps, man, back in the hotel room.

Lou Barlow: When I knew him he never really skied very much but he always said he did. I never saw him ski, I never saw his skis, I never saw him leave for a ski trip. But he had ski gloves and he would have the tags from the lifts, so I guess he did.

J Mascis: I like skiing, just because I've skied since I was four. I still ski, just because I can do it. I just do it because I know how to do it.

Allison Anders: I talked to him about doing a project I had going with Redd Kross, Duran Duran's John Taylor and [*Married With Children*'s] Christina Applegate, so he was interested.

J Mascis: Doing the soundtrack was fun: you just watch scenes and play along to the TV.

Jonathan Poneman, Sub Pop: Before he agreed to do the single for us he made us take him to the restaurant in the space needle. Making you go and have dinner in the space needle is like — remember *Pee Wee's Big Adventure*? — having somebody make you go to the basement of the Alamo in San Antonio. The guy's exposed to too much popular culture.

Bill Janovitz, Buffalo Tom: J came to one of our shows in England. He was doing the Rollercoaster tour and we were hanging out backstage and he was telling me that he met all these famous people like Axl Rose. He was real blasé about it, you know how he is. Then Norm [actor George Wendt from *Cheers*] walked in and J jumped out of his seat. I'd never seen him so excited.

IV: THE FREED PIG

DINOSAUR'S JR.'S BASSIST MIKE JOHNSON first joined the group as a hired hand, but has since found his own identity. Last year's *Green Mind* was Mascis's solo project, but Johnson and drummer Murph plan to work on all future recordings. Before Johnson joined, various Dinosaur line-ups included Van Conner and Donna Dresch, both of Screaming Trees at one time or another; Dresch was part of the ill-fated five-piece version of Dino Jr. that also included Velvet Monkeys/B.A.L.L./Gumball guitarist Don Fleming and drummer David Spiegel. To old Dinosaur Jr. fans, however, there was only one authentic Dinosaur Jr. bass player: Lou Barlow.

Barlow has played with J since the days of Deep Wound, though he says the two were never close friends. Dinosaur was at its best when Barlow was still in the band; in addition to strength and volume, Barlow contributed melodic figures and chording that could have easily been mistaken for guitar overdubs, adding a depth to the songs and interesting wrinkles to Dinosaur's more experimental tendencies.

It's been claimed that Barlow and Mascis didn't speak a word to each other during the last two years Barlow was in the band. When he left, Barlow went on to pursue the home-taping projects he had been working on that evolved into Sebadoh. It was rumored that Dinosaur had broken up, and then that Barlow had been fired, all of which created fodder for many a fanzine interview, with Barlow venting his bitterness and indie hipsters taking sides.

dinosaur jr.

Gerard Cosloy: I don't really have any problem with J these days, but I don't exactly understand what happened with Lou, or why he left Homestead. I don't think J handled it very honestly, and his explanation — "It's nothing personal" — didn't go that well with me.

Lou Barlow: Actually, J didn't say anything to me, he wouldn't speak. They came to my house and Murph sat down and said, "Well, it's all over," and I said, "OK, that's cool." J just stood by the door and looked really afraid. Our communication had broken down at that point because he was just so completely irritable at that time, and so terminally annoyed at everything I did. And I was just oversensitive to it. They fed me this total bullshit and went off and said, "We kicked Lou out." It was just really lame, completely lame. He would shy away from confrontation but he was always one of the most confrontational people I ever knew.

> *I've got nothing better to do than to pay too much attention to you.*
> *It's sad, but it's not your fault...*
> *Self-righteous but never right/So laid back but so uptight...*
> *Right, I want success to bring you down*
> *Watching your every move, playing the little boy game*
> *Always with something to prove.*
> — Sebadoh, "The Freed Pig"

Lou Barlow: That was pretty much the very last song I ever wrote about it. People think that's very nasty about J, but to me it's just the most realistic thing I ever wrote. I wrote it because I thought it would be the only way to communicate to J, because I could never sit down and have a serious discussion with him about what happened. That, to me, has been incredibly frustrating, and it doesn't occur with other people I know, whether it takes huge explosions or horrible fights.

Sean Slade: J handles crises by going to sleep.

J Mascis: I've seen Lou a couple of times. He's not mad at me anymore.

Lou Barlow: I talk to him. I broke up with my girlfriend and I was just totally in a bizarre mind state, and I was like, fuck it. And I saw him and said hey... We talked about Nirvana. I haven't spoken with him since, but I traded him a *Sebadoh III* for his newest CD one night.

V. ZEN AND THE ART OF J

IT'S EASY TO DRAW THE SAME minimal insights from Mascis's lyrics as you would his conversations. The lyrics are like his comments: "There you are and here I stand..." "I don't know one thing to say to you..." "There never really is a good time/There's always nothing much to say..." "I'll leave the house when I'm less scared/Don't make me go I'm not prepared." His guitar playing not only articulates his feelings better than his words, but it also elevates the simplicity of his lyrics into overwhelming expressions of ennui, loneliness and fear. What seems sullen or disaffected on paper is fragile, hungry, heartfelt and hard-fought on record. Like Lou Reed or Neil Young, J Mascis makes a case for the superfluousness of interviews. It's all there in the music, he argues, no explanation required.

The recollections of his friends suggest that in many ways Mascis is exactly what he appears to be — that the clichés are true for a reason — but that's not all there is. Mascis is no more reflective about his music-making than he is about anything else, which is a comment on both the mysteries of his creativity and the depth of his vision.

Currently in a position to make his music with a fair degree of artistic freedom and financial success (with no rent or mortgage to pay, either), Mascis seems eager to pursue new musical directions. Whereas *Bug* was a rehash of the first two records, *Green Mind* and the *Gas, Food, Lodging* score tread newer, subtler ground. Music is the reason anyone is interested in J Mascis in the first place, and his music fascinates most of the people who agreed to speak for this article.

Allison Anders: I met him at a show. He was enormously charismatic onstage; he didn't say a word to anybody, but everybody was just focused on him. Then at the end nobody would talk to him. This is a really interesting J thing, how he can keep people away from him. All these people were pontificating to me — all these alternative music-philes, they knew everything about him and were avid fans — but they wouldn't talk to *him*. I just saw him walking around by himself and said, "Well, excuse me, I'm going to talk to this guy."

dinosaur jr.

Lou Barlow: I loved Dinosaur's songs. I think J is enormously talented, really intriguing and important, and I felt pretty privileged to be a part of the band. That's why I let everything build into this impossibly bizarre emotional situation, because I wanted to keep it together. It just seemed very important to me.

Dr. Mascis: It's great, I like all kinds of music. I used to play trumpet myself. I'd rather hear other music than that stuff, but the young people enjoy it. I went to one of his concerts a month ago and I had such a good time, just seeing the kids slamdancing. I've never seen people have such a good time.

Michael Mascis: I just like that mean, chunky sound he gets out of his guitar.

Sean Slade: When J would do guitar overdubs, literally all the knobs on the Marshall were turned up all the way. When he was playing, you could not walk into the room. It's really the key to the sound.

Steve Shelley: Dinosaur has influenced Sonic Youth quite a bit. I don't think our song "Teenage Riot" would have come out exactly like that if Dinosaur hadn't been around. I think J teaches Lee and Thurston a thing or two about the guitar.

Gerard Cosloy: We talked about J trying out for the Replacements once as a joke, how he'd be so much better than anybody in the band.

Sean Slade: Recording with J is always fun because he's relaxed about it and not neurotic at all. He doesn't sweat the details, which a lot of bands do. J is so talented that he makes it all seem effortless.

Dr. Mascis: People keep coming back and trying to find out about him. I get a lot of calls here at the office. One day last week this lady came in, an older lady, and she had a cover of the "Just Like Heaven" single, and she said, "You've got to do me a favor: Get this autographed."

Lou Barlow: He speaks very eloquently in his songs, and when I've heard *Green Mind* recently, I started really listening to the lyrics. He is trying to say what he feels.

Allison Anders: His music is so painfully, beautifully melodic and emotional, which is, once again, the interesting thing with J. Where it really comes out is in his work.

Steve Shelley: You should have seen J playing at the Reading Festival last summer. It was a really good bill that day: Nirvana, Babes In Toyland, Dinosaur and ourselves. Just watching J from the side of the stage, he seemed so at home playing guitar solos to 50,000 kids. That was one of the happiest times I've ever seen Dinosaur play. He could be such the rock star if he had a bigger mouth.

J Mascis: I just gotta do something. If I was happy just doing nothing I probably would. Gotta do something to get out of the house and music's just what I decided to sink energy into. It's just what I can do, so that's what I do.

May 1992

my bloody valentine

BEAUTY IN THE BEAST

BY **MARK KEMP**

WELCOME TO "GOD'S OWN COUNTRY," as a Texas politician recently decribed his home on the range, "where the grass grows tall and the wind blows free and anyone who says 'income tax' gets their mouth washed out with soap."

"Have you ever been to El Paso?" asks Ann Marie Shields, sister of My Bloody Valentine guitarist/singer Kevin Shields, and the group's tour manager. Her voice is full of concern. "We drove through it yesterday. It's this big city that's completely poor, just totally devastated." Bilinda Butcher, the group's other guitarist and singer, is wedged between the Shields siblings, providing echoes. "*Really* poor," she says.

"I'd never seen such a place in my life," Ann Marie continues. "It was just unbelievable — all those tiny, run-down shacks."

"Unbelievable," Butcher softly repeats.

It's a Friday, around supper time, and the members of My Bloody Valentine are squashed together in a rental van and barreling down one of Houston, Texas' many endless, flat streets. They're headed to sound check at the Vatican, a cavernous, cinderblock dive located at the corner of Washington Avenue and Cohn Street in the central part of town.

Houston is the fourth-largest city in the U.S., and a hotbed of violent crime. Last year, 671 people were murdered here, sometimes for nothing more threatening than an awkward glance. Residents are so frightened they've caused stock in handguns and home security systems to soar; in fact, folks saying "income tax" in Houston are as likely to get their mouths washed out with a .38.

Amid this eerie, violent Southwestern Americana, the Valentines will do a 45-minute set of otherworldly music tonight before a sold-out house on a package show with Dinosaur Jr. and Babes In Toyland. Two nights earlier, the Valentines stirred up so much energy at the Roxy in L.A. that kids were stagediving and slamdancing. That wouldn't be so odd except that My Bloody Valentine's sound is hardly music to mosh by.

EARLIER IN THE DAY, Kevin Shields sits at a poolside table at the group's hotel, a glass of iced tea beside him and 70 degrees of Texas sunshine all around. He's describing what it feels like to lasso a lifetime's worth of tension and spew it out to hundreds of people in a mélange of beautiful melodies and disturbing dissonance. Some folks, he says, just get out of hand.

"I'm not afraid of anyone coming up onstage and personally hurting me because I'm big enough to take care of myself." he says, glancing off into the pale blue afternoon. "It's *weapons* I worry about.

"There's always a few people who really, really resent it," he says of his band's music. "Some people get really aggressive, angry, mad. They feel like we're a bunch of wankers who have no right to do this. They take it personally, as a massive insult. Sometimes I think, shit, *anything* could happen."

At the moment, he's thinking about the gig in L.A. "I saw this big skinhead guy moving his way aggressively through the crowd," says Shields, who speaks and sings with an almost self-effacing gentleness, but makes his guitar yowl like a wounded beast. "I looked at one of the guys in the band and said, 'Watch it, there's someone coming towards us! But then he stopped about halfway through and stood there and stared. You just never know."

What sets off such intense reactions is a song called "You Made Me Realise," the emotional and psychological breaking point of every My Bloody Valentine show. For about an hour, the group coils through a set of noisy, ambiguous songs, like "I Only Said," "Soon" and "To Here Knows When," all marked by simple, delicate melodies and hushed male/female vocals, and wrapped up in wavering layers of textured guitar and drums. The result is a sustained roar of glorious experimental rock, with tiny pop sounds

my bloody valentine

occasionally peeking in and out, above and beneath the haze. A barrage of photographic images, circles, and flickering lights are projected onto a backdrop, adding visual punch to the musical chaos.

And then comes the onslaught of "You Made Me Realise," which, depending on the night and the mood of the band, can be up to 20 minutes and at least 100 decibels of pure, unrelenting, confrontational white noise, exacerbated by blinding strobe lights.

"It seems like such an odd thing to do, you know, to make a lot of noise," Shields admits. "But I think we take it way past the point of acceptedness. It takes on a meaning in itself. I don't know exactly *what* it means, but it basically transcends stupidity. For us it's genuinely..." He trails off, glancing again into the hazy Lone Star sky. "It's the most relaxing moment of the whole gig."

I HAD FOLLOWED THE VALENTINES to God's Own Country because they stood me up in Sin City. It wasn't out of meanness; apparently, a tire on their equipment trailer had blown out on the way from San Francisco to Los Angeles, and the weight of the equipment had damaged the rims, delaying their arrival. The group spent the entire next day in L.A. searching for a replacement truck that was so weighted down during the trip to Houston that it puttered all the way across the desert at less than 55. "It's been horrible," Kevin says. "But the good thing about it was that we were driving in the daylight and I got to see Arizona and New Mexico. I'd never been in the desert before."

In the last two years the Valentines haven't seen much daylight at all. They've spent their time holed up in various London studios in the middle of the night recording their latest album, *Loveless*. The album took so long to record that Shields says, "Everybody had completely lost faith in us." To be sure, the British music press was having a field day trying to predict what it would sound like. When the EP *Tremolo* came out as a teaser, some felt the band had lost its edge. "We weren't trying to make the perfect album or anything," Shields says defensively, in response to an article that suggested the group *had* been trying to do that. "The reason it took so long was because we had started out on the wrong foot and never got back on the *right* one. Right up to the last minute, we kept thinking we would be finished in a couple of months — *two years* of thinking we would be finished in a couple more months."

Like the group's live shows, *Loveless* flits back and forth between light, whimsical pop melodies and deep blotches of noise and wavering dissonance. The vocals are set way back in the mix — further back than ever before — and function more as added instrumentation than as verbal communication. Not to say the Valentines don't communicate feelings in their music; it's just that its feelings aren't especially tangible ones. Still, when Butcher hisses, "Midnight wish/Blow me a kiss/Hoping I'll see you," in the song "Blown a Kiss," you can feel the longing, even as her voice snakes in and out of the drone. It's just not the sort of longing that can be summed up in a "Dear Abby" column.

"It's not like we're thinking, 'Oh, I feel really bad or angry and I want to make something that will represent that,'" Shields says of the group's songwriting process. "It's done more in a really unfocused sort of way. The only time it makes sense is when it all comes together. When I write lyrics, I take liberties with them because I'm not particularly trying to convey anything to anyone in words. It makes sense to me and gives me enough conviction to sing the songs, but it doesn't necessarily make a lot of sense to other people.

"That's what all our music is like," he continues. "It's ambiguous, but in an ethereal, flowy way. It's kind of see-through. And the lyrics are only as substantial as the impression you get from the entire song."

KEVIN SHIELDS IS THE QUIET, sensitive type, almost to a fault. He has longish brown hair, and calm, gentle features that are enhanced by a pair of wire-rimmed glasses he wears when he's not onstage. With his prominent nose, small lips, and an ever-so-slight overbite, Shields looks a bit like John Lennon — only prettier.

Born on New York's Long Island, he was uprooted at ten and moved to Dublin, Ireland, forced to leave a cozy American childhood behind and acclimate himself to a new, completely alien culture. "I remember very vividly the day we moved," he says. "When something that traumatic happens, you remember every detail. I'd left everything behind me — not just my friends, but everything I was into as a kid. I had been really, really into things like Godzilla films and Saturday morning cartoons. Ireland had none of that; it was 20 years behind America back then."

It took time for Shields to get over his identifcation in the neighborhood as the American kid on the block, but he managed. For one thing, Ireland had English TV, which carried the popular music show *Top of the Pops*. "At that time it was suddenly completely blown over by glam rock," he says. "I hadn't come across that in America. When I was in America the only rock bands kids were into were, like, Three Dog Night, bands like that. In England, even *little* kids were totally into glam rock, like T-Rex and even Roxy Music. Because it was glam rock. It was pop music. It was on Saturday morning TV. It was like cartoons. All the kids in my neighborhood were into, like, Slade."

By the time he reached his mid-teens, Shields had befriended Colm O'Ciosoig, a shy, wiry kid a couple of years younger than himself who played drums. The two both shared an interest in punk rock and in thinking of themselves as rebellious. So like any other normal teenage misfits, they formed a band. "We had a lot of different bands together," says O'Ciosiog (pronounced o-COO-sak), "a punk band, a poppy kind of band. But then we just started experimenting and turned out this total dirge music. Once we went out to this shopping mall and plugged into an outside plug and made a lot of noise on a Sunday afternoon. We thought it was pretty rebellious. It was actually quite funny. We ran away before anything happened, though."

In 1984, Shields and O'Ciosoig formed My Bloody Valentine, which was named for a B-grade Canadian slice-and-dice flick. Though the music on the group's first EPs (variously on the Tycoon, Fever, Kaleidoscope Sound and Lazy labels) was much different from what the Valentines would become known for, their experimentation on those early releases contained the seeds of what showed up later on their Creation EPs, their debut full-length, *Isn't Anything*, and last year's *Loveless*.

The impression you get listening to My Bloody Valentine is of a group of ghosts inside a monstrously big machine, trying to sing and play their way out of it. But it's really not so spooky. In fact, Shields and Butcher are so normal they have a family life away from the band, raising an eight-year-old child, Toby, from Butcher's former marriage.

"He's a good kid," says Shields. "When we're out on the road or recording, he goes to this really great boarding school called Summerhill. It's so radically different from other schools that the kids are seen as kind of like a tribe, like a society of children. They actually have a vote on everything. They don't have to do anything, but they vote, so there are rules. But they're amusing rules because they come from a kid's point of view. Like, they can curse, but you can't call anybody a cucumber because the children don't want you to."

A SCREAMING COMES ACROSS THE CLUB. Shields and O'Ciosoig are standing onstage at the Vatican, working out the glitches in the sound system. On the walls surrounding them are graffiti from other bands: there's the Pixies logo in light blue, Nirvana in hot pink, and Primus in gaudy orange. Off in one corner, Kat Bjelland of Babes In Toyland holds a casual conference with her band, and in the mid-section of the club a cluster of Dinosaur Jr. roadies kicks a hackeysack around. Shields steps down to fiddle with an effects box while snippets of songs from *Loveless* blast out of the speaker columns with shrill feedback.

Bassist Debbie Googe, meanwhile, is standing with Bilinda Butcher at the front of the club, as far away from the noise as possible, talking about Butcher's first gig with the Valentines. "She had to hold Toby the whole time," Googe says, laughing. "He wouldn't let her go. When it came time for us to go onstage, he just wouldn't let go."

Butcher, whose long brown hair is tucked casually behind her small ears, giggles. She's the quiet, sensitive type, too. (It seems to be a requirement for membership in the band; in fact, all of the Valentines are so quiet and shy it's as if they're vying with each other to be the least noticed.) Butcher's arms are folded; a silly grin on her face accentuates her red jeans and gold, glitter-speckled red sneakers. "Toby was just three then," she says. "He was fine until I got on the stage and then he was like, 'whaaaa.' So I had to stand there and hold him. For about an hour."

The stress of being in a relationship with the leader of the band is something Butcher doesn't think about all that much, though it is hard for her to draw the line between their private life and the band itself because. "The band's always there," she says. "In

my bloody valentine

a way, our private lives do come into the band, but it's not in a very obvious way." She giggles again. "I mean, we're not often going off and snogging together before the gigs or anything. At least I don't think so."

She turns to Googe: "Do we do that?"

"*I* dunno," Googe says, slightly annoyed at the question. "It's not obvious if you do. I think I'd notice."

Shields describes Butcher and himself as a "typical band couple" — as opposed, say, to those "normal" couples. "I mean, we're together so much," he says. "Normal couples aren't together all the time. When you're in a situation like this, you can't live the life that other people live. You haven't got the same freedoms. I mean, you have *different* freedoms. But, like, we can't just go out and say, 'I gonna do *this* for a while.' Can't do that. Everything is tied into what we are doing with the band. But we don't talk about the band when we're alone, really."

Athough Butcher was the last to join the Valentines, today she practically defines the group. It's not that she's strikingly beautiful, in a quirky, arty way — though she is. And it's not just because, as one British music writer once noted, "she has eyes you could get lost in, and it would take you days to get out" — though that's true, too. Butcher's presence in the band is more enigmatic than that.

Her vocals supply the often-cited ethereal quality that launched a thousand new British indie bands who co-opted My Bloody Valentine's sound — like Lush, Chapterhouse, Ride, Slowdive... and the list goes on. It's a soft, airy voice which acts as the wind in the Valentines' turbulent tunnel. Shields and O'Ciosoig often sample her voice so they can regurgitate it digitally as the sound of a flute or other woodwind instruments. "It gives it the texture of a human voice," Shields says, "but doesn't sound particularly human."

UNFORTUNATELY, BUTCHER'S OMNIPRESENCE in the group, together with her amiable, soft-spoken manner and blurred, pretty voice, has made her the target of obsessed admirers. In L.A., a young, Morrissey-like fan leapt onstage during one song and hugged her. It was an awkward moment.

"It happened before, and it makes me confused," she says. "I

SO YOU DON'T HAVE TO

don't know whether to start playing the guitar or... hug them back. I don't know why they do it. It's like they just don't know quite what to do. It's like they get there and realize there's a guitar in the way."

"And they're up in front of loads of people," Googe interrupts. "They don't know quite what to do with themselves."

"For a second, they just seem a bit lost," Butcher continues. "It's quite sweet, though it's funny."

Shields sees it a bit differently; not that he's jealous, it's just that he's a bit protective. "It's slightly unnerving, but I don't think it's meant as harassment," he says. "In that sense I don't mind it too much — as long as they don't stand on the effects pedals, I *hate* it when they do that. But it *is* unnerving because you never know what somebody's going to do. You don't know what kind of person they might be. 'Cause someday someone could just walk up like that and" — he pauses, hardly daring to articulate the worst — "like, *knife* you or something.

"But anything is possible," he continues, "so I definitely wish someone would invent some kind of super-duper radar thing so that if anybody was to walk in with any kind of weapons, they couldn't get in."

Metal detectors, at a minimum, would have been particularly handy at a My Bloody Valentine performance in Germany, where the group performed a free concert before a dubious crowd. When they segued into "You Made Me Realise," Shields got scared. "There were guns and drug addicts everywhere," he says. "That time I was genuinely frightened. There were dodgy people all over the place. It was a bizarre crowd, the weirdest crowd we'd ever played for. It seemed like a brave thing to do to play that song at that show, but generally it's not bravery, really, it's just a bit intense."

That's true of all of My Bloody Valentine's music. At a time when "ethereal" has become the latest marketing catchword for a musical scene in London that's taken to celebrating itself, as they say, My Bloody Valentine has kept a distance from the crowd. During the two years it took them to record *Loveless*, other groups have incorporated the Valentines' techniques — but not its intensity.

On Lush's new *Spooky*, the group merely hammers out a set of

my bloody valentine

light pop songs with neatly plugged-in dissonance. In contrast, My Bloody Valentine has carved out a whole new territory of musical textures. "I don't like to talk about Lush because they're all friends of mine," Shields says, "but, like, we were doing this before they even knew what they *wanted* to do. I know that we would exist as we are whether this kind of music was hip or not."

But the Valentines didn't *invent* the stuff. "I'm defiinitely influenced by Sonic Youth," Shields admits. "They did an awful lot in terms of groundbreaking. Their attitude towards guitars paved the way for a lot of people — a *hell* of a lot of people. We get a lot of credit for being influential in England that they never got and deserved."

THE VALENTINES WERE ALSO INFLUENCED by the Cocteau Twins, though Shields's guitar textures are much richer and more inventive. Shields and O'Ciosoig have extended the boundaries of what mundane devices such as sequencers, samplers, guitars and drum machines can do. "I like music that's inventive," says Shields, "and I find that a lot of the current guitar bands in England who are influenced by the Cocteau Twins are quite uninventive. They're happy just to plug into a pre-programmed effects thing and make weird guitar sounds. I like to abuse the effects, to use them in ways they're not supposed to be used."

He also likes to combine modern computer technology with old-fashioned effects boxes — a daub of Hendrix with a pinch of Public Enemy. "A lot of the digital stuff has these pre-programmed beats," he says, "and rarely do you come across something that's pre-programmed that doesn't get boring real quick. After five minutes, it's like, 'uhh God, I'm sick of it.' Also, a lot the digital effects have built-in protective circuits where, if you try to overload things, it just stops. Whereas if you're messing around with the more analog-y type devices, they're just more open to abuse."

That gives the Valentines' music an older psychedelic feel filtered through '70s art rock and punk rock, but with more comtemporary ideas about rhythm, melody and dissonance. It has all the elements of older music without being "classic rock." "It's funny," Shields says, "the world has gone into this weird, like, time warp. You watch TV and hear people condemn bands for their '60s-isms, but it's honest because we still *hear* that music all the time. It's not like we're trying real hard to search it out and be retrogressive, it's just that it's always there in front of everybody's faces. It wasn't that way back in the '60s and '70s; the music of the '30s and '40s wasn't in everybody's faces back then. Modern-ness is down to context now more than the actual material that you're doing."

Shields would like to see My Bloody Valentine's sound more in the context of hip-hop and grungy American rock than in England's so-called "dream pop" trend. "I realize that hip-hop is very modern music in a way that ours isn't," he says. "If people in the '60s were to hear us they'd go, 'Wow, that band's kind of weird.' It might seem alien to them because of the technological precisionism in what we do. But we are in a machine age, so we kind of naturally imitate those machines. So that side of us would seem alien when put beside the Velvet Underground, who were all loose and flowing.

"But if you played hip-hop or house music to a '60s audience, people would go, 'Wow! That's weird, avant-garde wildness!' And that's kind of strange, because in the '90s it's totally commercial music. So, in that sense, hip-hop and house music is more modern than what we're doing; not that what we're doing is less relevant. It's realness that matters, and in England, it's trendy to be modern — to be hip-hop or house or ethereal, or this or that — whereas in America, it's pointless to be trendy."

But how does all that fit in with the music of My Bloody Valentine? "Well, it's not in the exact beats — though we do use some of the beats because they are good rhythms and suit what we do — it's more in the attitude."

In sharp contrast to Morrissey, who announced last year in these pages that "dance music has killed everything," Shields has another view. "Dance music has done a hell of a lot for people's perceptions of tune and hearing — of what it means to be 'in tune.' There's a lot of out-of-tune stuff in dance music because they just pile samples on top of each other which sound real good together, but are way off key. But because the bass is turned up so loud you can't hear that it's off key. That stretches people's attitudes towards what is right or proper.

"Dance music helps us," he says, "yet we have fans who hate

my bloody valentine

dance music, and that's really frustrating. I tell them, 'It's good. Just listen to it.' I think a lot of people don't realize that it's helped them to like us. It paved the way for us. I guess it's just that when some things are popular people tend to react heavily against it. To me, that's kind of silly; you'd think that people who listened to this kind of music would be more open-minded. Yeah, *right!*"

IT'S DIFFICULT TO DESCRIBE BEING in the middle of the pounding, incessant noise of My Bloody Valentines' "You Made Me Realise" unless you've actually seen the band live. After about 30 seconds the adrenaline sets in; people are screaming and shaking their fists. After a minute, you wonder what's going on. Strobe lights are going mad, and you begin to feel the throbbing in your chest. After another minute, it's total confusion. People's faces take on a look of bewilderment. The noise starts hurting. The strobes start hurting.

The noise continues.

After three minutes, you begin to take deep breaths. Some people in the audience stoop down and cover their ears and eyes. Anger takes over. A few people leave the room. After about four minutes, a calm takes over. The noise continues. After five minutes, a feeling of utter peace takes over.

Or violence.

"For some peolple," says Shields, "it's hypnotic. It's very organic. Others can't deal with it. It's just too much for them. For me, it's total experimentation, completely relaxing. I like watching what happens; looking at people and watching their reactions. Sometimes it's amusing and sometimes it's scary. It says a lot about people."

March 1992

nirvana

PUNK PHILOSOPHERS

BY **GINA ARNOLD**

SATURDAY AFTERNOON AT MCDONALD'S is the same across America. From Bellevue to Bangor, their parking lots are full of sullen teens in beat-up Mavericks, screaming children, or the obligatory Baptist choir on its way to a sing-off.

Saturday afternoon at the McDonald's on Dairy Mart Road in San Ysidro, California, rebuilt on a new site after an infamous massacre in the summer of 1984, is an exception. Around three o'clock its lot is often peopled by the members of some of the coolest rock bands in America. They're on their way across the U.S. border to Tijuana for gigs at Iguana's, a three-tiered nightclub in a *turista* shopping mall. Sometimes, when I'm down in San Diego writing a story on a band, I go to the parking lot of McDonald's and catch a ride with them over the border.

That lot was where I first met up with Nirvana. Trailed by a square yellow truck that was serving as the equipment van for headliners Dinosaur Jr. (J Mascis always drives separately, breeezing in at midnight, three minutes before his set), Nirvana pulled into the lot one hot afternoon in June. They were an hour late because of freeway traffic up in Orange County, and still looked half asleep. When their manager pushed me unceremoniously into their dirty, smelly van, no one even looked up to ask who I was. I glanced around disconsolately at the pizza crusts, candy wrappers, a cooler full of warm water and crushed cans; the grafitti all over the inside walls, and the pair of grotty high-top sneakers tied so that they hung out the crack of a window, presumably because they smelled so bad. The seats had been ripped out and replaced by the kind of torn plaid sofa you might see out on city sidewalks — the kind even halfway houses have rejected.

nirvana

I sat down gingerly on one of the seats, surrounded by baleful stares; the atmosphere was positively forbidding. The only person who wasn't near comatose was David Grohl, Nirvana's fifth drummer in as many years, who managed a semi-friendly "hi." Then, as we pulled out of the parking lot, I reached up nervously and turned my black baseball cap around, Sub Pop style, so the white K label insignia faced backward. There was a slight stir from the back seat, as 24-year-old guitarist and lead singer Kurt Kobain sat up and widened his eyes. "Where'd you get that cap?" he asked.

"Made it myself with Liquid Paper," I replied. He didn't answer. Then suddenly, very shyly, he thrust his arm under my eyes. On the back of the forearm was a tattoo of the K logo, a crude heraldic shield with a hand-lettered "K" inside. From then on, it was smooth sailing.

THIS WAS SUPPOSED TO BE a story about Dinosaur Jr., but since J Mascis can't talk, and since Nirvana pretty much blew Dinosaur off the stage at most of their shows together, the editors and I switched allegiance. After all, when I first heard Nirvana's debut album, *Bleach*, I had thought, "This band is kind of like the Pixies crossed with Soul Asylum." When I saw them play Tijuana that night back in June, I thought, "No, this band is the Pixies *times* Soul Asylum." In the two years since *Bleach*, Nirvana has sopped up so much power they positively glow. Onstage, they throw it off in enormous bursts, leaning over their guitars with the weight of their fury, and finally smashing the instruments to the ground, or hurling them at each other. It's as if Nirvana's guitars are possessed.

One night I saw Kobain leap on bassist Chris Novoselic's shoulders, forcing Novoselic to the floor — yet both were still playing.* Another time, Kobain leapt spontaneously into the crowd, which held him upright, their arms around each of his legs as he screamed the song without the benefit of a microphone, and continued playing his guitar. Nirvana's fervor is infectious.

---

* At the time this story was written, Cobain was using a corrupt spelling of his own last name. Later, he returned to its original spelling, though at times he used the first name "Kurdt." Novoselic later altered the spelling of his first name to "Krist."

SO YOU DON'T HAVE TO

What makes them not just good, but great — better than their grungy Sub Pop brethren like hometown pals the Melvins, better than college radio alternative bands such as Smashing Pumpkins or Urge Overkill, who play more melodic guitar rock — is their complete lack of affectation. And their songs. On their latest album, *Nevermind*, it's clear that this is the first band to cross grunge with the excitement of pure, unadulterated rock'n'roll; melody with noisy static, Black Sabbath and soul. Their songs are more intuitive than articulate, but their lyrics certainly aren't dumb. "On a Plain," "Lithium," "Drain You," and "Smells Like Teen Spirit" paint a pristine picture of a frenzied search for meaning among kids who have been given no tools for contemplation whatever — except, of course, electric guitars.

Kobain told me his favorite books are by philosophers — Bukowski, Beckett, anyone with a "B" — and that he once tried to tackle Nietzsche, but didn't understand a word of it. Still, you can't tell me the guy who wrote, "Love myself/Better than you/Know it's wrong/But what can I do," didn't absorb the tenets of *Man And Superman*, even if Novoselic jeers at the notion. "Oh yeah," laughs the 26-year-old bassist, "we're pocket philosophers." Adds Kobain defensively, "Well… blue collar ones, maybe."

NIRVANA HAILS FROM ABERDEEN, WASHINGTON, a town of almost 19,000 on Grays Harbor, about 100 miles southwest of Seattle. Kobain and Novoselic had been friends there since high school. The embodiment of small town stoners — the American equivalent of the kids in England who back in '77 angrily declared they had "no future" — the two discovered punk after giving up on mainstream hard rock (Kobain's first concert was Sammy Hagar; Novoselic's was the Scorpions.) Six years ago, they had typical small town jobs: Novoselic was a housepainter and Kobain was a fireplace cleaner at an ersatz Polynesian motel.

Their story begins in 1983, when Novoselic first heard punk rock on a compilation tape made by his friend Buzz, who today plays with the Melvins. "Buzz was the punk rock guru of Aberdeen," says Novoselic. "He's the guy who spread the good news around town, but to only the most deserving, 'cause a lot of people in Aberdeen would discount it. I tried to turn people on to it, but they'd be, like... One guy I know, I remember, he goes, 'Ah, that punk rock stuff, all it is, is: "Want to fuck my mom! Want to fuck my mom!"' And then I listened to *Generic Flipper* and it was a revelation. It was art. It made me realize it was art. It was valid. It was beautiful. 'Cause I gave things validity, like, 'Is it as good as *Physical Grafitti*?' And it was suddenly, like, 'Sure it is — if not better.'"

Another of the "deserving" people Buzz gave a tape to was Kobain. "I'd met Buzz probably around the same time you met Buzz," Kobain says, glancing over at Novoselic. "One night I went over to the Melvins practice before they were the Melvins and they were playing, like, Jimi Hendrix and Cream, stuff like that. I was really drunk and I thought they were the greatest band I'd ever seen. It was really awesome, and it was right around that time Buzz started getting into punk rock."

You can learn volumes about Nirvana just by hearing Kobain howl, "I'm a negative creep and I'm stoned" behind the band's wall of noisy rock — more, perhaps, than from actually talking to them. Still, I had a burning desire to find out if Kobain got that "K" tattooed on his arm because both his names begin with a K, rather than as a tribute to the hip indie label. "Oh no!" he says, aghast. "Not at all. That's not it at all. I really like the K label a lot and I admire what Calvin [Johnson, K's proprietor] is doing. They've exposed me to so much good music, like the Vaselines, who are my very favorite band ever. They remind me of how much I really value innocence and children and my youth — of how precious that whole world is. I think they're great."

Kobain's identification with how children behave and think is evident on Nirvana's 1990 Sub Pop single, "Sliver," in which the song's protagonist is a three-year-old. "I do love kids," he says, again. "I know that sounds weird, but I do. I have a little sister who's four years old. And I was a lifeguard, and I taught pre-school kids how to swim, and I worked at the YMCA and did day care, and I babysat during my teenage years. Which was a kind of a strange thing in Aberdeen, because mostly males don't babysit that much and sometimes when I was sitting and the lady's date would come over, he'd have this weird reaction when he saw me — like it wasn't right or something."

Those parents might be even more worried if they ever heard "School," on *Bleach*, with its "No recess!" chorus, and lines like, "You're on acid again," or "Floyd the Barber," wherein Kobain wails, "I've been shaved." But when they start seeing Nirvana's videos on MTV, maybe they'll be reconciled to it. As with many of the best bands, all this rock'n'roll brilliance couldn't come from less likely guys. They're the type of self-described "negative creeps" — sly, weasel-faced, introverted and witty — that Sean Penn immortalized with his Jeff Spicoli character in *Fast Times At Ridgemont High*. You get the feeling that they've slamdanced harder than kids in their audience ever have.

Nirvana's music comes from the kind of obsessiveness and determination that saw the band, in its early days, travel up to Seattle time and again in a "van" that was really a Volkswagen with its seats torn out, packed with tiny amps and an old Sears trap set with cymbal stands that were converted from high school music stands. Their early equipment, according to Novoselic, consisted of the Melvins' second-hand scraps. It's the kind of obsessiveness that comes from the genuine misfit status that growing up on the outskirts of Aberdeen will give a kid with a brain: a craziness that can't be faked. Kobain and Novoselic didn't form Nirvana just because they wanted to — they formed the band because they *had* to. "I just can't believe anyone would start a band just to make the scene and be cool and have chicks," says Kobain in earnest. "I just can't believe it."

UNLIKE MANY GRUNGY, WHITE BOY college rockers of the '90s, Kobain and Novoselic come from pretty humble stock. They take great pride in the fact that they even graduated from high school. The two met in Aberdeen, the suicide capitol of Washington and the rainiest spot in an already very rainy climate. Both were attracted to people on the edge — misfits, outcasts, strangers with candy. But everything has changed. Geffen's DGC label signed them to a reported $400,000 deal after they'd released only one previous album, *Bleach*, on Sub Pop.

A month has passed since my Mexico road trip with Nirvana, and now the band is lounging by the pool of the elegant Beverly Garland Hotel in North Hollywood. It's a sunny July day, and

Nirvana is waiting for studio time to mix some of the final tracks on *Nevermind*. The contrast never seems to amaze, even embarass, Kobain and Novoselic. "The main thing is that we're just as happy playing our music now as we were when I was cleaning fireplaces in Aberdeen," says Kobain, looking furtively around the hotel pool. "There's still the same excitement, so the level of success we're on doesn't really matter to us. It's a fine thing, a flattering thing, to have major labels wanting you. But it doesn't really matter. We could be dropped in two years, go back to putting out records ourselves, and it wouldn't matter. 'Cause this is not what we were looking for. We didn't want to be staying at the Beverly Garland Hotel. We just wanted people to get the records. And we did do it on an independent label. That's the beauty of it."

Kobain clearly longs for the old days, when he was able to spend more time with his indie mates, such as the Melvins and other bands on Sub Pop and K. In fact, when he had to miss K's International Pop Underground Convention this summer in order to play the Reading Festival in England, he was genuinely disappointed. His eyes light up when he decribes the early music of his pals. He talks as enthusiastically about the Melvins as he does about his own band. "They started playing punk rock and had a free concert right behind the Thriftways supermarket where Buzz worked, and they plugged into the city power supply and played punk rock music for about 50 redneck kids," Kobain says. "When I saw them play, it just blew me away. I was instantly a punk rocker. I abandoned all my friends, 'cause they didn't like any of the music. Then I asked Buzz to make me that compilation tape of punk rock songs and got a spike haircut."

"Punk rock kind of galvanized people in Aberdeen," explains Novoselic. "It brought us together and we got our own little scene after a while. Everybody realized — all the misfits realized — that rednecks weren't just dicks, they were total dicks. And punk rock had this cool, political, personal message. You know what I mean? It was a lot more cerebral than just stupid cock rock. Dead Kennedys, MDC... Remember? We were never exposed to any radical ideas; all the ideas came from, like, San Francisco or Berkeley."

Kobain wanted to start a band right then. "I got an electric guitar and was really into it, but I couldn't find anyone in Aberdeen to be in a band with. I was lucky to find Chris at the time." After rehearsing for a while, the duo's pre-Nirvana band "sounded exactly like Black Flag," Kobain says. "Totally abrasive, fast, punk music. There were some Nirvana elements — some slow songs, even then. And there was some heavy, Black Sabbath-influenced stuff. I can't deny Black Sabbath. Or Black Flag."

FOR A WHILE, KOBAIN AND NOVOSELIC called themselves, ironically, Skid Row. Their first drummer, Kobain recalls, was "this stoner guy — but he had a drum set." Nirvana had lots of problems starting out, and didn't seem, as Kobain says, "as legitimate as we wanted to be. We'd play these parties. One of the best was in this town called Raymond, and all these rednecks were there, but they moved into the kitchen. They didn't like us at all. They were scared of us. We were really drunk, so we started making spectacles of ourselves, playing off the bad vibes we were giving to the rednecks — you know, jumping off tables and pretending we were rock stars." To top it off, he says, "Chris jumped through a window, and then we played Flipper's 'Sex Bomb' for about an hour. Our girlfriends were hanging on us and grabbing our legs and doing a mock lesbian scene. That started freaking out the rednecks."

Kobain thinks for a second. "It was such a great vibe," he says. "I mean, we were totally wigging the rednecks out! And that was the idea of punk rock in the first place — to abuse your audience. What better audience to have then a redneck audience."

During that period, the closest cool places to play were in the state capital of Olympia or in Tacoma, 70 miles away. Nirvana started getting booked in Olympia immediately because the clubs there relied entirely on local acts. But no one came to their shows. "There was this one show we did at the Central Tavern in Seattle," Kobain recalls, "where nobody came. We didn't even play. We just loaded up our stuff and left."

Drummer Grohl, who has been silently sunning himself by the pool for nearly an hour, suddenly looks up with tired eyes. "Really?" he asks. "Nobody came at all?" Kobain grins: "Not one single person — except Jon and Bruce."

Bruce was Bruce Pavitt, who by that time, 1987, had already started Sub Pop, the label he named after a column he wrote in

Seattle's monthly music rag, *The Rocket*; Jon is Pavitt's partner, Jonathan Poneman. Nirvana had raised enough money to hire another drummer and record a demo all in one day. Poneman heard it, liked it, and offered to put it out as a single. The song was a cover of Shocking Blue's "Love Buzz" — from 1969 — which Kobain says he heard randomly on an album he picked up at a garage sale. It was an inspired choice, but in fact, Kobain and Novoselic deny having any special knowledge of obscure '60s and '70s music. To top it off, they swear up and down that their favorite bands include Devo and the Cars as much as the Vaselines and the Melvins. (Indeed, a Devo cover will appear on a Peel Sessions album Nirvana recorded last year.)

When Nirvana started working on *Bleach*, Novoselic says, "We didn't know anything about Sub Pop. We just loved playing. It's just so totally fun. It was the most important thing in my life at the time. It was awesome." But wasn't it a pretty big deal for a tiny band like Nirvana to put out a record? "We were excited, yeah," shrugs Kobain, "but after a while the excitement kind of left us because it took over a year for it to come out. We waited for Sub Pop to get enough money to put it out and we ended up paying for the record ourselves — $600. Still, when we go on tour, kids come up to us in flocks, going, 'Where can we get the record? We can't find it.' That's the only reason we decided to go with a major; it's just the assurance of getting our records into small towns like Aberdeen."

Kobain seems to have a problem with the major label thing. He's personally a strong believer in the indie ethic, yet says, "What were we gonna do? Stay on Sub Pop? You couldn't even find our last record! And we were under contract to them. Somebody had to have the money to get us out of the deal. We ended up giving them $70,000 to get out of the contract." Still, Nirvana is not ungrateful to Sub Pop. "The Sub Pop hype thing helped a lot — you know, the Seattle sound thing," Novoselic says. "We just kind of got caught up in it." Adds Kobain, "In England, we were very popular. It's kind of an unusual thing for a band that's as young as us to have gone over there so soon, and Sub Pop did that for us."

The reported $400,000 advance that DGC gave Nirvana has been blown way out of proportion, if you ask Novoselic. "Taxes, production, stuff like that, ate it all up," he says, not even mentioning the money Sub Pop got for releasing the band. "We could actually have signed for a lot more elsewhere, but we didn't want to be that much in debt." Apparently, Sub Pop had been talking about signing a major label deal after Nirvana's first tour abroad, but it fell through. "It was all very up in the air," Novoselic continues, "so our lawyer started sending our tapes around and we started to get wined and dined." He smiles and pans the pool area. "And here we are today at the beautiful Beverly Garland Hotel."

IRONICALLY, THE LAST OF MY CONVERSATIONS with Nirvana took place while I was in Olympia, attending the International Pop Underground Convention. The Nirvana guys were down in Los Angeles preparing to go to England to perform at the Reading Festival. Kobain was depressed because he couldn't be in Olympia to perform with a side project he has with his girlfriend. The band was back at the Beverly Garland, gloomily getting ready to make a video — hardly the most appropriate creative outlet for such an energetic rock band.

Novoselic said he'd been picking up bad habits lately — "like alcoholism" — and suggested the band should make a made-for-TV movie, "to show everyone what a bore it all is." He yells at Kobain, "Who will play you?" A faint response comes back: "Ernest Borgnine. Who'll be you?" Novoselic laughs: "Someone tall — Kareem Abdul Jabbar?"

You can see it now: the love, the camaraderie, the letdowns, the triumphs... *The Nirvana Story*. In a melodramatic voice, Novoselic improvises dialogue for his movie: "'I'm in this band, too, and what I say goes!' We'll throw wine goblets through the window. And then there'll be a love part: 'Baby, I'm sorry, I've got to go out with the band.' Us onstage — 'booooo,' and we're getting shit thrown at us. It'll be directed like an *ABC After School Special*. 'You know I love you, baby, but I've got to put the band before anything.' 'Yes, I understand, but you'll live in my heart forever.'"

Kobain gets on the phone to stop this silly fantasy. "And then at the end," he says, "our manager will come by and go, 'You guys have been dropped, you're broke,' and the last line is: 'Hello... Give me Sub Pop.'"

October 1991

fugazi

MAJOR THREAT

BY **TAEHEE KIM**

"NO ONE EVER WRITES ABOUT FUGAZI for the music anymore," moans Ian MacKaye, frontman for the politically charged punk group Fugazi. "It's all, 'Oh, they only charge $5' — all these little novelty things. It gets incredibly tedious to me.

"I'm disappointed with a lot of writing that's going on, and I'm sick of the word 'cool,'" he continues. "I'm just not interested in being cool, and I don't want to be included in anything that's called 'cool.' I'm not interested in being part of any kind of classification or cheap novelty slant. Fugazi is a band and we should be taken as such."

IT'S ONLY 7:30 P.M. and the line outside the Sacred Heart Church has already snaked down the block, past the parsonage, beyond the ice cream vendor at the corner and around the neighboring softball field. The church, a whitewashed stone building with a cluster of pink geraniums out front, sits along 16th Street in the Mount Pleasant section of Washington, D.C., one of the District's few racially mixed neighborhoods. Just a month earlier, the shooting of an Hispanic man by local police led to three nights of intense rioting a few blocks away. Tonight, however, the area is calm, almost pastoral. As I stroll around the softball field, a man in a sleeveless T-shirt, sporting a thin goatee, taps my shoulder, more puzzled than alarmed. "Excuse me, miss," he asks. "Something is happening at the church?" Indeed, something is happening, but it's not a riot — and it's not your average Wednesday night prayer service. This crowd came to experience the fire and brimstone of Fugazi.

After the flock is let inside, the church basement teems with people — more than 1,400 of them, chatting, craning their necks to find their friends and picking over the piles of politically progressive literature spread out on large folding tables at the back. The tables were brought in by Positive Force, the punk concert promoters and grassroots activist group that organizes all of Fugazi's D.C.-area benefit shows. Tonight, the Force's presence is particularly appropriate, given the Supreme Court's recent decision restricting federal funding to clinics that counsel on abortion. Each of the three bands on tonight's bill — Canada's NoMeansNo, Dutch group the Ex and Fugazi — stress the need for a humane national health care policy, and the money raised by this show (nearly $5,000 after expenses) will go to the Washington Free Clinic, which operates out of another neighborhood church.

It's hot and humid enough in the basement to steam raw vegetables. The condensation of human sweat on the ceiling makes the entire space look like it was sprayed with a firehose. By the time Fugazi crawls to the bandstand, lead singer Ian MacKaye is barefoot, having removed his sneakers to avoid slipping on the brown slime (a mixture of sweat and grime) coating the stage.

Fugazi's live shows really capture the essence of this band — shows that are capable of restoring your faith in the energy and potential of punk rock even a decade after its decline. But tonight Fugazi is more subdued than usual, rooted to one spot for the duration of their set for fear of falling — or passing out from heat stroke. It's one of their more trying performances. As drummer Brendan Canty would later comment, "Everyone was bummed out at that show."

In spite of all this, Fugazi manages to convey the taut, powerfully original sound that's heard on all of its albums. Tonight, Fugazi focuses on selections from its latest LP, *Steady Diet of Nothing*. It's clear they are moving beyond the (mostly) anthemic writing of their first two EPs and more toward the musical complexity hinted at on 1990's *Repeater*. While the more experimental nature of *Repeater* was not always sucessful, songs from *Steady Diet* such as "Nice New Outfit," "Latin Roots," and "Reclamation," are more consistent, and rich with interplay between singer/guitarists MacKaye and Guy Picciotto. MacKaye's direct, resonant voice — sometimes chanting, sometimes screaming — alternates with Picciotto's raspy, less melodic style of singing. It is this musical democracy that characterizes Fugazi most. "We all contribute to writing music," Picciotto says, "but all the lyrics are written by either me or Ian, depending on who's singing. That's the only area where we're not *completely* democratic."

In the early 1980s, MacKaye's band Minor Threat, along with other D.C. bands such as Bad Brains, turned the nation's capital into a hotbed of hardcore. When Minor Threat broke up in 1983, MacKaye formed the short-lived group Embrace, along with former members of another D.C. outfit, Faith. In Embrace, MacKaye was effectively replacing Faith's former singer (who, incidentally, was his own younger brother, Alex). Embrace was MacKaye's transition from the tense, impassioned songs of Minor Threat to Fugazi's more expanded sound.

Fugazi was the result of a complete musical evolution. While their music retains every ounce of hardcore's anger and edge, the anger has become more tightly focused, and the edge is much sharper than that of most hum-drum thrash. The group lays elements of punk and heavy metal atop a distinctive, anchoring bass line, creating inventive, unpredictable progressions wherein grinding electric riffs suddenly transform into propulsive, major key anthems. Fugazi's music is so far advanced today that shortsighted pigeonholes like "hardcore" are not only simplistic decriptions, they are inaccurate.

"When people refer to us as 'hardcore,'" says MacKaye, "it's just their own convenient tag, not ours. It's what Kurt Vonnegut called 'the filing drawer concept.' People always used to call Vonnegut's work science fiction. It used to drive him crazy. It's just writing, it's just fiction. And what we play is just music."

A FEW DAYS AFTER THE SHOW, MacKaye sits at his dining room table sipping Perrier from a coffee mug. Although unfailingly polite, he shifts restlessly while speaking, indicating a discomfort with journalists. "Why don't I trust the media?" he muses, turning the question over in his mind. "Because the printed word, when it's typed up and looking nice, people think it's the truth. But most of the time it's incredibly slanted — it's written by misinformed writers, or it's just not telling the whole story. Like with this whole war coverage thing... I mean, *come on!*" Mackaye's voice rises. "They say things like 'a couple hundred casualties' and it's completely not true! And these articles were using words like 'we' and 'our.' That's not journalism, that's the party line. To be honest, the state of print media is pretty fucking abysmal right now. For instance, the *Washington Post* has gone down incredibly just in the past ten years. It's definitely gotten less satisfying, even during my lifetime. But traveling around, and seeing other papers out there, the *Post* is like" — he pauses — "the *Oxford English Dictionary* or something."

Rock journalism, MacKaye says, is just as bad. He mocks the typical comment made about Fugazi: "They're the Paul Reveres of rock'n'roll, ringing the bells of freedom..." He rolls his eyes in disgust. "That's the kind of stupid slant you see. Who wants to be the Paul Revere of rock'n'roll? I mean, *fuck* that. Or 'The Last of the Mohicans,' or whatever. There are all these cheesy kinds of slants. And it's weak."

MacKaye pauses to adjust the small red cap atop his shaven head. "Furthermore, it's not necessary."

Fugazi doesn't despise all media attention; it's just that the band seriously considers whom they talk to. A recent Fugazi "feature" in *Spin* devoted most of its verbiage to the writer's tale of chasing after the group without getting substantial comments from the band members. MacKaye and company have turned down opportunities to appear in higher-profile magazines such as *Rolling Stone*, but they make a special effort to talk to several dozen 'zines on every tour. "We think doing fanzine interviews is really important," MacKaye says.

Ironically, the band's pre-eminence on the underground music scene can be a hindrance, making normal, low-key encounters with fans difficult. "I think a lot of the kids are intimidated to approach us for interviews these days. They assume that we wouldn't do one," MacKaye says. "The physical layout of the room, the mechanics of approaching us backstage, is a whole different thing when you are playing to 1,500 instead of 50 people."

Lots of seemingly conscientious rock'n'rollers might *say* they aren't interested in media exposure, fame and fortune, but Fugazi means it. "It's not mandatory that everyone hear about us," says MacKaye. "People argue that we should welcome exposure in major magazines. There are people in Bangladesh that will never hear about us. Ever! And that's fine. It's perfectly OK if you've never heard about us. Life will still go on. The world will still turn."

MacKaye has supported himself with a lot of day jobs over the decade he's played in indie bands. He has worked at a record store, a movie theater, an ice cream stand, a pet store, a thrift shop, a theater company. ("I was a typist," he says. "I typed letters.") He once drove a truck for the *Washington Post*, delivered papers for the now-defunct *Washington Star*, carried equipment for a local concert promoter, and has worked hospitality for bigger shows — like Billy Idol, Depeche Mode and R.E.M. — that roll into D.C.

His lengthiest job, however, is the one he cares about the most — running Dischord, the independent record label that counts Minor Threat, Fugazi and a host of other local bands on its roster. Along with housemate Jeff Nelson, MacKaye launched Dischord ten years ago. "Jeff and I started Dischord when we were in the Teen Idles," a pre-Minor Threat band they formed in high school. "We had a tape of songs and we had saved up money from shows. So we said, 'Let's put out a record. No one else is going to do it for us.'"

THAT DO-IT-YOURSELF ETHOS has pervaded the way MacKaye has run the business ever since. His Dischord House is a sky-blue, two-story outpost in suburban Arlington, Virginia, where MacKaye and a few friends have lived and worked since he graduated from D.C.'s Wilson High School in 1980. Behind the kitchen is a small back room where a telephone with a separate business line rings every five minutes or so. In the front living room, titles of earlier Dischord releases line the walls in neat rows.

While MacKaye handles the Herculean tasks of managing Fugazi and booking all of the band's tours (typically six weeks long), he gets support from the small, salaried staff of Fugazi, Inc., a company the band formed last year. Those employees help with everything from finances to the flood of incoming calls. That's not all that makes this operation different from other corporations. "These are all friends of ours, people we know," Picciotto explains of the label's relationship with its artists. "Nobody has to sign contracts or anything like that."

One of the amazing things about Fugazi is that the group is able to stay on its home-grown, independent label and still have sales figures and concert turn-outs rivaling those of major label acts. In fact, the thought of marketing seems absurd in the context of Dischord's casual, personal approach to record-making. Mail-order a record from the company, and you get a friendly, handwritten note from an amiable Dischord employee. The company's success is a testament to the strength of the musical underground; it's also testament to the power of word-of-mouth. *Repeater* sold well over 100,000 copies without a marketing ploy, an advertising budget or a single press release.

With such sales figures, it's not suprising that Fugazi has attracted major label attention. "Some," says MacKaye, "are more persistent than others." But by now, it's common knowledge that Fugazi is simply not interested.

"We take the music seriously," says Picciotto, adding that the band would feel uncomfortable being manipulated by record executives. "All the mechanics of being an indie band are really just to facilitate playing better music. We don't feel a compulsion to entertain. We can put whatever we want on our record covers; no one else is responsible for our shit except ourselves."

"You don't need *everything*," MacKaye adds. "If something works, you should keep going with it. There's something incredibly wonderful about having your own thing. But I'll tell you one thing — if this band was selling only 5,000 copies, and we were happy playing, we'd still be together. We'd still be working day jobs and just doing what we want."

Most of the members of Fugazi have been actively involved in the D.C. punk scene since the beginning. MacKaye has sung and/or played bass in the Slinkees, Teen Idles, Minor Threat and Embrace. Picciotto and drummer Brendan Canty played together in Rites of Spring, One Last Wish, and Happy Go Lucky. But bassist Joe Lally lived too far outside the Beltway to catch on right away. Lally grew up in Rockville, Maryland, so his induction into the punk underground was haphazard.

"When the Dead Kennedys came to D.C.," Lally says, "I thought, 'I have to go.' When I saw them, I was way up front, and all these people were constantly jumping off the stage, five at a time. The club was so packed that these waves of people were jumping into the crowd like it was an ocean. I just sort of stood next to the wall, thinking, 'What the fuck?!'"

Lally is sitting on a wooden bench in the backyard of Dischord House. Surrounded by rows of tomato plants and raspberry bushes, he's staring pensively at a white porcelain basin that a housemate has whimsically attached to a tree trunk. "It doesn't work," he says of the sink. "It just seems to attract mosquitoes." Lally, 27 and softspoken, is searching his memory for some of his earlier experiences on the music scene. "Somewhere along the line," he continues, "I figured out that this music was called 'hardcore' or something, and I started to seek bands that were related. I guess if I had gone out and bought the right fanzines or magazines, I would have figured out a lot of what was happening. I remember thinking that the Cars were like, the weirdest thing." He laughs.

"I did own a copy of *Live At the Deaf Club* [a compilation of San Francisco punk bands], and I remember going to see the Cramps at the Ontario Theater when the Teen Idles were opening. Ian was playing, but I didn't really pay much attention to them. I thought the Cramps were like, the most incredible thing. Lux was totally drunk. As he was walking across the stage, he was taking his shirt off and his pants were falling down. And he had high heels on." He pauses, clearly awestruck by the performance. "At the end, he crawled around the drum risers with his pants around his ankles."

WHILE LALLY CONSIDERS THE SHOW a formative experience, punk rock still took a back seat to his main interest — a little-known heavy metal band from Maryland called the Obsessed. "I spent a lot of time going to hear them and not really knowing what was going on with the whole punk thing," he says. He had thoughts of actually growing his hair out and becoming one of the Obsessed, but a pivotal incident stopped him. "I went to see Rites of Spring and Beefeater. Seeing those bands was the greatest thing. Rites of Spring were so beautiful. I would try to get people from Rockville to go down with me, but no one was really interested. Maybe sometimes these younger guys who were into skateboarding would be interested, but for the most part I was alone, going down to D.C. to see these shows all by myself."

Punk rock, as the Minutemen once sang, had changed his life. "Seeing the shows made me think about what I was doing with my time, being stoned all the time, being bored, depressed… whatever."

Lally put his substance abuse behind him for good and started touring with Beefeater as a roadie. He also started experimenting with different diets (he is now a strict vegetarian). Most importantly, he summoned up the courage to leave his day job of four years. Lally had been a government contractor, working with computer tapes and driving a forklift in a storage facility until he had an accident in the warehouse. He displays two fingers that still have reddish scars at the tips. "The bone in one of them got chipped," he says, "and this guy sewed it up at first with the chip still inside."

Though he hated the job, Lally didn't quit right away. "I was raised to think that it would be ridiculous to leave a job where I was making so much money. I had this big thing back when I started seeing Rites of Spring that I really wanted to work at Dischord, but I never did anything about it. I just figured that, a small record label like that, they wouldn't be hiring, they'd just use their friends or something. It's funny because now I see it all the time — kids writing or approaching Dischord and wanting to work there — and I can totally identify."

THIRTY MILES SOUTH OF Washington, D.C., in rural Virginia, is the Lorton correctional facility, the sort of place that would make you think twice about breaking the law. It is surrounded by landfills where garbage constantly burns, all day long, day after day. It's a brutal, depressing sight. Yet while such hopelessness is the norm at the prison, at least one group of minimum security inmates got a taste of the surreal last Christmas: a private performance by the four screaming white guys of Fugazi. It was likely the first time any of the prisoners had seen such an act; it certainly was a far cry from the occasional gospel or jazz outfit that ventures inside the prison walls.

"It was totally different from any of our other concerts, where kids are familiar with us and know practically every other syllable of our songs," says MacKaye, who was reluctant at first to talk about the experience. He walks into the kitchen and pulls out a slim, well-designed fanzine called *Uno Mas*, which features a photo essay of the show shot by Jim Saah, a friend who accompanied Fugazi to the prison. The pictures, all in black and white, show

Fugazi playing before a few dozen black men with bewildered looks on their faces. "They were pretty freaked out," says MacKaye, pointing to one of the photographs. "They'd never heard anything even remotely like us before."

"They were really nice guys," Canty says. "They were the same kind of kids I might of known when I was at Wilson High. You could tell that it was such a shaft that some of them were in there."

"They had a great sense of humor about the whole thing," adds Picciotto. "I mean, we were playing music that they thought was kind of humorous, really. I don't think they could understand why we weren't playing David Bowie covers."

IF ONE OF PUNK ROCK'S most important tenets involved breaking rules to reinvent them in more creative ways, Fugazi has taken punk ethic to its logical extreme. The group's penchant for playing unusual spaces is one of the ways the band operates outside the conventions of the rock industry. While most of Fugazi's benefit shows in Washington are in church basements, the group has also played in an old Safeway grocery store, a group house in Arkansas and a sprawling structure that was once a community rollerskating rink.

Fugazi's club shows always draw massive crowds; their two nights at a downtown club in D.C. sold out within an hour on a chilly afternoon last winter. One of their most memorable gigs was an outdoor concert in the rain at Lafayette Park, a small grassy area facing the White House, on the day Congress declared war in the Persian Gulf. "We always welcome new ideas," says Picciotto, "anything that will break the conventional ways of putting on shows."

Sometimes that ethic inspires incidents which more conventional harcore fans find weird — like the Charlie incident. A PETA (People For the Ethical Treatment of Animals) accountant by day, Charlie becomes a freeform dancer by night at many of Fugazi's D.C.-area shows. He jumps onstage with the band and dances in a short skirt, wearing nothing underneath. "We have never asked him to come up onstage," says MacKaye. "But he just did it, and it was fine. But before one show, this kid said, 'Are you going to have your hippie dancing tonight?' I said, 'My what?! My *hippie*?!'" MacKaye crooks his index finger. "I said, 'Come here.

That guy is more punk than you will ever hope to be. He's breaking rules that you haven't even *thought* of yet.' Another time, someone said, 'Hey, why don't you get that guy off stage? Man, we don't want to see his dick.' Well, if you don't want to see it, then don't look! It's a free country."

THE CONVENTIONS OF HARDCORE — stagediving, slamdancing — have even become an area of conflict at Fugazi shows. In spite of (or perhaps *because* of) the band's persistent pleas for a more tolerable concert atmosphere, most of their shows outside D.C. still suffer to varying degrees from band/audience antagonisms. "You get jaded after a while because it's become such a custom for there to be bone-headed violence at the periphery of our punk shows," says Picciotto, in a phone conversation from the Mount Pleasant group house he shares with Brendan Canty. "It's kind of a drag to have to be cop at your own show, and it's kind of frustrating when you just want to play a show and there's all this other stuff going on. We play loud, electric guitar music, and you'd hope that it doesn't mean you have to act like an asshole."

First, there's a purely practical reason Fugazi chooses to dissuade its crowds from slamming and diving: they want to protect innocent bystanders trying to concentrate on the music from getting kicked in the head. Secondly, to Fugazi, who pride themselves on innovation, stagediving and slamming are hopelessly retro. "I mean, it's *old* — that kind of dancing is ten years old," says Lally.

Finally, there's the nemesis of "straight-edge" that follows them everywhere. Straight-edge hardcore is a movement in which adherents do not smoke, drink or do drugs. Many of them are so violently opposed to the alcohol/drug lifestyle that they physically and verbally attack those who aren't with the program. The straight-edge scene was spawned by an early Minor Threat song called "Straightedge," which espoused a moral asceticism. Yet MacKaye adamantly refuses to take credit for the movement, or be defined by it.

"When people see me, they see all this baggage — straight-edge this, straight-edge that. 'Straightedge' was *one song* among many others. It had some pretty important points, mainly saying take responsibility for your life. But it was just a song; it was never intended to be a movement."

Straight-edge or not, Fugazi does live a cleaner rock'n'roll lifestyle than many other bands. Paperback books and mineral water accompany the band on tours, and all of the members eschew drugs and alcohol. This makes the flipside of the lifestyle misconceptions that surround the band particularly hilarious. "We get so many strange questions from people that think we're, like, living in some kind of Led Zepplin fantasy," says Canty. "The misconceptions of us as a band are more incredible."

"Some people think we are completely hardline straight-edge," he adds, "or some people think we might sit in the back and do speedballs. Some kids might think we're too fucking arty. People come with their own baggage. But then, we only give them so much. We don't try to represent ourselves in any sort of outfit." That's the real, naked point of Fugazi — they support the individual's freedom to chose what to believe. "In the end," Canty says, "they're free to think what they want to. And they probably will."

September 1991

mekons
DAMNED, DAMNED, DAMNED

BY **GORDON ANDERSON**

EVER WONDER WHAT IT'S LIKE to be cursed? I don't mean just *sworn* at, I mean something plague-like, permanent, postitively Biblical. It happened to me and about 1,500 other New Yorkers one unbearably hot June day in Central Park. We had gathered there to see the Mekons kick off their feverish American mini-tour (NYC-Frisco-Boston-Washington-NYC-NYC-Hoboken, all in 12 days) in support of their new, import-only album, *The Curse of the Mekons*. For an hour, we had been treated to tried-and-true Mekon anthems like "Hard To Be Human," "Memphis, Egypt," and "Blow Your Tuneless Trumpet," rendered about as tightly as you could expect, given the savage weather. But now the band looked soaked, spent. Jon Langford, one of the two remaining original members, and singer Sally Timms both appeared ready to faint, an angry red flush riding up their cheeks. Tom Greenhalgh, the other founding Mekon, had disappeared for a lengthy stretch. Only Susie Honeyman, their comely, unflappable fiddler, seemed relatively fresh.

When Langford, after introducing the "disco dance" section of the show, executed a few kickboxing moves and left the scene, it looked like things were about to peter out entirely. The stage flooded with roadies and dancers, as various musicians joined Ruth Cochran and John Langley (the Mekons' short-term rhythm section, on loan from the Blue Aeroplanes) in laying down a throbbing groove. Then, without any visible cue, the beat shifted to something more... more menacing. Greenhalgh stepped forward, and in an eerie falsetto, recalling the Band's late Richard Manuel, began to sing:

mekons

He's a sorcerer, he's a bourgeois sorcerer
Miraculous and magical
His world is also demonic
Terrifying, swinging wildly out of control
Oooh! The abyss is close to home...

I got shivers down my spine; apocalyptic shivers, the kind I hadn't had since I saw John Lydon and PiL back in '82. It was a moment worthy of an outfit that once dubbed itself a "Dance Band On the Edge of Time," made all the more powerful by the sheer artlessness of singing on a stage full of bobbing bodies. The sun sat like a fat man on the back of my neck, and as I looked at the dark, silent, sentry-like skyscrapers towering through the noxious, white haze just beyond the outer fringes of the park, it seemed not just that it could all go up in smoke at any moment, but that maybe it had already begun to. It could have just been the heat, but the Curse of the Mekons is strong stuff indeed.

This curse, this message-cum-celebration of doom, cuts both ways, because the '90s have not been the best of times for the Mekons. In fact, in the space of a year and a half, one of the world's great rock bands lost its American record label and its rhythm section. Now they have a new album out that you'll probably have a hard time finding. How this came to pass says a lot about what the music business is, and about who the Mekons are.

IT'S NOON ON A THURSDAY, a few days after the Mekons' Central Park sorcery, and — of all days, of all dates — it's July 4, the Mekons' favorite holiday. Jon Langford and Tom Greenhalgh are looking not-so-fresh from a 7 a.m. arrival back in New York City from a gig in Boston the night before.

"It was a stupid joke, really," chuckles Langford about his band's choice of a name. "It comes from this comic called *The Eagle*. One of the characters in it was called Danny Dare," Greenhalgh further explains. "He was a space pilot of the future, and his arch enemy was the Mekon, who had a big, green head and sat in a flying saucer and went around doing evil deeds."

"He was like sort of a Nazi-stroke-Communist bogeyman," continues Langford, who is beginning to wake up a bit, due in no small part to a brick of firecrackers that just went KER-POW-POW-POW-POW-POW-POW outside the window. "And Dan Dare was like a Battle of Britain fighter pilot who somehow got into outer space — sort of a British imperialist fantasy." Perhaps it's not surprising the Mekons chose to identify with the villain in this space opera. But such irreverence comes naturally to a band with roots in the late '70s British punk explosion; in fact, the Mekons are among the *only* bands from that lot who are still going without an interim "comeback."

"There was the Anarchy tour of the Sex Pistols, the Clash, Johnny Thunders and the Damned," says Greenhalgh. "It was like a package, and it came around to Leeds in about December of '76, and it was the first punk thing... and then about May of '77 we had a band. Suddenly, it seemed possible."

Langford was inspired mostly by the punk attitude. "The things the Sex Pistols said in interviews, and the things that were said in the papers, were maybe more interesting than English punk rock music," he says. "It was just the idea of the possibility of being able to do it, because before, bands were like the Rolling Stones and the Who, which were massive and came around once a year. And then there were all these stupid punk rock bands, which we liked."

Thus a scene was born. The Mekons joined Gang of Four and the Delta 5 in making Leeds a hotbed of arty, dissonant punk. It was a close-knit scene; the three groups shared a rehearsal space and collectively built a PA system. It was maybe even a little too close-knit. *The Quality of Mercy Is Not Strnen*, the Mekons' maiden 1979 release, is notable not only for its humor, intelligence and determined lack of melodicism, but also for the picture of Gang of Four on its back cover. Grouses Langford, "People always thought that was us; Virgin obviously did when they put that record out without even talking to us about it. 'Here, have a picture of the Gang of Four on the back of your record.'" It would be the first gaff in a career remarkable for its back luck with record labels.

It is a commonly held misconception that *Fear And Whiskey*, their fiddle-drenched 1985 masterpiece, represented some sort of miraculous stylistic departure for the Mekons, a sudden embrace of Hank Williams by a band previously known for its inchoate amateurism and political acumen than for its interest in country music. It is true that the Mekons emerged from a recording hiatus of several years with something approaching stability for the first time ever. "That's when we were actually working on trying to get a band together, 'cause that's when the miners' strike was on," recalls Langford. "We were trying to do benefits for the coal miners."

Fear And Whiskey does sport a revamped line-up anchored by ex-Rumour drummer Steve Goulding, bassist Lu Edmonds and a full-time violinist in Susie Honeyman. But the band did not, as Mekons acolyte Robert Christgau would have it, coalesce willy-nilly out of some anarchist commune. "That's bullshit," scoffs Greenhalgh. "It's in a lot of things and I don't know why. There were various people sort of, like, in and out of the band, but that was just due to the fact that we couldn't really pay anybody anything, so it was just that people did it when they could."

AS FOR THE NEW INSTRUMENTS on *Fear And Whiskey*, violin had appeared on Mekons records from as far back as 1980, albeit more as rhythmic instruments than anything else. Beginning with 1982's *The Mekons Story* — which, according to Greenhalgh, has "a lot of bits and pieces that kind of link up this period to later" — it became apparent that the band wasn't just fiddling around with the notion of hillbilly music. And with the 1983's *The English Dancing Master* EP, the idea of adding a violin as a permanent component of the Mekons had crystallized. "John Gill played violin on *The English Dancing Master* in particular, and it was that sound..." Greenhalgh trails off, pondering, then adds, "John couldn't always play with us live, so that's why Susie joined."

Fear And Whiskey took on an unsuspecting underground rock world by storm. The album's greatness came not only from the power of its songs, but also from the cumulative sense of dread that these were quite possibly the last ravings of a band of lost souls in a world gone mad. "For us it was definitely about England, and about the Thatcher years, and about the miners' strike," says Langford. "So a lot of it is pretty depressing. It was right after the strike collapsed and things looked pretty bleak. They still do."

That sort of depression might drive the average person mad, though the Mekons have made a career of it. Still, it was only natural that the band's next record should signal a bit of a retreat. *The Edge of the World* is a subdued, even sad affair, awash in fiddle and accordion (from deputy Mekon Rico Bell), and notable for the first recorded appearance of vocalist Sally Timms (she sang with an earlier line-up in 1982). Both records were released on the Mekons' own Sin label with money scraped together from gigs, as their previous label, the Leeds-based CNT, had gone belly-up by 1984. Both records had been recorded in a hurry; Langford reports that the second side of *Fear And Whiskey* was actually recorded and mixed in one day. News of a label deal, then, was well-earned and welcome, even by this gang of unregenerate do-it-yourselfers.

The Mekons signed with Twin/Tone in 1987, right about (or just after) the highwater mark of the American independent label scene. Bands like Sonic Youth and Hüsker Dü had yet to make the jump to the majors, so, not coincidentally, labels like SST and Twin/Tone were still going strong. But the rot had set in, and within two years the Mekons were to feel the effects of a sub-industry in collapse.

"We played in 1988 when the album *So Good It Hurts* was out," says Langford. "We did a lot of touring that year. It seemed really futile because we went to San Francisco and you couldn't buy the record! At least we were doing our job properly; for once, we were trying to be vaguely professional." Adds Greenhalgh, "It wasn't their fault; their distribution collapsed. Somebody they were using on the entire west coast" — typically, neither Greenhalgh nor Langford knows who — "just went bust when the album came out. The whole thing was such a piss-off that when Twin/Tone made a deal with A&M it seemed worth a try — at least from the point of view of getting better distribution, if nothing else."

So the most determinedly non-professional band in the music business found itself again with a major label's resources at its fingers. But success didn't go to their heads; true to form, the group's immediate impulse was to self-destruct. "We had an idea to do a very straightforward concept album, and the title of each track was going to be like, 'The Agent,' 'The Manager,' 'The Roadie,'" says a grinning Greenhalgh. "'The Journalist' was also one of them.

"We were going to name names and everything — a savage critique of the music business which would probably be the last record we'd ever make."

mekons

WITH ALL THE BAD INTENTIONS in the world, the Mekons nevertheless rewarded A&M with their second classic album of the decade. *The Mekons Rock'n'Roll* points a steady finger at the ravenous maw that is the music biz. "The battles we fought were long and hard/Just not to be consumed by rock'n'roll," Langford bellows in "Memphis, Egypt." And "Empire of the Senseless" is a hilarious, deadpan indictment of the values (or lack thereof) of American business and politics. Yet, in spite of itself, *Rock'n'Roll* also features three instant anthems: "Memphis," "Blow Your Tuneless Trumpet," and "Amnesia," with arrangements and songwriting more self-assured than ever before. It also marks the real emergence of Timms — on tracks like "Learning To Live On Your Own" — as one of the most enchanting female vocalists in rock.

Ah, but here's the sad part of the story. Actually, the Mekons' trouble with A&M began even before the album came out. First, there was the number of tracks. The Mekons had 14. A&M wanted 12. A&M won. And then there was the album cover. The Mekons wanted Elvis. A&M was afraid the King's estate might sue. The corporation won again. The American cover is a weird, splotchy pastiche ("A dog's breath" is how Greenhalgh describes it) with His likeness completely obscured. The import version on Blast First, their independent English label, includes both the orignal cover concept and all 14 tracks.

After *Rock'n'Roll* came out, there was the nasty matter of disappointing sales, corporate indifference and inexplicable business practices. And, perhaps, even downright deceit. The course and causes of the events about to be related are the subject of some dispute — there are, of course, two sides to every story — but here, without mincing words, is how the Mekons say they ended up without an American record deal.

"They were completely fucking useless," Greenhalgh says of A&M. "They didn't have a clue what they were doing. We were in Los Angeles on December 17th of '89, and we said we should come back and do more touring [to support *Rock'n'Roll*], and they said yes." But the record company didn't assist the Mekons in regard to that at all; in fact, according to Greenhalgh, the company kept mum all through January and February. "We were continuously asking them for money so we could come back and tour, and then eventually they said the album had died." Greenhalgh gets exasperated just thinking about this stuff. "And then," he exclaims, "they said, 'Here's some money to make another record!'"

The happy result of such "brilliant" decisions was *F.U.N. '90*, a four-song EP (of course, there were six tracks on the English version), which pays tribute to some Mekon heroes, alive and dead, with covers of the Band, Kevin Coyne, and a ghostly taped appearance of the late rock writer, Lester Bangs, moaning in the background Hank Williams' words, "When the Lord made me, he made a ramblin' man," out of tune, in a mix rhythm of tracks, dance beats and a snaky Arabic vocal sample. The record was a brilliant riposte to the dance music sweeping England. Says Langford, "We thought it was really good, but it didn't sound like *Rock'n'Roll*, so they just went, like, 'What the fuck's this? We're not interested.'" He grimaces. "They wouldn't give us any tour support to do any gigs, or do a video, or promote it. And there's no press. So we said we will come over and sort this thing out."

Just whom the Mekons would sort things out with is unclear. A&M had been bought out by Polygram, and most of the old contacts had fled. "Basically, they hated us and they hated our manager, Paul Smith," says Langford. "They had a real thing about him." Yet when the group came over to the States in November of 1990 to ask out of its contract, A&M refused. Point blank. "Their response was, like, damage limitation," Langford adds. "They just kept telling us what a good job they were going to do, and how everything would be great if Paul Smith were run over by a car."

MEANWHILE, THE MEKONS had almost completed work on a new album, cut with advances from Twin/Tone and Blast First. "We were saying we don't want to give you the album because we've no confidence in you to do the job," says Greenhalgh. "And they said, 'No, no, no!,' and they kept sending us plans. It was all nonsense." Says Langford, "So we said, 'How much are you gonna spend on the marketing, tell us?'" Langford's stocky build and sharp wit would make him a formidable opponent in any confrontation. "We had to sort of make up a marketing plan and try and give it to them."

As Greenhalgh adds bitterly, "In the end, we just said, 'OK, we've got no alternative, we'll make the record.' So we give them the record and they drop us."

(A&M product manager Celia Hirshman was the person whom Langford and Greenhalgh had dealt with on the label's marketing plan. "We didn't drop them," she claimed in a later telephone conversation with me. "They're still under contract with us, and they will be until November. We just chose not to put that particular album out.")

All this back and forth with the record company took a toll on the band. Drummer Steve Goulding, who'd been around since *Fear And Whiskey*, had become depressed by recent events. He had already planned to get married, and, according to Greenhalgh, "decided that he had better things to do with his time." When Goulding packed it in, so did bassist Lu Edmonds.

But if A&M couldn't sell something as instantly infectious as *Rock'n'Roll*, how would it sell this — this *Curse*? The final twist to this tortuous tale is that *The Curse of the Mekons*, the album that's available from Blast First only, is among the band's best. In fact, its grim humor — the liner notes read as if they were written by Eric Idle and Aleister Crowley — and the apocalyptic imagery of songs like "Sorcerer," "Funeral" and "The Curse," conjure the demons of *Fear And Whiskey*, except that the Mekons seem a little less inclined to romanticize their precarious stance on the edge of the world.

"This is my testimony/A dinosaur's confession," Langford sings before going into a defense of socialism, and presciently anticipating the use of smart bombs in the Persian Gulf. After 12 years of the music business and Margaret Thatcher, any quixotic cast to their politics has been drummed out. What remains is an unapologetic world view and a steely pessimism. "I'd say there's no cause for optimism whatsoever," says Greenhalgh, himself a "nonperson" in the British government's eyes, since he failed to pay his poll tax. "Anybody who says otherwise, what's their evidence?"

How about the new Mekons album? It's a fun record — fun in a sort of painfully stimulating way, like watching yet another Republican victory at a presidential returns party with a group of drunken socialists. "Lyric" is as eloquent and plaintive an expression of despair at an amoral world as you could find, and "Secrets" is a chilling probe inside the mind of a Nazi expatriate set to return to her East German home. But Langford, in modest fashion, downplays their wordsmithing talents. "We all bring a load of lyrics we've got on scruffy bits of paper and stick them together and see whether they work or not."

That haphazard process surfaces in the music, too. Unlike the records of so many so-called alternative groups, Mekons albums (and *The Curse*, despite its surefootedness, is no exception) never sound sterile or over-produced. There's a reason for that. The Mekons take real pride in their status as part-time rockers. "We write to order when we get kind of a deadline," says Langford, proudly. "That's why the songs are often quite good; because they didn't exist till days before we recorded them." And they keep the songs simple — so simple, in fact, that any number of people can play on them. "Quite often there's quite a few people who want to come and play," complains Greenhalgh, good-naturedly. "So they're queueing up outside, and then they'll come and play over every song and we have to, like, spend hours mixing them out."

"We've been trying to be more disciplined," he adds. And you can tell, because the songs — written, as always, by Langford and Greenhalgh, with additional help this time from John Gill and longtime Mekon Ken Lite — sail easily into unchartered waters, from Sally Timms's rustic folk reading of "Wild And Blue" to the acid house mutation "Sorcerer." And if it lacks the anthemic crunch of *Rock'n'Roll*, the songs' lyrical acuity has never been sharper.

Such creative anarchy sometimes sparks fireworks, and not the kind still popping outside the window here in honor of America, baseball and apple pie. "There's thunderstorms in the studio," says Langford. "It's a process of, like, pain and pleasure. Stroking and scolding."

"Sally likes to be told what to do," Greenhalgh adds off-handedly, and Langford completes the thought: "Like clean the oven out."

Langford's politically incorrect comment calls for something of an explanation. He and Timms have been an on-again, off-again couple for years. Lately, according to secret sources, they're of an "off-again" status. This was evident during two of the Mekons performances in New York City.

mekons

AT THE CENTRAL PARK GIG, in the midst of the chaos, Timms was playfully throwing things at Langford. A week later, during the band's performance at the downtown Tramps nightclub, a sullen, black-wigged Timms flipped Langford the bird after he made a comment to the effect that rock'n'roll was a great hair-restorer. And things can get rather stormy with the violin-playing female Mekon as well. "We try to tell Susie what to play," says Greenhalgh, "and she refuses absolutely and plays something else and we go along with it, really."

Indeed, for two leaders of a band wracked by personal problems, Langford and Greenhalgh seem fairly blithe about any intra-Mekon squabbles. In true Mekon fashion, they are inclined to turn bum situations into their own creative uses. "In the pipeline, as they say, is an album with a theme to it," says Greenhalgh. He pauses, smiling in the direction of Langford. "I dunno whether we should lift the wraps off, but actually it's a bit similar" — he points at the "I Luv NY" coffee cup in my hand — "to that mug. There's some Mekons stickers, 'I love Mekons.' We're going for sort of a generic look."

"'Cause we're all in love at some point... we're all in love," Langford cuts in, dripping sincerity. Greenhalgh finishes his mate's sentence: "With people!"

"We love people," Langford emphasizes. "We do love people."

"'Cause there's a lot of love in this band," Greenhalgh adds. "Not between members of the band, I *hasten* to add" — the emphasis is for Langford's benefit — "but members of the band and other people. Everybody in the band hates each other, but we're finding love outside."

July 1991

contributors

Steve Appleford is a former editor of *Option* and a Los Angeles-based free-lance writer and photojournalist.

Chuck Crisafulli has contributed to *Request*, *Musician* and the *Los Angeles Times*; he has also written books on the Doors and Nirvana.

Larry Kanter is an ex-rock critic and a senior reporter at *Los Angeles Business Journal*.

John Lewis is a new dad as well as a free-lance music journalist based in Baltimore.

Holly George-Warren is a new mom and an editor at Rolling Stone Press.

Gina Arnold is the author of *Route 666: On the Road To Nirvana* (St. Martin's, 1993) and *Kiss This: Punk In the Present Tense* (St. Martin's, 1997). She teaches springboard diving to adolescents in the San Francisco Bay Area.

Mark Kemp is a former editor of *Option* who is now a vice president of music development at MTV.

Eddie Huffman has written for *Rolling Stone*, the *New York Times* and other publications. He lives in the town of Elon College, NC.

Jason Cohen, a contributing editor at *Texas Monthly*, is at work on a book about minor league hockey in Texas.

Lorraine Ali was named 1997 Music Journalist of the Year; her stories have appeared in *Rolling Stone*, the *New York Times* and *GQ*. She lives in L.A. where she is at work on a book.

contributors

John Corbett is the author of *Extended Play: Sounding Off From John Cage To Dr. Funkenstein* (Duke University Press, 1994); he teaches in the Sound Department at the School of the Art Institute in Chicago.

Jason Fine is an associate editor at *Rolling Stone* and a former *Option* editor; he is researching a book on Bay Area jazz.

Gordon Anderson is director of the Chicago-based Collectors' Choice Music label, which reissues everyone from Fred Neil to Staff Sgt. Barry Sadler.

Scott Becker founded *Option* in 1985. He lives in Los Angeles with his wife and an assortment of other critters.

David Shirley and **Taehee Kim** – phone home: optionmag@aol.com

acknowledgements

Immeasurable thanks are due to *Option*'s former editors — Steve Appleford, Jason Fine, Mark Kemp and Richie Unterberger — as well as senior editors Erik Pedersen and Sandy Masuo. Finally, this book would not exist were it not for the contributions of all the *Option* writers whose works have not been included here, the photographers and designers who made the original pages of the magazine jump, and everyone who in some way made *Option* a home for great writing about great music.

INCOMMUNICADO PRESS

BOOKS

Steve Abee KING PLANET 146 pages, $12.

Dave Alvin ANY ROUGH TIMES ARE NOW BEHIND YOU 164 pages, $12.

Dave Alvin THE CRAZY ONES 156 pages, $12.

Elisabeth A. Belile POLISHING THE BAYONET 150 pages, $12.

Iris Berry TWO BLOCKS EAST OF VINE 108 pages, $11.

Beth Borrus FAST DIVORCE BANKRUPTCY 142 pages, $12.

Pleasant Gehman PRINCESS OF HOLLYWOOD 152 pages, $12.

Pleasant Gehman SEÑORITA SIN 110 pages, $11.

Barry Graham BEFORE 200 pages, $13.

R. Cole Heinowitz DAILY CHIMERA 124 pages, $12.

Hell On Wheels Edited by **Greg Jacobs**, 148 pages, $15.

Jimmy Jazz THE SUB 108 pages, $11.

Michael Madsen BURNING IN PARADISE 160 pages, $14.

Peter Plate ONE FOOT OFF THE GUTTER 200 pages, $13.

Peter Plate SNITCH FACTORY 182 pages, $13.

Scream When You Burn Edited by **Rob Cohen**, 250 pages, $14.

The Spacewürm I LISTEN 160 pages, $13.

Jervey Tervalon LIVING FOR THE CITY 185 pages, $13.

Unnatural Disasters Edited by **Nicole Panter**, 256 pages, $15.

We Rock, So You Don't Have To Ed. by **Scott Becker**, 261 pages, $15.

Incommunicado also releases spoken word CDs and distributes select CDs from New Alliance Records and Ruby Throat Productions. See our website for audio clips and the full list.

Available at bookstores nationally or order direct: Incommunicado P.O. Box 99090 San Diego CA 92169 USA. Inside the U.S., include $3 shipping for 1 or 2 items, add $1 for each additional item. Outside the U.S., $7 shipping for 1 or 2 items, add $2 for each additional. For credit card orders call 619-234-9400. E-mail: severelit@aol.com. For online ordering, book excerpts and audio/video clips, go to the website: http://www.onecity.com/incom/
Distributed to the trade by Consortium Book Sales and Distribution.
Please help us destroy American Publishing. Thank you.